Parapsychology
and the Nature of Life

'With these words I indicate what seems to me the greatest danger of the present, the greatest threat of the future. This danger has already taken shape in America, where, in the name of science, many thousands of young people are every year taught to believe that man is literally nothing more than a piece of mechanism, without power or influence on his destiny. Against this fatalistic dogma, so destructive of aspiration and so weakening to all higher effort, I have not ceased to wage war in my own little corner since I first began to write.'

WILLIAM MCDOUGALL,
Character and the Conduct of Life (1927)

Parapsychology
and the Nature of Life

John L. Randall

1817

HARPER & ROW, PUBLISHERS
New York   Hagerstown   San Francisco   London

FIRST U.S. EDITION

LIBRARY OF CONGRESS CATALOG CARD NUMBER: 75-30341

Library of Congress Cataloging in Publication Data

Randall, John L
    Parapsychology and the Nature of Life.
    Includes bibliographical references and index.
    1. Psychical research. 2. Biology. I. Title. [DNLM: 1. Parapsychology. BF1031 R188p] BF1045.S35R36 1975 133.8'01'57 75-30341
ISBN 0-06-013509-3

To my father

Contents

A section of photographs follows page 128

Preface

Towards the end of the Second World War there appeared on the bookstalls a remarkable little paperback entitled *The Personality of Man*. Its author, G. N. M. Tyrrell, was a distinguished British physicist, mathematician, and psychical researcher, who at one time worked with Marconi on the development of radio communication. In assessing the human situation Tyrrell wrote as follows:

'It is vitally important that we should know in which direction the facts of experience point. We have to ask ourselves whether it is true, as seems to be popularly supposed, that scientific knowledge has rendered materialism almost a certainty. It is a curious fact that the general conclusion to which the *whole* body of knowledge points is unknown.'

During the thirty years that have elapsed since Tyrrell wrote there have been many scientific advances which are relevant to the problem of the nature of man. We have seen the rapid development of computer technology and the study of 'machine intelligence', cybernetics and information theory, molecular biology, neurophysiology, and brain chemistry. Many of these advances seem to reinforce the materialist viewpoint; yet there have been others, no less striking, which appear to go *against* a purely materialistic interpretation of life. The most important of these lie within the field of parapsychology, which during the last decade has begun to occupy an increasingly prominent place among the life sciences. Now that a growing number of professional scientists are turning their attention towards this subject it is no longer possible to dismiss it as a mere hobby for a handful of eccentrics. Parapsychology must find a place in any serious assessment of the nature of human personality, and of life in general.

It is towards such an assessment that this book is directed. Part I outlines the development of those sciences which have contributed most directly to the mechanistic theory of life, and attempts to evaluate their overall effect on human life and thought. Part II—the major section of the book—deals with the problems, failures, and successes of parapsychology. Part III, the most speculative part of the book, approaches Tyrrell's problem of determining the general conclusion to which the whole body of knowledge points. In this section, and particularly in Chapter 16, I have permitted myself the luxury of speculating rather freely about the nature of things. If I am accused of stepping outside the boundaries of a strictly scientific approach I can only plead guilty, and respectfully suggest that my critics should confine their reading to the purely factual sections of the book. I have provided a fairly comprehensive list of references for those who wish to explore further, and these are referred to in the text by means of numerals enclosed in brackets. Chapters 10 and 14 are largely taken from articles by me which have appeared in the *Journal* of the Society of Psychical Research; I am grateful to the Society and to the editor of the *Journal*, Miss Renée Haynes, for permission to quote from these articles and from other material printed in the Society's publications. I am also grateful for the help and advice of many people, including Drs Ted Bastin, John Beloff, Robert E. D. Clark, J. B. Rhine, Helmut Schmidt, and Rupert Sheldrake. Except where their writings have been specifically quoted they must not, of course, be held responsible for any of the opinions expressed in this book.

For permission to print extracts from copyright material I am indebted to the following: Academic Press and Drs J. Brooks & G. Shaw (*Origin and Development of Living Systems*); Messrs Collins and Alfred A. Knopf Inc. (Austryn Wainhouse's translation of *Chance and Necessity* by Jacques Monod); Dr J. B. Rhine and Dr Helmut Schmidt; Laurence Pollinger Ltd and the Estate of the late Mrs Frieda Lawrence (poem by D. H. Lawrence on page 58); Mr Arthur Koestler; Edinburgh University Press (*Towards a Theoretical Biology*).

For the photographs I am grateful to Dr J. B. Rhine, Marie H. Avery, Graham Watkins, Helmut Schmidt, and Peter Davis.

Warwick   John L. Randall
July 1975

Introduction

This book is in all important respects of such quality as to need no preface to bolster it. As it is, I add this prefatory note to the American edition only because it is a genuine pleasure to introduce it and its young author to readers on this side of the Atlantic.

John Randall has the advantage of being a biologist. In dealing with parapsychology this gives him a broader perspective on the new field than any of the other sciences could provide; and he very well shows this advantage throughout the book. The author's qualifications as a teacher show up in the clarity and grasp of his exposition. Furthermore, his successful experience in actual research is evident in the insight and discriminative judgment shown in his review of the experimental work of this broadening field.

As a British scientist, John Randall pays full respect to the "opposition," the criticism of parapsychology (which seems to flourish best in that tolerant country which founded parapsychology). On the other hand, he ventures to speak out on the larger meaning he sees in the findings of psi research for the nature of life itself.

Armed thus with courage in one hand and caution in the other, this teacher-researcher-thinker has written a book that should win its way through many editions and be kept in good step with the continuing advancement of both parapsychology and the sciences of life.

—J. B. Rhine
*Foundation for Research
on the Nature of Man*

Part 1: Mechanism Triumphant

1. The Descent of Man

In the year of the Great Exhibition, 1851, a government census was taken of all the people who attended church in Britain on a particular Sunday. The date chosen for this exercise was Mothering Sunday, March 30th, and the statistics collected by the hard-working census-takers showed a total church attendance of 7,261,032 persons. No census on this scale has been undertaken in the twentieth century, but there can be no doubt that, if it were, it would reveal a very much lower church attendance than in those early days of Queen Victoria. Church statistics show that in 1970 only 5.1% of the population made their Easter Communion in the Church of England, whereas on the day of the 1851 census some 21% of the population attended Anglican churches alone. No doubt the figure would have been even higher if the investigators had performed their task on Easter Day.

If anyone had ventured to predict in 1851 that religious belief and practice would steadily decline over the next hundred years, he would probably have been met with that sort of tolerant smile which is reserved for eccentrics and cranks of all kinds. Life must have seemed remarkably stable in early Victorian Britain. At the centre of a great Empire, the Victorians looked forward with confidence and pride to a future of unimpeded social and economic progress. The Christian churches were undergoing a period of expansion unparalleled since apostolic times. In 1836 Bishop Blomfield launched a scheme for the building of fifty new churches in the London area; ten years later this number was found to be too small. While the Tractarian movement had raised the standard of worship in almost every church throughout the land, the Evangelical revival had brought the practice of daily Bible reading and prayer into thousands of homes. Slavery had been abolished throughout the Empire, and strenuous attempts were being made to improve the lot of the workers at home. The religious orders were being re-founded: monks and nuns could be seen in the streets of the big cities for the first time since the days of Henry VIII. It seemed as though Church and State would go forward in partnership for ever, to the salvation of man's soul and the advancement of his physical well-being.

Of course, not everyone accepted the belief-systems of the day. There were certainly sceptics and atheists, some of them men of very high intellectual calibre, such as John Stuart Mill. Nevertheless, the majority of Englishmen lived in a world which they believed to have been created by a benevolent God. William Paley, in his *Natural Theology* (first published in 1802), argued that the living world showed very clear evidence of design; and design implied the existence of a Designer. Paley's book became a theological classic, and ran into many editions. The young Charles Darwin read it when he went up to Cambridge in 1828, and later wrote in his autobiography that he was 'charmed and convinced' by the long line of argumentation used by Paley. Not only did the natural world seem to reflect the mind of a Creator, but man himself, according to the Book of Genesis, was made in God's image. Destined for eternal fellowship with his Maker, man was envisaged as an immortal soul embedded in a physical body, and if life was frequently short and brutish, there was always the prospect of a better world beyond the grave. Despite a great deal of poverty and pain (chloroform was not discovered until 1847!), early Victorian man still felt that life was essentially meaningful, and God was in control of His world.

Such was the thought background of the age upon which Darwin's *Origin of Species* fell like a bombshell in 1859. The theory of evolution put forward in that famous book was first launched upon the scientific world in a joint paper by Darwin and Wallace read before the Linnaean Society in London in 1858. The book came out on November 24th of the following year, and every single copy of the edition of 1,250 was sold on the same day. The Victorian world was scandalised, and yet fascinated by the picture presented by Darwin. Looking at nature in the light of Thomas Malthus' *Essay on Population*, he saw all living creatures locked in a furious life and death struggle for existence. Where Paley had seen evidence of the work of a benevolent Creator, Darwin saw only the law of the jungle. The beautiful and multitudinous adaptations of living creatures to their surroundings were attributed to the accumulation of a vast number of small, random changes over long periods of time. Only those changes which happened to increase the organism's chance of survival were preserved; the unfit were ruthlessly eliminated before they were able to reproduce. Evolutionary progress was thus shown to be the result of 'blind chance', working through the suffering and death of countless millions of creatures trapped in a relentless battle for survival.

There can be little doubt that the rise of Darwinism played an important part in undermining Victorian religious beliefs. True, there had been evolutionary ideas in the air long before Darwin: theories of a quasi-evolutionary nature can be traced back to the ancient Greeks, and in the century immediately preceding Darwin evolutionary concepts had been propounded by Jean Baptiste Lamarck, Geoffroy St-Hilaire, Erasmus Darwin (Charles' grandfather), and others. Yet none of these writers captured the popular mind in the way that Charles Darwin did. This was partly due to the enormous quantity of evidence which he had patiently collected in support of his theory; it was also in no small measure the result of the aggressive propaganda of Thomas Henry Huxley. Styling himself 'Darwin's bulldog', Huxley set out not only to convince the scientific world of the truth of the theory, but to use it as a stick with which to beat the Church. When the British Association for the Advancement of Science met at Oxford in 1860, Huxley seized the opportunity it presented with both hands.

Exactly what was said at that famous meeting will never be known, for no verbatim record was kept. For this reason, the accounts given in various books must be regarded as preserving no more than the general atmosphere of the meeting. What is certain is that Bishop Wilberforce, in trying to be witty at the expense of the Darwinian theory, suffered a crushing defeat at the hands of Huxley. From that time onwards Darwinism became a major topic of conversation in civilised society. Educated people divided into pro-Darwinians and anti-Darwinians, with some eminent churchmen and scientists in each camp. Although many atheists and agnostics (a word coined by Huxley) liked to represent the conflict as a battle between ecclesiastical dogmatism and the freedom of thought represented by science, the evidence hardly supports such a view. Quite a number of eminent churchmen accepted and praised Darwin's work: for example, F. J. A. Hort, R. W. Church (later Dean of St Paul's), and Charles Kingsley. Even Cardinal Newman seems to have been half converted to the Darwinian viewpoint. On the other hand, there were some eminent biologists in opposition to the theory. Sir Richard Owen, one of the greatest anatomists of the day, wrote that Darwin's book 'left the determination of the origin of species very nearly where the author found it.' Adam Sedgwick, Woodwardian Professor of Geology at Cambridge, described the Darwinian theory as 'a dish of rank materialism cleverly cooked and served up merely to make us independent of a Creator.'

Why did our Victorian forebears react so violently to the theory? In his book *Evolutionary Theory and Christian Belief* (84), David Lack points out that Darwinism was believed to conflict with Christian teaching in at least four different ways:

(1) It contradicted the creation story in Genesis, which was at that time taken literally;

(2) It undermined the popular rational argument for the existence of God based on the presence of design and purpose in the animal body (Paley);

(3) It denied the occurrence of the Fall, implying that man had risen from the beasts rather than fallen from a state of blessedness;

(4) It suggested that man's higher mental faculties had evolved from those of animals, in which case there seemed no reason to suppose that they had any ultimate significance.

Of these four points of conflict, only the first can be regarded as more or less resolved, even today. It is now generally accepted by most Christians that the creation story in Genesis is not (and was probably never intended to be) a literal account of the formation of the earth and the development of living organisms. The strongly literal interpretation of the Bible adopted by fundamentalist Christians is not a necessary part of the Christian faith; many of the early Church fathers, such as Irenaeus, Clement, and Athanasius, regarded the Fall as allegorical, while Augustine believed that the earth was created in a single instant rather than in six days. However, even if we accept that a literal interpretation of the scriptures is not an essential part of the Christian faith, there still remain important points of conflict between Darwinism and Christianity. A careful study of Lack's book (which is sub-titled *The Continuing Conflict*) should be sufficient to convince anyone that this is by no means a dead issue, as some modern writers would have us suppose. In fact, Darwin's theory not only removes the necessity for a Creator, as far as the living world is concerned; it also removes entirely the concept of *purpose* in nature. It is a purely *mechanistic* theory, and this is undoubtedly the reason for much of the opposition it has provoked down to the present day. Not only Christians, but many other people as well find the Darwinian picture depressing in the extreme; for it attributes the whole of life upon this planet to the interplay of mindless, purposeless forces.

Following the early triumph of Darwinism, several scientists began to make careful statistical studies of the small continuous variations in living things, which according to Darwin were the raw material of evolution. Sir Francis Galton (Darwin's cousin) showed that most measurable characteristics of organisms follow a frequency distribution known as the *Gaussian* or *Normal* distribution; and in order to detect relationships between characteristics he developed the use of correlation coefficients. Galton was particularly interested in human inheritance, and he studied a number of continuous variables in man, such as height, susceptibility to disease, and intelligence. Finally in 1897 he put forward a theory of blending inheritance, according to which the inheritance of each individual is half determined by each of his two parents, a quarter by each of his four grandparents, and so on. Galton's ideas were eagerly seized upon by some of the younger Darwinians, who saw in them a possibility of providing a mathematical basis for the Darwinian theory of Natural Selection. Out of their efforts grew the science of *biometrics*, the application of measurement and statistical analysis to the study of variation in living things. Biometrics has since become one of the main pillars of twentieth-century biology.

In their belief that natural selection (that is, the 'weeding out' of the unfit) operated upon the small, continuous variations which are always present in populations of living organisms, the Galtonians were of course following Darwin. Yet some years before Galton put forward his theory of heredity Darwin's faith in the principle of natural selection had been severely shaken. In 1867 the *North British Review* carried an article which so disturbed him that it led him to make considerable changes in all the later editions of the *Origin*. The article was by Fleeming Jenkin, a Scots professor of engineering, who argued that if a new characteristic occurred in an animal as a result of some genetic change, it would quickly become diluted in the subsequent breeding of the species until it had no further effect. Only if the variation occurred simultaneously in a majority of the organisms could it become established, but such a widespread simultaneous change would be something very different from the small, random changes postulated by Darwin. So impressed was Darwin by this argument that he almost abandoned his principle of Natural Selection and reverted to the ideas of Lamarck. This eighteenth-century evolutionist had suggested that a species acquired new characteristics by constantly striving to adapt to its surroundings, and then passed these acquired characteristics on to its offspring. Lamarckism thus implied a purposeful striving on the part of the animal, as distinct from Darwinism which made the animal a more-or-less passive victim of the environment. In order to evade the force of Fleeming Jenkin's arguments, Darwin inserted Lamarckian passages into the later editions of his book. Yet had he but known, the answer to his difficulties was already in print. In 1866 the *Proceedings of the Natural History Society of Brünn* (now Brno, Czechoslovakia) carried a paper by a little-known Augustinian monk on the hybridisation of garden peas. It was destined to revolutionise the study of heredity, and infuse new life into the Darwinian theory.

Johann Gregor Mendel was born on July 22nd 1822, in the Moravian village of Heinzendorf. As a boy he learnt fruit-growing in his father's garden, and developed a love for natural history which remained with him all his life. At the age of 21 he joined the monastery at Brünn, where he was permitted to carry out botanical experiments, and also attend courses in mathematics, physics, and zoology at the University of

Vienna. For a time he taught in the local schools, although he never succeeded in obtaining a regular teacher's licence. The reason for this, surprisingly enough, was that he failed to satisfy the examiners in natural history, although he passed those parts of the examination concerned with the physical sciences. After two unsuccessful attempts to qualify Mendel gave up trying, although he continued as a substitute teacher for some years. From 1856 onwards he began to devote more and more of his time to plant-breeding experiments, and in 1856 he read his epoch-making paper to the local natural history society.

Detailed descriptions of Mendel's experiments are given in many modern text-books, so that there is no need to repeat them here. His great achievement lay in demonstrating that hereditary characteristics are determined by unitary factors (later called *genes*), which are passed from parent to offspring in the reproductive cells. He also showed that one form of a gene may be *dominant* over another form. If a child receives, say, the gene for brown eyes (B) from his father, and the gene for blue eyes (b) from his mother, he will be a *brown*-eyed child, since B is dominant over b. Thanks to Mendel, we now know that hereditary characteristics do not blend together as Fleeming Jenkin and Galton thought, becoming increasingly diluted generation by generation. Instead, the genes controlling these characteristics are constantly being reassorted without being lost, so that a particular character may suddenly reappear after a lapse of several generations.

Mendel was an extraordinarily well-read man, and followed carefully all the developments in evolutionary theory. It is said that he bought all of Darwin's books the moment they were published. Darwin, on the other hand, had no idea of the important work being done in the monastery garden at Brünn. Mendel's paper remained virtually unnoticed in the west until 1900, by which time its author had been dead for fourteen years. Towards the end of his life Mendel became increasingly occupied with administrative matters (he was elected Abbot in 1868), to the sad detriment of his scientific work. Although among scientists he will always be remembered for his work on the hybridisation of peas, he also carried out a number of other researches, including an investigation into sunspots, and a study of the behaviour of bees.

Towards the end of the nineteenth century it was becoming clear even to the most ardent supporters of Darwin that the theory of natural selection was in grave difficulties. Attempts to produce new kinds of organisms by selecting out some particular characteristic over a number of generations had failed. Following Galton, Karl Pearson and the school of biometricians had made a careful study of the continuous variations which the Darwinians believed to be the basis of evolution, and the results seemed to show that these variations were not inherited. An alternative school of thought formed itself around William Bateson, a distinguished naturalist who had at one time been a Lamarckian. Bateson had no use whatever for correlation coefficients and frequency distribution curves: he believed that evolution occurred by sudden sharp changes in the heredity of an organism, rather than by the small continuous variations studied by the biometricians. A furious battle of intellects took place between the two schools, soon reaching an almost incredible level of spitefulness. By 1900 the two chief exponents of the biometric view, Karl Pearson and W. F. R. Weldon, had been ousted from the scientific establishment and founded their own journal (*Biometrika*) to carry the results of their experiments.

In 1900 three scientists, De Vries of Leyden, Tschermak of Vienna, and Correns of Berlin, independently rediscovered Mendel's paper of 1866. De Vries had already noticed sudden genetic changes in the American evening primrose, and had coined the word 'mutation' to describe them. Now, in the light of Mendel's experiments, the pieces of the picture began to fit together. Suppose that Darwin's natural selection acted not upon the small continuous variations of the biometricians, but upon sudden, discrete changes occurring at random in the genes. Such changes would not be diluted as previous evolutionists had supposed, but would be passed on in the manner described by Mendel. This Mutation Theory was first published by De Vries in 1901; and in England it added fuel to the already fiercely burning flames of the battle between the supporters of Bateson and the biometricians. Pearson and Weldon refused to accept the Mendelian theory, and Pearson used his very considerable influence with the editor of *Nature* to prevent Bateson's views being published. Bateson, finding himself attacked in the pages of *Biometrika* and denied the right to reply, responded by having his views privately printed and bound in a cover which was the exact replica of the cover of *Biometrika*! Both sides carried out numerous experiments to try to establish their points of view : while Bateson looked for evidence of Mendelism in the breeding of sweet peas, poultry, and rabbits, Weldon studied continuous variables in moths, mice, and poppies. For six years the battle raged until, with the death of Weldon in 1906, most of the spirit went out of the biometric attack on Mendelism.

While the arguments over heredity were going on in England, a young Austrian biologist was carrying out a series of extraordinarily ingenious experiments which were destined to involve Bateson in yet another acrimonious dispute. Paul Kammerer, working with salamanders, sea-squirts and toads, claimed to have obtained evidence in favour of a Lamarckian type of inheritance. Bateson, who had himself failed to find any evidence for Lamarckism, attacked Kammerer mercilessly. Arthur Koestler (80) points out that Bateson saw in Kammerer an imagined facial resemblance to his old enemy Pearson, and this, combined with a certain amount of straightforward jealousy, may account for the bitterness of the attack. However that may be, it is certain that in those unsettled years around the First World War a battle was being waged for the establishment of a new scientific orthodoxy based upon the combined theories of Darwin and Mendel. Such orthodoxies can tolerate no heretics. Hounded by the scientific establishment under Bateson and accused of faking one of his experiments, Kammerer finally committed suicide in 1926. His name was so effectively obliterated from the biological texts that few modern biologists had even heard of Kammerer until the publication of Koestler's brilliantly written biography in 1971.

The distinguished American embryologist Thomas Hunt Morgan was at first highly sceptical of Mendelism. In 1908 he agreed with Pearson that there was no really convincing proof that the Mendelian theory applied to any living organism. However, the following year he began searching for a suitable animal species with which to carry out breeding experiments. After trying out aphids, rats, mice, and pigeons he finally settled upon the little fruit-fly *Drosophila*, whose Latin name means 'lover of dew'. This small creature is found in refuse dumps all over the world, and is said to be particularly fond of wineries, being attracted by the smell of fermentation! Morgan soon found that *Drosophila* was an almost ideal animal for genetic experiments. The little flies can be kept quite easily in milk bottles, feeding upon such delights as mashed bananas, corn-meal, and black treacle. Under favourable conditions their life-cycle is completed in ten days, making it possible to follow the transmission of inherited characteristics through many generations of flies in only a few months' work. Even more important, the cell nuclei of *Drosophila* contain four pairs of large *chromosomes*, which are easily visible under the microscope in preparations made from the salivary glands of the insect. These thread-like chromosomes later came to play a central role in the modern theory of genetics.

In April 1910 Morgan discovered his first mutant: a fruit-fly with *white eyes* (the eyes of a normal *Drosophila* are red). By the end of the same year he had no less than forty mutant forms of the insect: flies with grey wings, yellow wings, or no wings at all; flies with yellow, black, or ebony bodies; eyeless flies, hairless flies, and so on. By repeatedly crossing the various types with each other he was able to show that the genetic characteristics fall into certain distinct groups, the characteristics within each group tending to remain together during the crossing experiments. By 1914 it was clear that all the characteristics of *Drosophila* fall into exactly four such linkage groups, corresponding to the four pairs of chromosomes seen by the microscopists. Now at last, almost 50 years after the publication of Mendel's original paper, a physical basis for inheritance was beginning to become clear. Morgan took the bold step of postulating that Mendel's 'hereditary factors' are actual material structures situated on the chromosome threads within the cell nucleus. One of his pupils, A. H. Sturtevant, further suggested that these factors or genes were arranged along the chromosome in straight lines, like the beads on a string. By means of careful breeding experiments it even became possible to construct 'gene maps' showing the relative positions of the various genes along the chromosomes. Although no one had actually seen a gene, microscopic observations of the behaviour of the chromosomes tied in so well with the results of the breeding experiments that it was hardly possible to doubt the validity of the gene theory. From now on, the invisible gene would become as fundamental to the thinking of every biologist as the equally invisible atoms and molecules were to the thinking of the chemists and the physicists.

Lancelot Hogben has put forward the view that in two hundred years from now Morgan's name will be mentioned more often than Darwin's. Certainly Morgan's achievements were immense. The little fruit-fly which he introduced to the genetics laboratory has become part of the stock-in-trade of the geneticist, and millions of the creatures are now sold every year to laboratories all over the world. Morgan's great breakthrough—the discovery of the link between chromosomes and genes—came when he was over forty years old, and he devoted the remainder of his long life to the investigation of the genetics of *Drosophila*. He gathered around him a dynamic team of fellow experimenters, including his wife Lilian and his students H. J. Muller, A. H. Sturtevant, and C. B. Bridges: it has been said that the Morgan laboratory probably did more than anything else to establish the present-day approach to science as a team activity rather than an individualistic one.

By 1930, the battle between rival schools was over. Darwinism, allied with the genetics of Mendel and Morgan, passed into the text-books as the only permitted diet for all students of the biological sciences. Biometrics, which had once seemed antagonistic to this neo-Darwinian synthesis, was quietly assimilated into it through the work of J. B. S. Haldane and Sir Ronald Fisher. Lamarckism, once the chief rival to Darwinism, was ridiculed so successfully that few young biologists dared allow themselves to be seen taking an interest in Lamarckian experiments. To this day Kammerer's experiments have never been repeated, although even his strongest opponents could not claim that he faked all of them. It seems that in science as in religion, once a belief-system has been established as a result of a period of in-fighting, there is a powerful reluctance to even think about anything which might conflict with the system. To illustrate the strength of this feeling, Koestler cites remarks by two eminent biologists: the geneticist C. D. Darlington, who referred to the Lamarckian theory as 'a disreputable and ancient superstition', and the embryologist Sir Gavin de Beer, who called 'attempts to impugn' Darwin's teaching an 'exhibition of ignorance and effrontery' (80, p. 32). Thus, seventy years after the first printing of *The Origin of Species*, Darwinism became enshrined as the biological orthodoxy of the twentieth century.

2. Life in the Test-tube

Historically, there have always been two diametrically opposed approaches to the problem of the nature of life: they are usually known as *mechanism* and *vitalism*. The mechanist believes that all living things are completely explicable in terms of the laws of physics and chemistry. To him, organisms are nothing more than highly complex machines. Of course, he would not deny that we are a very long way from actually achieving a complete explanation of the working of these machines in physico-chemical terms; nevertheless, he holds that such an explanation is possible in principle, and he believes that a truly scientific biology cannot operate on any other assumption. The vitalist, on the other hand, denies the possibility of a fully mechanical explanation of living organisms. He believes that there is something distinctive about living matter which places it in a class above the level of the mere machine, no matter how complex the machine may be. To this distinctive 'something' vitalists down the ages have given a variety of names: *entelechy, élan vital, vis essentialis, vital force*. In the field of medicine vitalistic ideas led to the assumption that living tissue contains an innate healing power, the *vis medicatrix naturae*, and the duty of the physician was not so much to heal the patient as to provide the right conditions for this mysterious force to operate.

As with so much of our modern thinking, the concepts inherent in both mechanism and vitalism can be traced back to the ancient Greeks. The term '*entelechy*', used by the later vitalists, is derived from Aristotle, who found it necessary to postulate an extra-physical organising principle to explain the facts of development, or embryology as we would call it today. Just as the statue 'exists' in the mind of the sculptor before it is realised in stone, so Aristotle believed the structure of the living organism to exist in some ideal form prior to its actual development. He also suggested that three kinds of 'soul' occur in living organisms : plants possess only the lowest kind, the 'nutritive' soul, but animals have in addition the 'sensitive' soul, which enables them to feel and move. Man alone possesses the third kind of soul, the 'reasoning soul' (*nous*), which is divine and confers on him the power of intellectual activity. To Aristotle the soul is the organising principle, or *entelechy*, of the body, and the possession of a soul is what distinguishes the living from the non-living.

For many hundreds of years soul-theories such as Aristotle's were perpetuated through the great religions of mankind. However, they were not without their difficulties, of which the most important was the problem of the *origin* of the soul. Everyone could see where the physical body came from; but how did it acquire a soul? Within the Christian Church the 'creationist' theologians argued that God creates a fresh soul out of nothing at the conception of each human individual, while their opponents, the 'traducianists', maintained that the soul is transmitted from parents to children in the act of inter-course. Such was the domination of thought by religion during the Middle Ages that few people stopped to ask themselves whether, in fact, the soul existed at all. The first resurgence of the mechanistic view began with the French philosopher René Descartes (1596-1650), who is said to have discovered the principles of coordinate geometry while lying in bed in the morning. In his *Tractatus de homine*, published in 1662 but written thirty years earlier, Descartes formulated a theory of animals and men as machines. He described a theoretical model of a mechanical man, constructed on the same principles as the machines of his time : artificial fountains, mills, and clocks, which 'though made by man, yet have the power of moving in various ways' (70, p. 88). According to Descartes, muscles were supposed to move through being inflated with a fluid which was sent out from the brain and travelled down the nerves!

At about the same time as Descartes was constructing his mechanistic theories of life another distinguished scientist, Galileo, was suffering humiliation at the hands of the Church for daring to suggest that the earth goes round the sun. It is not surprising, therefore, that Descartes decided to play safe and stop short of a full-blooded mechanistic theory. While treating all other animals as entirely mechanical, he preserved the uniqueness of man by allowing him to retain his immortal soul. According to Descartes the human body is as much a machine as are the bodies of the animals; but it differs from them in that it is directed by a soul implanted by God. Unlike the animals, man possesses the gift of free-will, which is a property of the soul, and he is therefore responsible for his actions in a way which makes him qualitatively different from any animal. This theory, ridiculed by one twentieth-century philosopher as the 'ghost-in-the-machine' theory (115), had at least the merit of providing some sort of a basis for ethics, which is more than can be said for the theories of the later mechanists.

Following the lead given by Descartes, a number of eighteenth-century thinkers began to adopt a mechanistic approach to life. Prominent among these was a French physician, the Chevalier Julien de la Mettrie, whose denial of the existence of the human soul provoked a great deal of hostility among his contemporaries. Accused of heresy, La Mettrie was forced to flee to Holland, where his book *L'homme machine* was published anonymously in 1748. A year later an anonymous pamphlet attacking La Mettrie's views appeared in London, bearing the title *Man Not a Machine*. Cynical rumour suggested that it had been written by La Mettrie himself, presumably in a fit of remorse! However that may be, La Mettrie's work became immensely influential, inspiring the writings of a whole generation of mechanists, particularly the French philosophers C. A. Helvetius (1715-1771) and P. H. T. d'Holbach (1723-1789). The aggressive atheism of men such as these played an important part in stimulating the anti-religious feeling which was one of the features of the French Revolution.

From the advanced standpoint of the twentieth century it is easy to see that the eighteenth-century attempts to construct a mechanistic theory of life were wildly premature. Living organisms are clearly *not* machines in the same sense that an eighteenth-century clock is a machine; and we now know that no plausible mechanistic theory could have been constructed prior to the development of organic chemistry in the nineteenth century and biochemistry in the twentieth. If living organisms are to be described as machines at all, the components of those machines must be atoms and molecules, not cog wheels and escapement mechanisms. In fact, the very crudity of the theories of Descartes and his successors provoked a vitalist backlash, for it was possible to point to innumerable biological facts which the mechanists had simply ignored. It is not surprising, therefore, to find that most of the great biologists of the eighteenth century were vitalists. Among them we find Albrecht von Haller (1708-1777), the Swiss anatomist, physiologist, botanist, and medical historian. G. R. Taylor describes Haller as a man of 'fantastic erudition' (137, p. 84). At the age of nine he is said to have written Latin verse, studied Chaldean, and compiled a Greek and Hebrew dictionary. Among his 49 most important books are listed two encyclopedias, four treatises on anatomy, twelve on physiology, seven on botany, five on bibliography, two theological works, four historical novels, and a book of poems. Whatever else may be said about the vitalists, it cannot be denied that they had among their ranks some of the finest intellects of their day.

Towards the end of the eighteenth century vitalism often included an assertion that chemical substances extracted from living organisms could never be made in the laboratory, since they required the operation of the 'vital force' for their formation. One of the supporters of this view was the great Swedish chemist Jöns Jakob Berzelius (1779-1848), the originator of our modern system of chemical symbolism and the first man to extract lactic acid from muscle tissue. 'In living nature,' wrote Berzelius, 'the elements seem to obey laws quite different from those in inorganic nature.' This belief was rudely shattered in 1828 when Friedrich Wöhler, a former pupil of Berzelius, succeeded in making an organic substance, urea, from an inorganic substance, ammonium cyanate.* It soon became clear that there are no essential differences between organic and inorganic substances, and by 1860 Kekulé was able to define organic chemistry as simply 'the study of carbon compounds'. Retreating to their second line of defence the vitalists began

---

* Some recent historians have challenged the generally accepted view of this discovery as a serious blow to vitalism. Cf. Coleman, W.: *Biology in the Nineteenth Century*. Wiley & Sons, 1971, pp. 146-7.

to insist that it is not the organic compounds themselves but the *method by which they are made inside the living body* which must remain forever mysterious. Thus, Berzelius wrote: 'The highest knowledge which we can attain is the knowledge of the nature of the products, whilst we for ever are excluded from the possibility of explaining how they are produced' (70, p. 69). Unhappily for the vitalists, this position also turned out to be untenable.

Baron Justus von Liebig (1803-1873), known to every schoolboy as the inventor of the Liebig condenser, probably did more than anyone else to open up the study of the chemical processes occurring within living organisms. By careful quantitative experiments he was able to show that the heat produced by the bodies of animals is derived from the food they eat, and he introduced the modern classification of foodstuffs into proteins, fats, and carbohydrates. When Liebig's book *Animal Chemistry* was published in America in 1845 it aroused considerable disquiet because of its mechanistic tone. Charles Caldwell, professor of natural sciences at Philadelphia University, wrote: 'When the chemist declares that the same laws which direct the crystallisation of spars, nitre and Glauber's salts, direct also the *crystallisation* of man, he must pardon me if I neither understand him, nor believe him' (137, p. 263). Notwithstanding such protests, the disciples of Liebig continued to press forward with their attack on the chemistry of life throughout the second half of the nineteenth century, making Germany famous for her schools of organic and biological chemistry. In 1862 Ernst Hoppé-Seyler obtained the first pure crystalline sample of haemoglobin, the red colouring matter of blood, and demonstrated its ability to combine reversibly with oxygen. Emil Fischer (1852-1919), one of the greatest chemists of all time, later determined the structural formulae of many of the carbohydrates and also of the group of substances known as *purines* (which includes the caffeine found in tea and coffee). For his extensive work in these fields Fischer was awarded a Nobel Prize in 1902. He also proved that protein molecules are composed of long chains of amino-acid units, thereby laying the foundation of much of the biochemistry of the twentieth century.

In 1897 there occurred one of those accidental events which

occasionally mark a turning point in the history of science. It had been known for centuries that yeast is capable of turning sugar into alcohol and carbon dioxide (the process of fermentation), and Louis Pasteur had proved that this is an activity of the live yeast cells, which feed upon the sugar as they grow and multiply. Eduard Buchner (1860-1917), together with his brother Hans and a laboratory assistant, were trying to prepare a cell-free extract of yeast for medical use. They ground up the yeast with sand in order to break open the cells, added kieselguhr, and squeezed the mixture through a press. The problem then arose of how to preserve the resulting brown, sticky liquid. Ordinary antiseptics could not be added, as these were far too poisonous for human consumption. The laboratory assistant, remembering how sugar is used in jam-making, suggested adding a large quantity of sugar to the mixture. This was done, and, to everyone's astonishment, the brown extract began at once to convert the sugar into alcohol. For the first time in the history of science a biochemical substance had been found to bring about the same reaction *outside* the cell as it did in the intact living organism. Vitalism had received yet another severe blow.

By the end of the nineteenth century those who believed that life was more than a mere 'fortuitous concourse of atoms' were in full retreat. The organic chemists had proved conclusively that the materials found inside living cells differed from other substances only in their degree of complexity; Buchner had shown that the processes of life could be made to occur in the test-tube; and Darwin had suggested how highly complex organisms could have arisen through the operation of Natural Selection on chance variations. There seemed to be nothing much left for a 'vital force' to do. However, vitalism was not quite dead. It reared its head for a final fling in the field of embryology, perhaps the most difficult of all the biological sciences. Hans Driesch, a young German biologist, divided a sea urchin's egg into two halves at an early stage of its development and found that he obtained two *complete* animals. Astonished at this, Driesch began to wonder how any kind of mechanistic theory could possibly account for such a strange fact. What kind of machine could be cut into pieces, each one of which could restore the whole machine again? He set out to try further mutilations on the developing eggs, to see how much interference the developing 'machine' could take without spoiling the final product. He tried separating the individual cells when the egg was at the four-cell stage and found that 'one of the first *four* blastomeres is also capable of performing a whole organogenesis, and three of the first four blastomeres together result in an absolutely perfect organism' (36). By raising the temperature or diluting the sea-water he was able to alter fundamentally the cleavage stages of the developing egg, but still obtained a typical larva (known to the biologist as a *pluteus*). He tried pressing the eggs of the sea urchin between glass plates so as to prevent the normal formation of two rings of four cells each; he thereby obtained a single flat plate of eight cells, quite unlike the normal two-ring structure. 'But the next cell division occurred at right angles to the former ones, and a 16-cell stage, of two plates of eight cells each, one above the other, was the result.' It seemed as though some intelligent force was trying to counteract the effects of the experimenter's interference.

Driesch found the results of his experiments 'uncanny', and they caused considerable excitement throughout the biological world. For a time it looked as though vitalism would make a dramatic come-back, for it seemed impossible to imagine any kind of mechanical structure which would continue to yield the same product in the face of such drastic mutilation. Driesch was able to prove that the development of each individual cell depends upon its position in relation to the whole organism; somehow it 'knows' which of its many potentialities are needed in that particular situation in order to produce a perfect organism, and it responds accordingly. Driesch reintroduced Aristotle's term *entelechy* for the mysterious something which he believed directed the overall development of the embryo. Towards the end of his life his writings became increasingly philosophical, and he devoted a great deal of his time to parapsychology.

In 1924 the German embryologists Hans Spemann and Otto Mangold carried out an experiment which threw a great deal of light upon the mysterious properties of developing embryos. Taking a small piece of tissue from the dorsal lip of one embryo, they transplanted it into the ventral side of another embryo which was in the *gastrula* stage. At this stage the embryo is in the form of a hollow cup-shaped structure, the walls of the 'cup' consisting of a double layer of cells. The result of the operation was that the tissue in the vicinity of the transplant began to fold inwards to form a second nerve tube. When they subsequently dissected the embryo, the experimenters found that other tissues had formed around the transplanted piece, amounting in some cases to an almost complete secondary embryo. It thus became clear that the transplanted piece of tissue was somehow acting as an *organiser*; that is, it was *inducing* the neighbouring tissues to develop in a particular way. Spemann himself tended to take an almost vitalistic attitude towards his discoveries, but it was not long before his pupils showed that the action of 'organiser' tissues could be accounted for without invoking any vital forces. In 1932 J. Holtfreter and others demonstrated that the organiser did not even have to be alive to carry out its work : pieces of dead tissue could produce very similar effects.

These discoveries seemed to show that it *is* possible to explain embryonic development in physico-chemical terms, without resorting to the mystical ideas of Driesch. Clearly, the development of a particular patch of cells into nerve, muscle, bone, or other kinds of tissue depends upon some sort of influence emanating from the neighbouring tissues, and biologists naturally assumed that this influence must be chemical in nature. In view of the tremendous triumphs of biochemistry in other fields it is rather surprising to record that so far the attempt to isolate specific chemical agents from organisers has met with very little success. Indeed, Waddington and his co-workers put the cat among the pigeons by demonstrating that a variety of chemical substances which do not occur in the normal embryo at all are nevertheless capable of acting as inducers or organisers when they are introduced into it (150). One such substance is the well-known dye *methylene blue*, which many generations of microscopists have used for staining their specimens. Facts such as these are very puzzling, and there is no doubt that we are still a very long way from being able to give a fully mechanistic explanation of the development of embryos. Nevertheless, few present-day biologists doubt that such a complete explanation will one day be achieved. Driesch's vitalism, which caused such a stir at the beginning of the century, is now largely forgotten, and it is likely that the majority of young biologists have never even heard his name. To all intents and purposes, twentieth-century biology is completely mechanistic.

Undoubtedly the greatest triumph of the mechanistic approach to life is displayed in the meteoric rise to power of the molecular biologists, those scientists who probe the nature of the chemical reactions occurring in the innermost parts of living cells. Their science, which hardly existed before the Second World War, now dominates the pages of scientific journals such as *Nature*, ousting even the nuclear physicists from their position in the forefront of public interest. Already there is a considerable amount of anxious discussion going on about the consequences of the new knowledge. Terms such as 'genetic engineering' are being bandied about, and we are warned that it will not be long before the researchers are able to alter the genetic properties of animals and plants at will, perhaps even creating totally new types in the test-tube. Writers such as Gordon Rattray Taylor (136) have warned us of the possible consequences to mankind if this new-found knowledge is carelessly employed, and some American scientists have proposed a world wide prohibition of certain types of experimentation.

To understand the growth of this extraordinary subject, we must return to the early part of the century. By the end of the First World War Morgan and his team had established that the genes—the carriers of heredity—are actual material structures situated along the thread-like chromosomes inside the cell nucleus. The genes, therefore, must be composed of some chemical substance capable of forming a blue-print, or a kind of coded message, which can direct the development of the organism. Since living organisms are extremely complicated structures it follows that the instructions for their formation must be encoded in a chemical substance of some complexity. For many years the geneticists believed that the code existed in the form of protein molecules, since proteins are among the most complex constituents of living cells. Then in 1928 an English bacteriologist, Fred Griffith, carried out an experiment which turned out to be of far-reaching importance.

Griffith's research was concerned with the killer-disease pneumonia, which is caused by a spherical bacterium known as the *pneumococcus*. The deadliness of the pneumococcus is known to be due to a sticky coat, or capsule, on the outside of the organism which prevents the natural defence mechanisms of the body from attacking it. However, mutant forms of pneumococci had been discovered which lacked the ability to grow a protective coat: these forms, therefore, were quite harmless. One day Griffith injected into the bodies of his laboratory mice a curious mixture consisting of: (a) live, mutant pneumococci without coats, and therefore non-lethal, and (b) normal pneumococci which possessed coats, but which had been killed by heating. Neither of the two components of this mixture ought to have produced any noticeable effect on the animals, but Griffith found, to everyone's surprise, that the mice developed severe pneumonia and died. Somehow, the ability to grow a protective coat had been transferred from the dead, normal pneumococci to the live, mutant ones. It was as if the ability to grow a tail had been transferred from, say, dead rats to live guinea-pigs! Later it was shown that the transference of genetic abilities from one kind of bacterium to another could be brought about even in a test-tube.

In 1944 after ten years of difficult research using the most advanced biochemical techniques available, O. T. Avery, C. M. MacLeod and M. McCarthy at the Rockefeller Institute in New York succeeded in isolating the substance which carried the instructions for capsule-making from one pneumococcus to the other. It turned out to be a chemical known as *deoxyribonucleic acid*, or DNA for short. It had been known to chemists ever since 1862, when F. Miescher had extracted it from sperm cells, but no one had considered it to be of any importance. Now it became clear that the key to heredity lay not in the proteins, but in the nucleic acids, particularly DNA and its partner, RNA (*ribonucleic acid*). Careful measurements of the amounts of DNA in the cell nuclei of different species showed that each species of animal and plant carries its own fixed quantity of this substance. Furthermore the sex cells, which were known to have half the number of chromosomes contained in the ordinary body cells, also had half the amount of

DNA. Both in Britain and America, teams of physicists, crystallographers, and biochemists set to work to determine the exact chemical structure of this substance, which seemed to hold the key to the very nature of life itself.

In 1952 Maurice Wilkins and a team of researchers at King's College, London, investigated the structure of the DNA molecule by the methods of X-ray crystallography, and showed that the DNA samples from different sources all produced similar diffraction patterns. Working from the results of the X-ray analysis, and taking into account certain theoretical considerations, Francis Crick and James Watson put forward the now famous 'double helix' model for the structure of the DNA molecule in 1953. Whereas the work of most scientists is accepted only after a period of dispute and criticism, the Crick-Watson theory fitted all the known facts so beautifully that it was accepted almost immediately and hailed as one of the most important discoveries of the twentieth century. The double helix model provided the stimulus which led to the almost incredibly rapid expansion of molecular biology over the following twenty years. In 1962 Crick, Watson, and Wilkins received a well-earned Nobel Prize for their efforts.

The way in which DNA controls the chemical reactions taking place inside the living cells is a highly complicated business, and we shall not attempt to describe it in detail. Technical accounts are given in many advanced text-books, and for the general reader there is an excellent description by Taylor (137, pp. 327-344). Here we are principally concerned with the implications of these discoveries for our view of the nature of life, and for their impact on the vitalist-mechanist controversy; for there is no doubt that in the twentieth century the greatest challenge to any kind of vitalist or supernaturalist view of life comes not so much from Darwinism as from molecular biology. Indeed, Sir Francis Crick is reputed to have said that many scientists take up molecular biology out of a desire to refute vitalism! We must therefore examine the Crick-Watson discovery a little more closely, in order to understand why it is considered to provide strong support for a mechanistic interpretation of life.

Perhaps the most startling feature of the double helix model is that it shows how a mere molecule can be *self-reproducing*.

Reproduction was always considered to be one of the essential properties of living cells, not capable of imitation by any man-made machine. Indeed, it was very difficult to imagine how a machine, however complex, could construct exact copies of itself. Crick and Watson dispelled much of the mystery by showing how the ordinary known laws of chemical attraction could account for the replication of DNA molecules. Each strand of the double helix contains a sequence of four bases: adenine, cytosine, guanine, and thymine, or A, C, G, and T for short. These are arranged in a complicated pattern which forms the genetic code. The bases can, in fact, be regarded as the letters of a four-letter alphabet, and the 'words' they form provide the instructions for the cell's activities. Opposite each base on one strand there is a corresponding base on the other strand, and it is found that A is always paired with T, while C is always paired with G. This specific pairing is a consequence of the shapes of the molecules and the nature of the hydrogen bonds which hold them together. Now suppose the two strands are pulled apart: each strand can form a replica of its missing partner by attracting to itself the appropriate bases from the surrounding medium. Since A and T attract each other, and so do G and C, it is not difficult to see that the result of this process will be *two* molecules of DNA, whereas initially we had only one (see figure 1). In this way the genetic code is copied and passed on from one generation to another.

From the above greatly simplified account, it will be clear to the reader that it *is* possible to imagine a process whereby complex molecules can replicate, without invoking anything beyond the ordinary laws of chemistry. Experimental support for the theory came in 1957 when Arthur Kornberg of Washington University succeeded in demonstrating DNA replication in the test-tube. Surrounded by the right kind of 'soup' containing the four nucleotides, the enzyme DNA-polymerase, and the energy-providing substance adenosine triphosphate (ATP), the DNA molecules were able to construct

Fig. 1: A self-copying DNA molecule. When separated into two complementary strands, each strand can make a copy of its missing partner by attaching to itself the appropriate nucleotides. This leads to two identical copies of the original molecule.

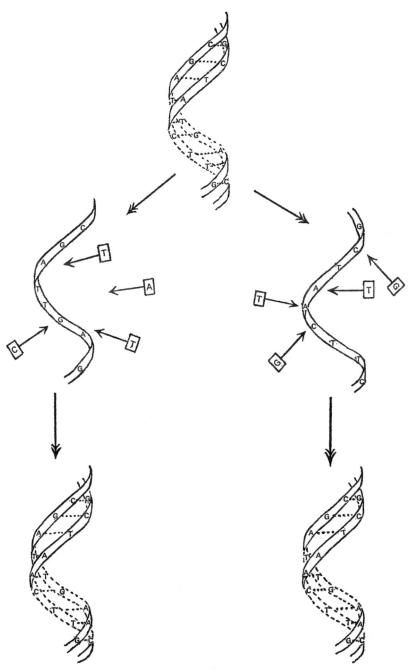

Fig. 1

exact replicas of themselves in the total absence of living cells. Even more startling were the experiments reported by H. Fraenkel-Conrat and R. C. Williams in 1955. These workers succeeded in taking a virus to pieces and reassembling it again in the test-tube. The virus in question was TMV, the tobacco-mosaic virus, which infects the leaves of tobacco plants. Chemical analysis showed it to consist of a nucleic acid (RNA) and protein. By careful treatment with mild alkalis and detergent the two components were separated, and it was shown that neither of them was capable of infecting a tobacco plant on its own. Fraenkel-Conrat then mixed the two separated components together and found, rather to his surprise, that the resulting mixture was highly infectious. If we consider viruses to be 'alive', then he had succeeded in dismantling a living creature and restoring it to life again, a feat previously attributed only to the semi-legendary St Nicholas of Myra!

The experiments of Fraenkel-Conrat and his collaborators triggered off an exceptional amount of excitement in the popular press. SCIENTISTS CREATE LIFE IN A TEST-TUBE, screamed the headlines. This was, of course, something of an exaggeration. However, ten years later Sol Spiegelman of the University of Illinois carried the work a stage further by actually putting together the RNA message which forms the core of the virus. From this he synthesised a virus which does not occur in nature. The artificial virus was able to multiply in exactly the same manner as a natural one, and appeared to be indistinguishable from the 'real thing'. Although no one has yet succeeded in putting together a living cell (viruses are much smaller than cells), it certainly looks as though it is only a matter of time before this final miracle is achieved. In the fields of nuclear energy and space travel man has already arrogated to himself some of the powers of the gods; it seems not unlikely that the next to be seized will be the power to create life out of non-life.

As a result of the intensive efforts of the molecular biologists we now know an enormous amount about the chemical processes occurring inside living cells. As we have explained, the coded message or 'blue-print' is carried by the DNA molecules which form the genes. These genes remain within the cell nucleus, but their message is copied on to molecules of RNA (known as 'messenger' RNA), and then transported outside the nucleus into the cell cytoplasm where it arrives at the protein-making factories, the *ribosomes*. Here the code is read and translated into the sequences of amino-acids which make up the proteins, the basic structural materials of all living cells. The whole procedure is controlled by a complex series of feed-back devices, so that the different parts of the message do not act in isolation from one another, but form a harmonious whole. For example, some genes do not themselves determine the structure of proteins, but instead act as controllers, causing other genes to be switched on or off according to the needs of the cell. Thus the apparently purposive way in which cells adjust to varying circumstances, which so impressed Driesch and others, is now attributed to the interlocking of chemical processes which occurs within the cell. Jacques Monod, who has carried out a great deal of brilliant work on this aspect of the story, likes to refer to the study of these interlocking processes as 'molecular cybernetics'.

We have come a long way from the vitalist-mechanist controversies of the seventeenth and eighteenth centuries. The verdict of modern science would seem to be inescapable : living things are nothing more than highly complex mechanisms. Throughout all the investigations carried out in the fields of genetics, biochemistry and molecular biology over the past fifty years nothing whatever has emerged which required the hypothesis of a 'vital force'. On the contrary, as the frontiers are pushed back, properties which were once thought to be characteristic of life are shown to be fully explicable in physical and chemical terms, and may even be demonstrated with non-living materials in the test-tube. The ability to reproduce has been shown to be a property of certain complex chemical substances such as DNA; the purposive or 'teleological' nature of organisms which so impressed the vitalists can apparently be explained in terms of the cybernetic concepts of feed-back and homeostasis, operating not only in the organism as a whole but at the molecular level within each individual cell. The *homme machine* of Descartes and La Mettrie operated on the simple mechanical principles of the seventeenth and eighteenth centuries : our present-day models are far more sophisticated, depending upon the shapes, sizes, and chemical interactions of giant molecules. Nevertheless the underlying philosophy of life is the same: modern biology is entirely mechanistic in all its thoughts, words, and deeds.

Yet there remains one aspect which we have not considered. By introspection we are aware of ourselves, not as mere machines but as conscious, thinking beings with hopes and fears, longings and strivings. Furthermore (though this may be an illusion) we have the impression that we are able to change the future to some extent through the exercise of free-will. The vitalist, compelled to abandon one position after another, is still entitled to ask his mechanist opponent: 'How do you explain the *mind* of man?' Is it possible to conceive of a machine which has the property of *curiosity*; a machine which is capable of wondering about itself and the universe; a machine which possesses both the ability and the incentive to carry out experiments in molecular biology? These questions lie within the fields of psychology and philosophy rather than biology, and will form the subject matter of our next chapter.

3. Exile of the Soul

'Perhaps this is the most important book ever written,' wrote the enthusiastic reviewer of the *New York Herald Tribune*, 'one stands for an instant blinded with a great hope.' The book which aroused such intense religious fervour was J. B. Watson's *Behaviourism*, first published by the University of Chicago Press in 1924 and since revised and reprinted many times (155). In this work Watson set out to demolish, once and for all, the concept of man as a conscious, thinking being possessed of freedom of choice, and replace it with the image of the machine-robot, responding mechanically to all the stimuli it receives. The scientific behaviourist, according to Watson, must drop from his vocabulary 'all subjective terms such as sensation, perception, image, desire, purpose, and even thinking and emotion as they were subjectively defined'. He must confine his activities to the observation of behaviour, all of which must be made to conform to the pattern of stimulus and response. The ultimate aim of the behaviourist is to learn so much about the conditioning of human and animal responses that eventually he will be able to 'control man's reactions as physical scientists ... control and manipulate other natural phenomena'. At least a part of Watson's dream has been horribly fulfilled in the brain-washing techniques of the prison camps; and without doubt there is more still to come.

The word *psychology* literally means 'the study of the soul'. In the previous chapter we have described how the soul theory of man, handed down through the centuries of religion, was incorporated into the dualistic theory of Descartes, and thus came to achieve a certain measure of philosophical respectability. While it seemed fairly obvious that the bodies of men were largely mechanical, it seemed equally obvious that some of the phenomena which they observed by looking into their own minds could not be attributed to any conceivable kind of machine. How could a machine be aware of its own existence?

How could consciousness, will and emotion be associated with mere configurations of atoms? The *mental* and the *material* seemed to be totally different in kind. The only common-sense way of describing the situation was by some kind of dualist theory: an immaterial 'soul' or 'mind' interacting with a material, machine-like body. Then, following the triumphs of Darwinism in the mid-nineteenth century, religion gradually began to lose favour among intellectuals, who became increasingly uncomfortable over the use of words with a semi-religious connotation, such as 'soul', 'spirit', and 'ghost'. Psychology therefore came to be regarded as the science of the *mind*, a term which sounded a little more scientific than *soul*, although in practice it often meant much the same thing. Yet even *mind* seemed somehow too abstract, too unobservable, and in 1892 William James started off his *Briefer Course* in psychology by defining his subject as 'the description and explanation of states of consciousness as such' (68). By 'states of consciousness', explained James, are meant such things as sensations, desires, emotions, cognitions, reasonings, decisions, volitions and the like. No normal human being could deny the reality of such phenomena, since we all have direct awareness of them in ourselves. The chief instrument of the psychologist was introspection: a person would be given a particular task to perform, such as carrying out a calculation, and would then be asked to describe what had gone through his mind while he was doing it. 'Introspective observation,' wrote James in his *Principles of Psychology*, 'is what we have to rely on first and foremost and always. The word introspection means ... looking into our own minds and reporting what we there discover. Every one agrees that we there discover states of consciousness. So far as I know, the existence of such states has never been doubted by any critic, however sceptical he may have been.' The book in which these words occur was published in 1890: fourteen years later James himself was to describe consciousness as 'the name of a non-entity ... a mere echo, the faint rumour left behind by the disappearing "soul" upon the air of philosophy' (11, p. 187).

Even before the emergence of behaviourism as a distinct school of psychology, there was a marked increase of scepticism towards anything which could not be weighed, measured or confined to a test-tube. The first psychological laboratory was established at Leipzig in 1897 under the directorship of Wilhelm Wundt (1832-1920), who was one of the first psychologists to argue against the reality of the soul. He was convinced that our awareness of a 'self' or 'ego' is nothing more than the sum total of our various bodily feelings and images, and that careful introspection fails to reveal anything in the nature of a soul over and above these. In his laboratory work Wundt studied such phenomena as vision, memory, attention and the emotions, carrying out careful measurements of the reaction times of subjects in various test situations. By the end of the nineteenth century pupils of Wundt had established similar laboratories in more than a dozen universities all over the USA, overwhelming the older philosophical psychology by their clean-cut experimental approach. Britain, with its academic conservatism and fondness for traditional philosophy, at first paid little attention to the new science, but the pioneer work of the British psychologist C. Lloyd Morgan on learning in dogs helped to lay the foundations for the subsequent development of animal psychology in America. Another British psychologist, Sir Charles Spearman, developed the theory of intelligence-testing and factor-analysis which was later to play a central role in the field of educational psychology. In view of the mushroom growth of experimental psychology during this period, it is staggering to find Watson later referring to 'the 30-odd barren years since the establishment of Wundt's laboratory'. Like so many of the prophets of new religions, the behaviourists often sought to further their cause by belittling the work of their predecessors.

From about 1900 onwards the animal psychologists became increasingly influential in American psychological laboratories. The most prominent of them was Edward Lee Thorndike (1874-1949), who had been a pupil of James at Harvard and who later became professor at Columbia University. Thorndike initiated systematic research into the behaviour of fish, chickens, cats, dogs and monkeys, and is famous for having discovered the principle of the conditioned reflex (he called it 'the law of effect') independently of Pavlov. Among his best known experiments are those in which he placed a hungry cat inside a puzzle box, from which the animal could escape only by pulling a string or turning a door button. Food outside the box provided the incentive to escape. The behaviour of the animal was carefully watched, and the time taken to achieve success was recorded. By repeating the experiment over and over again the animal's progress could be charted as a 'leaning curve'. Such experiments are of course *behaviouristic*, in that what is being observed is the response of the animal to a contrived situation; nevertheless the early animal psychologists were very far from being behaviourists in the Watsonian sense. They did not deny the existence of consciousness in either man or animals, and Thorndike repeatedly used words such as 'pleasure', 'satisfaction' and 'discomfort' in referring to his laboratory animals, a failing for which he was later roundly rebuked by Watson. Margaret Floy Washburn in her book *The Animal Mind* (1908) argued that it is possible to infer the existence of consciousness in animals from their behaviour, and that animal experiments could thus legitimately be used to throw some light on human psychology.

John Broadus Watson (1878-1958), the founder of Behaviourism, was born on a farm near Greenville, South Carolina. His parents, who were very religious, originally intended that he should enter the ministry, but the young Watson seems to have revolted against all forms of authority from quite an early age. He was constantly involved in fights, and was twice arrested by the police, once for using firearms within the city boundaries. His teachers described him as lazy, argumentative and insubordinate; nevertheless, he managed to achieve an MA at Furman University by the age of 21. His interest in philosophy led him to undertake a course of postgraduate study under John Dewey at the University of Chicago, but he found Dewey 'incomprehensible' and changed to psychology instead. After obtaining his doctorate in 1903 he joined the teaching staff of the university, where he established one of the earliest of the animal psychology laboratories. In 1908 he obtained a professorship at Johns Hopkins University, and in 1912 he launched the behaviourist revolution in a series of public lectures at Columbia University, following this up with an article in the *Psychological Review* in 1913. Later he wrote several books, of which *Behaviourism* is the best known. Watson's materialistic doctrines were well adapted to the mood of the age, and he rapidly became famous, being elected to the presidency of the American Psychological Association in 1915. However, in 1920 his academic career came to a sudden end: divorce proceedings brought against him led to a nationwide scandal which resulted in his resignation from Johns Hopkins, and he never again held a full-time academic post. From 1921 onwards he became active in the field of advertising, although he still continued to write semi-popular articles and give occasional lectures on psychology. A year before his death he was presented with a citation by the APA in acknowledgement of his work, which was described as being 'one of the vital determinants of the form and substance of modern psychology'. Watson's influence has certainly been immense, although in retrospect it appears to have acted more as a strait-jacket than as a stimulus to progress.

Watson and his followers were impatient with what they regarded as the slow growth-rate of psychology. In Watson's own words, 'they saw their brother-scientists making progress in medicine, in chemistry, in physics. Every new discovery in those fields was of prime importance ... one need only mention wireless, radium, insulin, thyroxin, to verify this.' Why then, were there not similar rapid and striking advances being made in psychology? A possible answer would have pointed to the youthfulness of psychology compared with the other sciences. After all, physics, chemistry and medicine all took several hundred years to reach the point where their devotees began to reap a rapid return for their efforts. This explanation would not do for Watson. He attributed the slowness of advance in the study of psychology to its contamination by ancient superstitious, magical and religious beliefs, holding it back from becoming a true science. Chief among these was the belief in the reality of *consciousness*, which to Watson was simply an oblique way of expressing the old religious idea of a soul. To admit the existence of the soul would be to open the flood-gates to all those parental beliefs which he had revolted against in boyhood:

> Human beings do not want to class themselves with animals. They are willing to admit that they are animals but 'something else in addition'. It is this 'something else'

that causes the trouble. In this 'something else' is bound up everything that is classed as religion, the life hereafter, morals, love of children, parents, country, and the like (155, p. v).

Because of his fear of getting involved with such 'religious' aspects of man's nature, Watson set out to banish from psychology all reference to mental events. As Koestler cynically pointed out, this left the psychologist with little to study except rats: 'for the last fifty years the main preoccupation of the Behaviourist school has been the study of certain measurable aspects of the behaviour of rats' (79, p. 7). Since there are few aspects of human nature which can be investigated without relying on introspective statements by the subject, the Behaviourist 'had to choose as objects of his study animals in preference to humans, and among animals rats and pigeons in preference to monkeys or chimpanzees, because the behaviour of primates is still too complex.'

The American behaviourists drew much of their early inspiration from the Russian schools of 'reflexology', particularly that of Vladimir Bechterev (1857-1927) who studied the conditioning of motor responses. If a person's hand is placed upon a metal grid and subjected to an electric shock, the hand is automatically withdrawn. This is a simple reflex, similar in kind to the well-known 'knee-jerk' reflex tested by doctors. If the experiment is repeated a number of times, and a buzzer is sounded each time the shock occurs, the muscular response soon becomes *conditioned* to the buzzer. From now on, the subject's hand will move whenever the buzzer is sounded, even though no shock is administered. Such a reaction is known as a *motor* conditioned response, to distinguish it from the *glandular* conditioned responses studied by Bechterev's better known rival Ivan P. Pavlov (1849-1936). Pavlov's most famous experiment—the conditioning of a dog so that its mouth watered each time a bell was rung—was only one of a vast number of experiments carried out by that extraordinary man. He won the Nobel Prize in 1904 for his researches into the functioning of the digestive system, and he also investigated the nerves of the heart. It is said that some 200 collaborators came to work with Pavlov, and his laboratory at St Petersburg was enormously influential. Like Watson, Pavlov was highly contemptuous of the psychology of his day, and refused to allow himself to be called a psychologist. Nevertheless, his reflexological approach to the behaviour of man and other animals became one of the most important elements in the psychology of the western world.

Watsonian Behaviourism rose to power with almost incredible rapidity, soon becoming the dominating influence in American psychology. One of the most brilliant minds to fall under its spell was that of Clark L. Hull (1884-1952), who became a research professor at Yale in 1929. Hull was a fine mathematician as well as a psychologist. Before he became attached to the behaviourist movement he had already done outstanding work in the fields of aptitude testing and the development of statistical techniques, even inventing a machine for computing correlation coefficients. His ten-year study of hypnosis and suggestibility was marked by the publication of some 32 papers, and culminated in a book which was published in 1933. Hull seems to have become enamoured of behaviourism after reading Pavlov's work in 1929. From then onwards his major interest became the working out of a theory of human behaviour based upon the principles of conditioning. In 1940 he published, together with five of his colleagues, a work entitled *Mathematico-Deductive Theory of Rote Learning: A Study in Scientific Methodology*. Although this was praised as a great achievement, it has been described as 'seldom read, less often understood, and unproductive of research ... an idealised but relatively fruitless model of psychological theory construction' (Marx and Hillix, quoted by Schultz, 124, p. 227). Even so, Hull became the leader of an immensely influential neo-behaviourist school of thought.

Burrhus F. Skinner (b. 1904), a younger contemporary of Hull, is usually regarded as the chief spokesman of the behaviourist movement today. Whereas Hull was to a large extent a theorist, Skinner avoids theory and approaches his work in a strictly empirical manner. He is chiefly famous for the notion of 'operant' conditioning, so called to distinguish it from 'respondent' conditioning (sometimes called 'classical' or 'Pavlovian' conditioning). In a typical Skinnerian experiment a rat is placed in a special box (known as a Skinner box) containing a hinged bar coupled to a device for delivering a food pellet. Sooner or later in the course of its exploratory wanderings the rat accidentally presses the bar, and thereby receives the food 'reward'. This reinforces the bar-pressing behaviour, which henceforth becomes more and more frequent. This kind of experiment differs from Pavlov's in that the animal *operates* on the environment instead of merely waiting passively for the stimulus to occur. Skinner believes that such operant behaviour therefore provides a more relevant approach to the study of human beings, who do not normally sit around waiting to be stimulated by Pavlovian scientists!

In describing the rise of behaviourism we have referred to its twin origins in Russia and America. At first sight it may seem strange that two countries so ideologically opposed should give rise to such closely similar attitudes to the problems of life. Pavlov, although he was openly critical of the revolution and wrote dangerously angry letters of protest to Stalin, nevertheless received generous government aid for his research, and eventually became 'the pope of soviet science whose infallibility it was henceforth a punishable heresy to dispute' (Beloff, 11, p. 44). Watson, as we have seen, was hailed almost as a new messiah, who left his contemporaries 'blinded with a new hope'. Obviously both men were well attuned to the spirit of the age: they preached a gospel which the world was only too willing to hear. The late nineteenth century had witnessed an unprecedented attack on religion and morality, following the triumphant ascent of Darwinism. Materialistic philosophies were in the ascendant everywhere. The youthful protagonists of the new thought saw themselves as casting off the centuries of religious domination, breaking the shackles of the mind to usher in a brave new world of progress. Mankind was coming of age, and from henceforth would take control of its own destiny. The disillusionment of the great world wars was yet to come. Behaviourism expressed the complete rejection of the non-physical and the supernatural. It also held out the hope of absolute power, the totalitarian dream of the complete control of human life:

To a technologist, science means mastery over nature; to a behaviourist, psychology means, above all, power over people's minds. I do not think it was just coincidence that the two nations on whom behaviourism made its greatest impact were the United States and Soviet Russia. Knowledge for its own sake is alien alike to the American and the Marxist ideal. (Beloff, 11, p. 44)

While behaviouristic doctrines were gaining ground in Russia and America a very different, though no less influential, approach to the problems of the mind was taking shape in Europe. Sigmund Freud (1856-1939), the founder of psycho-analysis, was the son of a Jewish wool merchant. Born in what is now Czechoslovakia, he spent most of his life in Vienna, where he studied first at the gymnasium and later at the university. As a boy Freud was interested in Biblical history, civilisation, human culture and relationships, even military history, rather than the natural sciences. It seems to have been Darwin's theory of evolution which first awakened his interest in science, and the influence of Darwinism remained with him throughout life, as is clear from some of his later writings. After receiving his MD in 1881 Freud went into private practice as a neurologist, and soon struck up a friendship with Joseph Breuer (1842-1925), a distinguished physician who was already well known for his work on respiration and his discovery of the function of the semicircular canals. In 1895 Breuer and Freud published a joint work entitled *Studies in Hysteria*, and this is usually considered to mark the foundation of psycho-analysis.

The partnership between Freud and Breuer did not last. Within a few years of the publication of their book the two men separated and, as far as is known, their friendship was never renewed. The cause of the breach seems to have been Freud's determination to see sexuality at the root of all mental disorders. During the last decade of the nineteenth century Freud was busy developing his concept of the unconscious mind as a kind of refuse dump. According to this idea, impulses and desires which are too painful or unpleasant for the conscious mind to acknowledge are 'repressed' into the unconscious, where they continue to make their presence felt in various ways. Not only the symptoms of neurosis, but also such rela-tively commonplace phenomena as slips of the tongue and the fantasy-images of dreams are attributed to these unconscious urges in the Freudian system. Freud presented his views in two important works, *The Interpretation of Dreams* (1900) and *The Psychopathology of Everyday Life* (1904), but they were largely ignored by contemporary psychologists. His insistence on repressed sexual desires as the sole cause of neurosis later cost Freud the support of two important followers: Alfred Adler (1870-1937), who broke with him in 1911, and Carl Gustav Jung (1875-1961), who left him in 1914. Both these men subsequently developed their own schools of 'depth psychology' based on the notion of the unconscious, but without the Freudian emphasis on sexuality.

It has been said that psychiatry was conceived in the insane asylum and brought to birth on the battlefields of the First World War. That terrible and long-drawn-out conflict generated vast numbers of casualties of a type unknown to the average medical practitioner. Men who had spent month after month in the hellish conditions of the trenches, often compelled to stand by while their companions were blown to pieces, returned from the front hysterically blind, deaf, or crippled. Physical medicine was unable to cure such cases: there arose an urgent need for some kind of psychotherapy. In the years following the war Freudian psychoanalysis gradually reached the peak of its fame as a system of treatment, and from about 1920 onwards Freud began to develop it as a comprehensive theory for the understanding of all human behaviour. The mainstream academic psychologists remained aloof from Freudianism, but they had nothing to offer in its place. Soon the notions of sexual repression, the unconscious mind, the Ego and the Id were being bandied about in intellectual circles all over Europe and America. Freudian concepts came to exert a profound influence not only upon psychiatry but upon art, literature, philosophy and religion. They became part of the folk-lore of the twentieth century.

At first glance, psychoanalysis and behaviourism seem to have little or nothing in common. Certainly Freud made no attempt to avoid the mentalistic concepts so strongly condemned by Watson. On the contrary, he created a vast superstructure of theory upon them ('metapsychology', he called it), supplementing the notions of the conscious and unconscious minds with new concepts of his own: Ego, Superego, Id. Such unobservable entities were, of course, anathema to the behaviourists. Even so, the Freudian and Watsonian approaches to the problems of human behaviour do have certain features in common; and it is these features particularly which have had such a powerful impact upon modern man's attitude towards himself and his fellows.

In the first place, both psychoanalysis and behaviourism assume that the living organism always acts in such a way as to reduce tension. To Freud, pleasure always arises from 'the diminution, lowering, or extinction, of psychic excitation', and discomfort or distress from an increase of it (51). Behaviourism, particularly in the form developed by Hull, sees 'drive-reduction' as the basic motivation of both animal and human behaviour. Whenever an organism's survival is threatened it is considered to be in a state of need which appears as a drive-stimulus: the organism then acts in such a way as to reduce the drive, and thereby return to the optimum conditions for survival. While there is undoubtedly an element of truth in this idea, it is by no means universally applicable, even at the animal level*, and applied as a model of human behaviour it is woefully inadequate. Clearly, there are many pleasurable human activities which involve a deliberate *increase* in tension: witness, for example, the teenager at a Dracula film, clutching the arms of his chair in sheer terror! More seriously, we may recall the very many instances where human beings, so far from acting in such a way as to satisfy their biological needs, have deliberately foregone such satisfaction in the interests of others, or in response to some ideological principle. The reader may decide for himself whether 'the pleasure principle' or 'drive-reduction' is capable of accounting for the behaviour of a Father Damien or an Albert Schweitzer. At any rate, it is clear that through their commit-

---

* For example, researchers have found that male rats find copulation rewarding, even when they are prevented from carrying the act to completion. In this case the animal acts in such a manner as to lead to a *heightened* drive state. Cf. Sheffield, F. D., Wulff, J. J. & Backer, R: Reward value of copulation without sex drive reduction. *J. of Comp. & Phys. Psych.* 1951, 44, pp. 3-8.

ment to a thoroughly hedonistic view of man, and their denial of any motives other than the purely biological, both psychoanalysis and behaviourism have tended to undermine all systems of morality and religion.

A second feature of the two systems is their *determinism*. Both Freud and Watson regarded man as little more than the prisoner of his early conditioning. Freud's psychic determinism allows no scope for the exercise of free will: all spontaneous actions are ascribed to unconscious causes, which in turn are determined by earlier experiences. Watson, even more aggressively deterministic than Freud, threw out a claim which even he had to admit went somewhat beyond the available facts:

> Give me a dozen healthy infants, well-formed, and my own specified world to bring them up in and I'll guarantee to take any one at random and train him to become any type of specialist I might select—doctor, lawyer, artist, merchant-chief and, yes, even beggar-man and thief.... (155, p. 104)

Such a thoroughgoing determinism inevitably raises the question of *creativity*, which to most of us must surely seem to be one of the most striking properties of the human mind. If our behaviour is all predetermined, how can anything new, such as a great work of art, possibly appear? In the one passage devoted to this topic (155, p. 247), Watson quickly disposes of the creative activities of the painter and the poet, who, he thinks, merely manipulate their materials until they obtain a satisfying result. He denies that they have any kind of image or idea of what they are trying to achieve: their activities are identical to the trial-and-error behaviour of the laboratory white rat in search of food! Predictably enough, Freud regarded all artistic and cultural activity as the result of sublimated sexuality. 'Wherever, in a person or in a work of art, an expression of spirituality (in the intellectual, not the supernatural sense) came to light, he suspected it, and insinuated that it was repressed sexuality,' wrote his one-time disciple Jung (73, p. 172). 'I protested that this hypothesis, carried to its logical conclusion, would lead to an annihilating judgment upon culture. Culture would then appear as a mere farce, the morbid consequence of repressed sexuality. "Yes," he assented, "so it is, and that is just a curse of fate against which we are powerless to contend." '

Yet of all the activities of man it is religion which has suffered the most in the hands of the psychological theorists. We have already mentioned Watson's contempt for all religious ideas, including the notion of the soul: 'no one has ever touched a soul, or seen one in a test-tube,' he complains (155 p. 3). The religious man who engages in such practices as prayer or Bible reading is simply in the grip of a 'religious habit system' (p. 273)—his behaviour has no deeper significance than this. Beliefs and practices which have dominated the human mind for centuries are thus dismissed in a few paragraphs, along with art and morality. Freud was much more thorough in his attack. In *The Future of an Illusion* (1928) he traced the origin of religion to the childhood desire for an all-powerful protective father. He pointed out that the young child regards its parents as omniscient and omnipotent beings who not only protect and feed it, but also punish it when it does wrong. Later, when it comes to realise that its parents are *not* omnipotent, it seeks to compensate for the feeling of loss by projecting the image of the all-powerful father into the external world. God is thus a projection of the earthly father, and is invested with all the properties which we attributed to our parents when we were very small. Religion is a kind of childish hangover which we must all learn to grow out of. Mankind must be 'educated to reality', and this education can only come from the application of scientific method:

> The scientific spirit engenders a particular attitude to the problems of this world; before the problems of religion it halts for a while, then wavers, and finally here steps over the threshold. In this process there is no stopping. The more the fruits of knowledge become accessible to men, the more widespread is the decline of religious belief, at first only of the obsolete and objectionable expressions of the same, then of its fundamental assumptions also. (52, p. 48)

Although Freud takes religious feelings more seriously than Watson, he nevertheless believes that they belong to a primitive stage of human development. 'Man cannot remain a child for ever; he must venture at last into the hostile world.' The

Freudian psychoanalyst, despite his use of an apparently mentalistic terminology, is as fundamentally opposed as the behaviourist to any kind of spiritual interpretation of life.

In Britain psychologists were (and still are) very much less numerous and less influential than their counterparts in America. Nevertheless, Britain has also made her contribution to the almost universal tendency of twentieth-century thought to emphasise the purely physical aspects of reality and denigrate the spiritual. During the late 1930s British philosophy came to be dominated by the Oxford school of logical positivists, who set out to demonstrate that all metaphysical propositions are nonsensical. Following the Second World War the influence of this school became widespread, and helped to provide a philosophical basis for the growth of behaviourism in America and elsewhere. In 1949 Gilbert Ryle, then Wayneflete Professor of Metaphysical Philosophy at Oxford, launched a powerful attack upon the whole notion of an immaterial 'soul' or 'mind' in human beings. This notion he referred to (with deliberate abusiveness) as 'the dogma of the Ghost in the Machine' (115). He set out to show that the idea was entirely false, 'not in detail but in principle ... it is one big mistake, and a mistake of a special kind. It is, namely, a category-mistake.' According to Ryle, when a person refers to 'my mind' he is making the same kind of statement as when he refers to 'my digestion'. We do not suppose that, if we dissected his body, we should eventually come upon an actual object or organ called 'the digestion'. The word refers, not to a *thing* but to a *function*. Ryle describes an imaginary foreigner visiting Oxford or Cambridge, and upon being shown the various colleges, playing-fields, libraries, museums etc., asks 'but where is the University?'. It then has to be explained to him that the University is 'not another collateral institution, some ulterior counterpart to the colleges, laboratories and offices which he has seen. The University is just the way in which all that he has already seen is organised' (115, p. 16). In the same way, the 'mind' or 'spirit' is not a thing which can be separated from a person's thoughts, actions, motives etc.; it is the name we give to the sum total of those activities. If Ryle is correct, then mankind has wasted an incredible amount of time and effort, over the past few thousand years, in trying to comprehend something which has no real existence.

Pavlov, Watson, Skinner, Freud, Ryle: all these men exercised a powerful influence upon the thought of the twentieth century. Although they differed greatly from one another, both in their fundamental assumptions and in their methods, they had at least one feature in common—they all denied the reality of the human soul as a distinct non-physical entity. To Ryle the soul was merely a category mistake; to the behaviourists it was a non-observable, and therefore meaningless, concept; to Freud it was part of that old religious system of beliefs which he regarded as just a childish hangover. Psychology, once the 'science of the soul', was no longer permitted to use that word : the soul had been banished from polite society. Even terms such as 'consciousness' and 'mind' were rejected by the strict behaviourist. In 1962 Sir Cyril Burt wittily summed up the situation in an oft-quoted passage :

> Nearly half a century has passed since Watson proclaimed his manifesto. Today, apart from a few minor reservations, the vast majority of psychologists, both in this country and America, still follow his lead. The result, as a cynical onlooker might be tempted to say, is that psychology, having first bargained away its soul and then gone out of its mind, seems now, as it faces an untimely end, to have lost all consciousness. (Quoted Koestler, 79, p. 6)

To anyone whose education has been largely in the physical sciences, reading the writings of the great psychological system-builders is a strange and rather disturbing experience; for the manner in which these latter-day materialists propagate their doctrines is very much more reminiscent of a religious than of a scientific approach to knowledge. Time and again we find *facts* ignored or suppressed in obedience to *dogma*. Pavlov presided over his laboratory like an Old Testament prophet, permitting no heretical ideas to penetrate its sanctified walls. It is reported that the great reflexologist even *fined* his laboratory workers if he caught them using psychological (that is, mentalistic rather than materialistic) terminology (124, p. 162). Freud likewise presided over his movement with patriarchal authority, excommunicating anyone who dared to deviate from his Gospel of Sex. Watson, seventeen years after the foundation of his movement, quite openly boasted that he had never replied to a criticism in all those years (see preface to 1930 edition of *Behaviourism*, 155). Such a claim would, of course, put him beyond the pale in any normal scientific community. Rather than the disinterested pursuit of truth we seem to find in these men a passionate attempt to establish a new orthodoxy, to replace the dogmas of the old religions with a no less dogmatic, if atheistic, religion of their own invention.

Those would-be disciples who find it difficult to accept the tenets of behaviourism are given a typically religious piece of advice by Watson:

> It is advisable for the time being to allay your natural antagonism and accept the behaviouristic platform at least until you get more deeply into it. Later you will find that you have progressed so far with behaviourism that the questions you now raise will answer themselves.... (155, p. 10)

In other words, have faith now and later all truths will be revealed! One is reminded of St Augustine's *credo ut intelligam*; believe first, and later you will understand. Freud's insistence that his followers should undergo a complete psychoanalysis before being allowed to practise within his movement is a similar demand that the individual commit himself fully in advance, with the promise of enlightenment later.

If these psychological systems are indeed more like religions than sciences, it is not surprising that they show considerable hostility towards the already existing religions. We have mentioned Watson's contemptuous references to religious concepts, and we have seen that Ryle wrote 'with deliberate abusiveness' (his own phrase) about the soul theory. It is possible that both Watson and Freud were reacting against an over-strict religious upbringing: certainly Freud seems to have had an almost pathological dread of anything supernatural. Indeed, Jung held the view that Freud's obsession with sex was a kind of defence mechanism, by which Freud protected himself from his own religious impulses:

> I can still recall vividly how Freud said to me, 'My dear

Jung, promise me never to abandon the sexual theory. That is the most essential thing of all. You see, we must make a dogma of it, an unshakeable bulwark' .... In some astonishment I asked him, 'A bulwark—against what?' To which he replied, 'Against the black tide of mud'—and here he hesitated for a moment, then added—'of occultism'. (73, p. 173)

Jung adds that what Freud seemed to mean by 'occultism' was virtually 'everything that philosophy and religion, including the rising contemporary science of parapsychology, had learned about the psyche'.

The word 'psychology' has many meanings. As Beloff has pointed out (12), psychology is not so much a single science as a 'collection of more or less loosely affiliated disciplines each with its own peculiar concepts and laws.' Even so, the various 'psychological sciences' (some of which, we have argued, seem more like religions than sciences) have had an enormous impact on the climate of modern thought. Before the advent of the psychological sciences man saw himself as an incarnate immortal soul, possessing freedom of choice over his own actions, and destined to survive the dissolution of his physical body. Today he tends to regard himself as a mere automaton, the victim of heredity and environment, the slave of his animal instincts. Psychology, for all its internal dissensions, has wrought a profound change in the outlook of the human race.

4. The Existential Vacuum

We have seen how, a little more than a century ago, most people believed in a God-centred universe, and a soul-centred theory of man. Sceptics such as La Mettrie had worked hard to propagate atheistic and mechanistic views, but with only very limited success. The ancient religions still held powerful sway over the minds of men, and the ideas of the early mechanists seemed too crude, too far removed from the obvious facts of everyday experience, to gain much support. Then, following the publication of Darwin's *Origin of Species* in 1859, the movement towards mechanism began to gather momentum. By 1930 the mechanistic philosophy was thoroughly entrenched as the orthodoxy of the twentieth century, with neo-Darwinism and Watsonian Behaviourism dominating the twin sciences of biology and psychology. Man's concept of himself and his relationship to the rest of the living world had suffered a drastic change; but it was an enlightenment for which human society had already begun to pay a terrible price.

Soon after the publication of Darwin's theory, Sedgwick wrote that if the theory were to become accepted, mankind would 'suffer a damage that might brutalise it, and sink the human race into a lower grade of degradation than any into which it has fallen since its written records tell us of its history' (Clark, 26, p. 96). Darwin, evidently finding the remark amusing, referred to Sedgwick as a 'prejudiced old bird'. Later, when a reviewer pointed out that the Darwinian theory had shown every criminal how to justify his actions, Darwin called the accusation a 'good squib'. In fact, as Clark has pointed out, the 'squib' turned out to be more like a bomb: its impact on all aspects of human thought and behaviour has been deep and lasting, and the echoes of the explosion remain with us today.

The first effect of the Darwinian revolution was the steady destruction of traditional religious beliefs. By about 1870 it was becoming obvious that attendances at churches of all denominations were decreasing throughout Britain. After the end of the Second World War Hensley Henson, Bishop of Durham, wrote:

> We see in our land tens of millions of men and women who acknowledge no connection with religion, and, as a result of this, a large proportion of our children are growing up without religious influence or religious teaching of any sort. (Spinks, 134, p. 198)

Darwinism was not the only factor contributing to this decline of religious belief, although it played a major part. Another important influence was the attack on the authority of the Bible carried out by Biblical critics such as David Strauss, whose sceptical *Leben Jesu* was translated into English just twelve years before the publication of Darwin's *Origin*. The study of primitive and ancient religions, epitomised by the publication of Frazer's *Golden Bough* in 1900, added still more fuel to the flames. Through Frazer, Christianity came to be regarded as just one of the many 'mystery religions' which flourished during the later stages of the Roman Empire. The thought of the late nineteenth century came to be dominated by the concept of a universe which ran itself according to inflexible predetermined laws, permitting no supernatural interference. Rationalistic exponents of the Bible, such as Matthew Arnold, T. H. Huxley and J. E. Renan, denied the possibility of miracles on the ground that they are contrary to the fixed laws of nature. Since the biblical writings contain numerous accounts of miracles, it follows from this point of view that the scriptures must be unreliable. Thus the belief in a mechanistic universe led to a belief in the unreliability of the Bible, and religion came to be dismissed as a mere superstitious relic of a pre-scientific age. Since science had uncovered the secrets of nature, there was no further need for a God.

As Sedgwick had foreseen, the doctrine of the Survival of the Fittest provided a perfect excuse for all manner of actions which would previously have been acknowledged as evil. Capitalists found in Darwinism a means of rationalising their exploitation of the workers; politicians found justification for brutal acts of aggression. The agnostic Herbert Spencer opposed such reforms as the Poor Laws, the introduction of state education and the regulation of housing conditions on the grounds that these things interfered with natural selection. 'If men are sufficiently complete to live, they *do* live, and it is well they should live. If they are not sufficiently complete to live, they die, and it is best they should die' (*Social Statics*). Although Spencer wrote these words before the publication of Darwin's book, it would be hard to find a more apt expression of the principle of the Survival of the Fittest. Later, Spencer found in Darwinism the perfect biological excuse for his anti-humanitarian views.

In the USA wealthy industrialists welcomed the writings of Darwin and Spencer. The absorption of small companies into bigger ones was regarded as the inevitable working out of nature's own laws. Andrew Carnegie, at first very troubled by the un-Christian methods of big business, later came to accept them on evolutionary grounds. A similar attitude was taken by J. D. Rockefeller. In Germany, Nietzsche was busy proclaiming his doctrine of the Superman, who climbs to power by trampling remorselessly over the bodies of those weaker than himself. Compassion for the less fortunate came to be regarded as an unnatural vice : the elimination of the unfit was necessary if the human race were to continue to make progress. Heinrich von Treitschke, a famous German historian, wrote : 'Ours is an epoch of war; our age is an age of iron. If the strong get the better of the weak, it is an inexorable law of life.' In the teachings of nineteenth-century 'Social Darwinism' are foreshadowed the horrors of Auschwitz and Buchenwald.

At the other end of the political spectrum, the early Marxists were also strongly influenced by Darwin. After reading the *Origin* in 1860, Karl Marx wrote : 'Darwin's book is very important and serves me as a basis in natural science for the struggle in history.' He requested permission to dedicate *Das Kapital* to Darwin, but the latter refused. Through the teaching of the Marxists, the poorer classes were encouraged to enter into a perpetual struggle against their rulers. Once again, the suffering generated by the class war was justified by an appeal to the Survival-of-the-Fittest principle : after all it was, apparently, nature's own way of doing things.

The twentieth century has inherited the grim legacy of

nineteenth-century materialism, with a vengeance. A philosophy which views human beings as nothing more than machines to be manipulated and conditioned at will leads inevitably to the brutalising of man, as that 'prejudiced old bird' Sedgwick saw only too clearly. The emotions which in earlier times were channelled by religion have become diverted into vast political systems such as Fascism, Nazism and Marxism, in which the individual is treated as a replaceable cog in the state machine. Throughout Germany whole generations were indoctrinated to believe that the only law is the law of the jungle, and that the strong have a duty to eliminate the weak. Both Hitler and Mussolini quoted Darwin frequently in their speeches, and the elimination of some six million Jews was but a part of the price the world had to pay for their belief in the Survival of the Fittest. During the brutal Stalinist regime in Russia, compulsory classes on Darwinism were given in the prison camps. All over the world the Christian ethic, which regarded each human being as made in the image of God and freely responsible for his own actions, has been replaced by a moral relativism which permits any kind of behaviour provided only that it is successful.

Few nineteenth-century thinkers saw what lay ahead. Most of the evolutionists of the late Victorian era believed in a golden age of progress just around the corner. They thought that natural laws, left to operate without the restricting hand of religion, would inevitably lead to the development of a better kind of society. Religious agnosticism, coupled with this naïve belief in the inevitability of human progress, became the fashionable attitude of the intelligentsia, until it was shattered on the battle-fields of the First World War. Yet there were some who found it impossible to accept the current view-point, and who saw the destruction of religion as a disastrous event which would one day have grave repercussions on the life of mankind. Such a person was Albert Schweitzer, who wrote in his autobiography:

> As early as my first years at the University, I had begun to feel misgivings about the opinion that mankind is constantly developing in the direction of progress. My impression was that the fire of its ideals was burning low without anyone

noticing it.... From a number of signs I had to infer the growth of a peculiar intellectual and spiritual fatigue in this generation which is so proud of what it has accomplished. (125, p. 173)

Following the First World War, the increasing mechanisation of life and the decline in religious belief brought an overwhelming sense of purposelessness. The twentieth century became the age of Colin Wilson's 'Outsider': the man who sees too much and too deep. The great wars fell upon a people which had no religion, no *Weltanschauung*: the only relief from the horror was the escapism of the cinema and the dance-hall. The dehumanising of man was poignantly expressed by the poets:

Oh, I have loved my fellow men—
And lived to learn that they are neither fellow nor men
but machine robots.

Oh, I have loved the working class,
Where I was born,
And lived to see them spawn into machine robots
In the hot-beds of the board-schools and the film.
                    (D. H. Lawrence, *Last Poems*)

By the end of the Second World War there was no trace left of the easy optimism of fifty years before. Instead, a great weariness seemed to settle over all the civilised nations. In Britain, H. G. Wells wrote his pessimistic analysis of the human situation, entitled *Mind at the End of its Tether*, while in France the gloomy writings of the existentialist philosophers became popular. The city streets soon began to witness the phenomenon of the rebel-without-a-cause, the mixed-up youth who must needs protest, though he does not know what he is protesting about. Mindless violence and vandalism began a steady increase; and millions came to rely upon soporifics and tranquillisers. Books presenting man as little more than a modified ape (and a rather nasty one at that) grew increasingly popular. Robert Ardrey, in his *African Genesis*, portrayed our ancestors as exceptionally aggressive animals with over-large brains, while Desmond Morris's best seller *The Naked Ape* took the lid off our most intimate patterns of behaviour. In the light of such depressing assessments of the nature of man, it is not surprising that more and more people turned to a purely hedonistic way of life, jettisoning the canons of traditional morality. In the western nations at least, an 'eat, drink and be merry' philosophy came to dominate the behaviour of millions, and the politicians and leader-writers coined the phrase 'the permissive society'. Yet no amount of self-indulgence or naked-apery could cure the deep-lying spiritual sickness of the age, or satisfy the need to find meaning and purpose in life. Viktor Frankl, Professor of Neurology and Psychiatry at the University of Vienna, has described modern man's lack of spiritual orientation as the 'existential vacuum':

> A psychiatrist today is confronted more and more with a new type of patient, a new class of neurosis, a new sort of suffering, the most remarkable characteristic of which is the fact that it does not represent a disease in the proper sense of the term ... I have called this phenomenon, which the psychiatrist now has to deal with so frequently, 'the existential vacuum'. What I mean thereby is the experience of a total lack, or loss, of an ultimate meaning to one's existence that would make life worth while. The consequent void, the state of inner emptiness, is at present one of the major challenges to psychiatry. (50)

Freud saw the drive to pleasure, especially sexual pleasure, as the principal motivation of man. His pupil Adler regarded the 'will to power', the urge to dominate, or to be someone important, as the chief factor. In contrast to both of these schools of thought, Frankl sets up the 'will to meaning', the need to believe that one's life has ultimate significance, as the centrepiece of his system of psychiatry, which he calls 'logotherapy'. It is the frustration of this need which, he considers, accounts for much of the misery of our time: 'More and more patients are crowding our clinics and consulting rooms complaining of an inner emptiness, a sense of total and ultimate meaninglessness of their lives' (82, p. 399). To discover just how common was this experience of an existential vacuum among the young, Frankl carried out an investigation among university students. He found that some 40% of his German-speaking students (Swiss, German and Austrian) admitted experiencing the feeling of total meaninglessness, whereas no less than 81% of his American students claimed to have done so. Frankl attributes this existential frustration to the crudely *reductionist* attitude of modern science, which sees man as 'nothing but' a collection of molecules, a programmed machine, or a naked ape:

> I well remember when I was a Junior High-School Student, how our science teacher used to walk up and down the class explaining to us that life in its final analysis is nothing but combustion, an oxidative process.... On one occasion I jumped to my feet and asked him: 'Dr Fritz, if this is true, what meaning, then, does life have?' At that time I was twelve. But now imagine what it means that thousands and thousands of young students are exposed to indoctrination along such lines, taught a reductionist concept of man and a reductionist view of life (82, p. 399).

Frankl was not the only psychiatrist to be alarmed by modern man's loss of a sense of purpose. Long before the Second World War C. G. Jung had noticed the increasing number of people suffering from what Frankl later came to call 'noögenic neuroses', that is, psychological disturbances caused by a lack of the sense of ultimate meaning in life. Jung attributed this to the decline in religious belief:

> How totally different did the world appear to mediaeval man! For him the earth was eternally fixed and at rest in the centre of the universe, encircled by the course of a sun that solicitously bestowed its warmth. Men were all children of God under the loving care of the Most High, who prepared them for eternal blessedness; and all knew exactly what they should do and how they should conduct themselves in order to rise from a corruptible world to an incorruptible and joyous existence. Such a life no longer seems real to us, even in our dreams. Natural science has long ago torn this lovely veil to shreds. That age lies as far behind as childhood, when one's own father was unquestionably the handsomest and strongest man on earth (72, p. 233).

The picture is, perhaps, somewhat overdrawn; for there was a good deal of fear in the religion of mediaeval man, including at times a hysterical dread of demons and witchcraft. Even so,

Jung is undoubtedly right in drawing attention to the very great loss sustained by mankind through the destructive effect of science upon religion. Some sort of religious belief seems to be necessary in order to escape the existential vacuum:

> During the past thirty years, people from all the civilised countries of the earth have consulted me.... Among all my patients in the second half of life—that is to say, over thirty-five—there has not been one whose problem in the last resort was not that of finding a religious outlook on life. It is safe to say that every one of them fell ill because he had lost that which the living religions of every age have given to their followers, and none of them has been really healed who did not regain his religious outlook (72, p. 264).

Aware of the widespread need for some kind of religion, certain writers have attempted to construct a 'Religion of Humanity', more or less loosely based on scientific principles. Those who belong to this school of thought would have us devote our religious energies to the worship of some aspect of the human race, and direct our efforts towards improving the environment for the benefit of future generations. Many of those who hold this kind of viewpoint are themselves psychologists or biologists, as for example J. B. S. Haldane and Julian Huxley (cf. *Religion without Revelation*, 1927). The difficulty with nearly all suggestions of this kind is that the concepts on which they are based lack the 'numinosity' of the old religious archetypes, and they therefore fail to evoke the same feelings of awe and devotion. Raymond B. Cattell, a British psychologist who settled in the United States, made an interesting attempt to solve this problem in his book *Psychology and the Religious Quest* (1938). According to Cattell, we must face up to the fact that science, particularly anthropological science, has completely destroyed religion. Psychoanalysis, he thinks, put the final nail in its coffin. Yet the price paid for this enlightenment has been high, with the emotions normally controlled by religion being diverted into such activities as Patriotism, Nazism, and Fascism:

> Men of affairs ... are aware that a bitter devastation has

been wrought, and that a heavy price in human happiness remains to be paid (22, p. 42).

Even ardent scientists, viewing the widespread destruction of happiness entailed, have ruefully admitted that truth can be entertained sometimes only at a prohibitive cost. Whilst those who thought that science would open a new paradise are already tired of their strange Messiah (22, p. 56).

Diagnosing our disease as 'social melancholia', Cattell goes on to suggest a solution based on a concept of a 'Group Mind' similar to that of Jung. The Group Mind, he claims, has properties closely similar to those usually attributed to God. Thus there is a sense in which we are all part of it, though it is greater than any one of us, and it contains all the accumulated wisdom of our race. We may attain a kind of 'immortality' by contributing to this store of knowledge, in the same sense that Plato may be said to be immortal through his works. By such considerations, we may come to have feelings of reverence for the Collective Mind which, thought of in this way, Cattell proposes to call the 'Theopsyche'. The worship and service of the Theopsyche will then become the religion of the future.

In practice, all of the attempts to construct a substitute religion whose postulates shall be acceptable to mechanistic science have proved abortive. No brand new Religion of Man has arisen to replace the old; instead we have a spiritual vacuum which seems to increase daily as the last remnants of the ancient faiths continue to decay. In the 1950s and 60s large numbers of the younger generation began to reject the materialistically orientated consumer society of the west, seeking for something to fill the existential vacuum which they felt so keenly. Hallucinogenic drugs, pop-star idolatry, Zen, Yoga, Transcendental Meditation and sex all became part of an underground culture which, thoroughly misguided as it often was, nevertheless served to spotlight the spiritual dilemma of modern man. Schweitzer's 'peculiar intellectual and spiritual fatigue', Cattell's 'Social melancholia', Frankl's 'existential frustration' are all merely ways of describing the same basic fact: the complete spiritual bankruptcy of twentieth-century man. To the question 'what is the meaning of life, why are we here?' mechanistic science answers: 'there is no meaning or purpose; life is nothing more than an accidental by-product of certain chemical reactions occurring on a minor planet; plants, animals, and men are no more than highly complex machines; while mind, consciousness and will are mere epiphenomena, of no more significance than the faint glow of the will-o'-the-wisp, flickering for a brief moment of time in the blackness of the marshes. Man sadly accepts this answer, for it seems to have all the massive weight of accumulated fact on its side; yet it fails to satisfy his deepest longings, and it leaves behind a horrible sense of emptiness. Is it not strange that a mere machine should have such a profound and ineradicable conviction that, somehow or other, it is more than a machine?

Part II: Counter-attack

Bacon foresaw the gradual victory of observation and experiment—the triumph of actual analysed fact—in every department of human study;—in every department save one ... I here urge that that great exemption need be no longer made.

F. W. H. MYERS, *Human Personality.*

5. Across the Threshold

Towards the end of the nineteenth century there were many intellectuals in England who felt the futility of the prevailing world-view very keenly. Among them was a small group of scholars and scientists who, at first separately and later as an organised body, sought to 'put the final question to the Universe'. These were the founding fathers of the Society for Psychical Research (SPR). Dissatisfied and depressed by the view of man as a mere machine, they set to work to investigate all sorts of phenomena which had been neglected by orthodox science, and which promised to throw more light on the true nature of man. The problem which occupied them more than any other, the 'final question', was: does any part of the human personality survive after the death of the body?

Those early founders of the SPR were men of very high intellectual calibre: Henry Sidgwick, later Knightbridge Professor of Moral Philosophy at Cambridge; F. W. H. Myers, classical scholar and poet; and William Barrett, a physicist who later received both an FRS and a knighthood. They had one thing in common: they were all seeking a way out of the mechanistic impasse into which nineteenth-century science had led them. Myers, in an address on Henry Sidgwick written many years later, shows something of the feelings which lay behind the movement:

> In a star-light walk which I shall not forget (Dec. 3rd, 1869), I asked him, almost with trembling, whether he thought that when Tradition, Intuition, Metaphysic, had failed to solve the riddle of the Universe, there was still a chance that from any actual observable phenomena—ghosts, spirits, whatsoever there might be—some valid knowledge might be drawn as to a World Unseen. Already, it seemed, he had thought that this was possible; steadily, though in no sanguine fashion, he indicated some last grounds of hope;

and from that night onwards I resolved to pursue this quest, if it might be, at his side (127, p. 285).

The phrase 'last grounds of hope' is worthy of note, since it reveals both the state into which Victorian materialism had got itself, and the primary impulse behind the founding of the SPR. Yet in spite of this obviously strong religious motivation, the members pledged themselves to 'examine without prejudice or prepossession, and in a scientific spirit, those faculties of man, real or supposed, which appear to be inexplicable on any generally recognised hypothesis'. It is important to point out that a strong motivation, even a religious one, is not necessarily incompatible with a strictly scientific approach to the subject matter of any field of enquiry. Some of the greatest scientists have been emotionally involved in their work to a very high degree, and probably all are to some extent, whether they recognise the fact or not. The early psychical researchers carried out their difficult task according to the very highest standards of scientific integrity and impartiality prevailing in their time. Although there were spiritualists among their ranks, the psychical researchers were careful to resist any attempt to identify the aims and ideals of the Society with those of Spiritualism. The latter is a religion, and therefore involves commitment to a system of beliefs, whereas psychical research, as a branch of science, must preserve the freedom to follow wherever the facts may lead.

Typical of the kind of phenomenon which interested the psychical researchers is the story of the Rev. Andrew Dukes, a Woolwich clergyman, who on Monday July 31st 1854 was staying in a house at Worksop. As he woke that morning he heard the voice of an old schoolfellow, who had been dead for several years, saying: 'Your brother Mark and Harriet are both gone.' According to the description given by Mr Dukes, the words were echoing in his ears at the moment of waking; 'they seemed to me like a voice from the unseen,' he said. So deeply impressed was the clergyman that he wrote the words down, there and then, on a scrap of old newspaper, having no other paper in the bedroom. Later in the day he entered an account of the incident in his diary, and also told the story to his wife. At that time he had no particular reason to be anxious about either his brother Mark, or his sister-in-law Harriet. The couple were then in America, and had been in good health when he had last heard from them. Even so, on August 18th he received a letter from Harriet, dated August 1st, saying that Mark had just breathed his last—of cholera—and that she herself was ill. Later he heard that she had died the second day after her husband, on August 3rd. It is interesting to note that at the moment when the Rev. Andrew Dukes heard the voice his brother was *not* yet dead; he died early the next morning, on August 1st. The message given by the 'voice' seems to have contained a precognitive element.*

Another incident, taken from the same volume of the SPR *Proceedings*, seems to suggest that impressions arriving by extrasensory means may reveal themselves in bodily symptoms. James Wilson, a student in his second term at Cambridge, was in the best of health and took part in football, boating and other physical activities. One evening he suddenly felt extremely ill, trembling for no apparent reason. He was frightened, for he said it did not seem to him to be a physical illness, or a chill of any kind. He tried to struggle with himself, resolving that he would ignore it and go on with his mathematical work, but it was of no avail. He became convinced that he was dying. He went down to the rooms of a friend, who exclaimed at his appearance before he spoke. The friend produced a bottle of whisky and a backgammon board to try to take James Wilson's mind off his symptoms, but he was unable to play the game. After some three hours of this strangely undefined yet distressing 'illness', he suddenly felt better, and went off to bed. The following afternoon he received a letter to say that his twin brother had died that very evening in Lincolnshire.†

During the years following the founding of the SPR in 1882, its members collected hundreds of such cases, carefully checking facts and interviewing witnesses. They also carried out a vast amount of valuable psychological research, including among their studies instances of multiple personality, hysteria, dreams and hallucinations, as well as the curious phenomena of spiritualism. Some of the 'inexplicable' things they investi-

* *Proc. S.P.R.*, 1884, Vol. 2, p. 129.
† *Proc. S.P.R.*, 1884, Vol. 2, p. 122.

gated have today become accepted by orthodox science (hypnosis, for example), and many of the early psychotherapists, including Janet, Freud and Jung, were members of the Society. For a time it looked as though psychical research would become incorporated into the fabric of modern science as a recognised branch of psychology, but this was not to be. As psychology became increasingly mechanistic and behaviouristic in the early years of this century, so its links with psychical research became more and more an embarrassment to it. Several of the great figures in academic psychology continued to show an interest in the despised field (William James and William McDougall are outstanding examples), but it became increasingly unwise for a young psychologist to do so. Even Freud could not entirely swim against the current, for in 1922 he succumbed to pressures from within the psychoanalytic movement and suppressed a paper which he had written on the subject of telepathy. Later, when he wanted to throw the weight of his movement behind the study of telepathy, he was prevented from doing so by Ernest Jones, who believed that such an action would be disastrous for psychoanalysis (145, p. xx).

The cavalier treatment meted out to psychical research in the early years of this century does little credit to the exponents of official science. Whatever else they may have done, the psychical researchers had at least amassed a great body of data relating to human psychology. Hundreds of dreams, hallucinations, instances of apparent telepathy, had been carefully documented and classified. Laboratory experiments on hypnosis, automatic writing, dowsing, clairvoyance and other topics had been conducted by methods which, though perhaps inadequate by present-day standards, were hardly inferior to those of the orthodox psychologists of the day. The primary claim that there exist in man faculties which transcend the normal sensory mechanisms of the body had not been *proved*, but a very strong case had been made out for its continued investigation. Why, then, did psychical research meet with so much opposition, amounting in some instances to open hostility? We have already seen how, from about 1860 onwards, mechanistic theories of life and of mind began to gain momentum, ousting the older religious views of the nature of man. Psychical research was almost the exact antithesis of this movement. While other branches of science carefully applied themselves only to those phenomena which could be fitted into a materialistic world-picture, psychical researchers deliberately and wantonly sought out those which could not. No wonder they were an embarrassment to the establishment!

The high-water mark of behaviourist psychology came around 1930, and this corresponds to about the lowest point in the acceptance of psychical research by officialdom. In the autumn of 1927 Dr William McDougall arrived in North Carolina to take up his post as head of the new department of psychology at Duke University, and from then onwards the fortunes of the psychical researchers began to change. McDougall was one of the few eminent psychologists to refuse to be seduced by the doctrines of Watsonian behaviourism. Born in 1871, he had already distinguished himself in the fields of biology, anthropology and medicine before settling down in 1900 to become a professional psychologist, first at London and later at Oxford. During the First World War he was a medical officer in the British Army dealing with cases of war neurosis, and when the war ended he became professor of psychology at Harvard. When the founding president of Duke University, Dr William Preston Few, invited him to undertake the formation of a new department there in 1927, McDougall was already well known as the author of many books and the founder of the hormic school of psychology.

Shortly after McDougall's arrival at Duke two young biologists turned up on his doorstep with a request to be permitted to conduct psychical research within the walls of the university. Dr Joseph Banks Rhine and his wife Louisa had read McDougall's great work *Body and Mind: a History and Defence of Animism*, and also his Clark University lecture *Psychical Research as a University Study*. They knew that McDougall was one of the few professors of psychology who were prepared to take psychical research seriously, and that the president of the university was also interested in the subject. Duke University was therefore an almost ideal place for the establishment of a psychical research program in 1927. With a dedication which McDougall described as 'magnificently rash', the Rhines threw up their careers as teachers of biology, spent a year at Harvard studying psychology and philosophy, and then joined the department of psychology at Duke to pioneer a new attack upon the problem of the nature of man. J. B. Rhine was gifted with a remarkable tenacity and perseverance, as well as a whole-hearted belief in the adequacy of scientific methods to solve the deep mysteries of existence. From among the heterogeneous collection of alleged phenomena which formed the subject matter of psychical research he sifted out a single item for attack : the belief that some people can acquire information from the outside world or from other people's minds without the use of the bodily senses. For this he coined the term *extrasensory perception*, or ESP. Probably because of the prevailing attitude towards psychical research among academics he also re-named his subject *parapsychology*, translating a term which had long been current in Germany.

With this new terminology and a brisk, empirical approach, Rhine and his co-workers set out to devise unambiguous tests for the existence of extrasensory perception. One of their first steps was to attempt to classify and distinguish clearly the three basic types of ESP : (1) *clairvoyance*, the extrasensory perception of a physical object or event; (2) *telepathy*, the extrasensory perception of another person's thoughts, and (3) *precognition*, the non-inferential awareness of a future event. To test for the existence of these faculties Rhine developed the now familiar card-guessing techniques, and applied the mathematics of probability to the results. After some six years of research involving hundreds of thousands of guesses, he considered he had enough evidence for the reality of both clairvoyance and telepathy to justify the publication of a monograph. Entitled simply *Extra-Sensory Perception*, the monograph was published in 1934 by the Boston Society for Psychic Research, and carried a foreword by Professor McDougall. The experimenters seem to have been naïvely unprepared for the storm of publicity which broke over their heads as a result. Instead of being largely ignored, as they expected it would be, the book became the centre of a violent controversy which raged on and off for years. Although Rhine had written it with no attempt at popular appeal, the book was seized upon by Waldemar Kaempffert, Science Editor of the *New York Times*, who gave it a highly favourable review, and before long many of the popular magazines carried articles on the research. 'ESP' became a household word, and card-guessing spread across America as a popular craze. Orthodox psychologists were outraged: not only was such publicity highly distasteful to them, but Rhine's discoveries seemed to undermine the whole mechanistic basis of modern science. They poured out a continuous stream of merciless criticism against the researchers, in some cases not stopping short of personal abuse. Strong pressures, both public and private, were put upon the Duke administration to have the experiments suppressed. Fortunately for parapsychology, neither Dr Few nor Professor McDougall were the kind of men to give way to such pressures. Through all the years of conflict they remained firmly behind the ESP researchers, ensuring a solid basis of support from which the young science could develop. To this day no other university in the world has sponsored parapsychology so strongly and so continuously as Duke. Even so, the intense publicity caused some tension within McDougall's department, and in 1935 Rhine asked for, and obtained, permission to set up his Parapsychology Laboratory as an autonomous unit on the Duke campus.

The years 1935 to 1940 saw the peak of the attack on the early Rhine researches: this was the great testing time for American parapsychology. The experimenters knew that they were on trial for their reputations as serious scientists. One of the most outspoken critics of this period was Professor Chester E. Kellogg, a psychologist at McGill University, who wrote in *The Scientific Monthly* for October, 1937:

Since Dr Rhine's reports have led to investigations in many other institutions it might seem unnecessary to prick the bubble, as the truth eventually will out and the craze sub-side. But meanwhile the public is being misled, the energies of young men and women in their most vital years of pro-fessional training are being diverted into a side-issue and funds expended that might instead support research into problems of real importance for human welfare. This has gone so far that a new *Journal of Parapsychology* has been founded.

(Quoted by Soal & Bateman, 132 p. 49)

Fortunately for the future of parapsychology, the professor's scandalised cry went unheeded. Despite the increasing volume of criticism the research effort continued to expand, although the funds available for parapsychology were modest compared with those devoted to other sciences. In 1938 Lucien Warner and C. C. Clark published a survey of opinion taken among the members of the American Psychological Association (APA), and found that no less than 89% regarded ESP as a legitimate subject for scientific enquiry, although only 8.8% felt that it was either a 'likely possibility' or 'an established fact' (152). Most of the APA members who considered that ESP was worth investigating at all thought that it should be studied within the province of academic psychology, as McDougall and Rhine had wished. Unhappily, the behaviouristically-orientated psychology of the day was in no fit state to receive such a heretical newcomer, so that the two fields of study became separated and have remained so ever since. Nevertheless, there have been many academic psychologists who, as individuals, have made valuable contributions to parapsychological research.

It would be misleading to give the impression that all the critics of the early Rhine work were abusive and ill-formed, although some certainly were. Others fulfilled a valuable function by pointing out weaknesses in the experiments which the researchers were then able to correct. Such healthy criticism is part of the normal routine of science. No doubt many of these critics hoped that as the experimental conditions were improved the ESP effect would disappear, thereby proving it to have been an artefact due to careless experimenting or bad observation. In the event, such hopes proved vain; ESP continued to display itself from time to time even under the most rigorous experimental conditions. By 1940 the critical attack had largely spent itself, and the Duke team then published a large volume* summarising and analysing all the results to date, and invited seven of the leading critical psychologists to contribute to it. Only three accepted, and of these, two seemed to be reasonably satisfied with the experimental methods then in use. It looked as though the case for ESP had been almost won. In a review of the controversy written for

* *Extra-Sensory Perception after Sixty Years*, by Rhine, Pratt, Smith, Stuart and Greenwood. Bruce Humphries, Boston, 1940.

the *Journal of Parapsychology*, Dorothy H. Pope and J. G. Pratt gave the following figures : there were five critical articles on ESP in 1935-36; forty-two in 1937-38; only twelve in 1939-40; and none in 1940-41.

Much of the early criticism was concerned with the mathematical procedures used by Rhine and his colleagues. In those days the application of statistical methods to the solving of scientific problems was still in its infancy, and few of the older psychologists were familiar with probability theory. It seemed natural to assume that there must be a fault in the mathematics. Speculation along these lines was brought to an abrupt end in December 1937, when the American Institute of Mathematical Statistics issued a press release declaring the statistical analysis to be essentially valid, and adding : 'If the Rhine investigation is to be fairly attacked, it must be on other than mathematical grounds.' Only slightly abashed, the critics next began to hunt for flaws in the experimental procedures : recording errors, leakage of information, faulty shuffling of the cards and so on. In each case the experimenters met the criticism by devising new and improved testing procedures; and still they continued to obtain evidence of ESP. While many of Rhine's preliminary experiments had been methodologically faulty (they were never intended to be anything more than exploratory) the really crucial experiments stood up so well to criticism that after 1940 most of the critics were forced into an uneasy silence. The majority of American psychologists still did not believe in ESP, but since they were unable to point to any specific flaws in the experiments there was little they could do to justify their scepticism.

One of the great classic experiments of this period is known as the Pearce-Pratt series. Hubert Pearce was a student in the Duke School of Religion, and in the Spring of 1932 he attended a lecture given by Dr Rhine, describing the research in parapsychology. After the lecture Pearce approached Rhine, and told him about certain psychic experiences which had occurred in his family. Rhine then asked whether Pearce himself had any psychic capacities, and he said that he had, although he was rather frightened by them. Rhine thereupon asked Pearce to report to J. G. Pratt for testing, and this he did. In the months that followed he proved to be one of the most gifted subjects in the whole history of parapsychology, repeatedly guessing the cards correctly to an extent far beyond anything that could reasonably be attributed to chance. In the Pearce-Pratt experiments, Pearce sat in the university library writing down his guesses while the cards were being turned over by Dr Pratt in a building on the other side of the campus. At the end of each session, Pearce made a duplicate copy of his guesses and handed it to Rhine in a sealed envelope, while Pratt did the same for the actual card order. When the two records were checked against each other, it was found that the odds against obtaining so high a score by chance were about 10^{22} to one—a result which the statistician would describe as 'highly significant'. Some of the sessions were carried out over a distance of 100 yards between Pearce and the cards, whereas others were carried out at a distance of 250 yards; in both cases the scores were statistically highly significant.

Because of the central importance of the Rhine laboratory in the history of parapsychology, there is an understandable tendency for both believers and sceptics to assume that most, if not all, of the experimental evidence for ESP stems from the Duke work. In fact, even before Rhine began his research there had been a number of isolated experiments in other universities, and some of these had produced very significant results. Probably because of the general climate of opinion none of these earlier studies continued very long, but the publication of Rhine's *Extra-Sensory Perception* naturally triggered off a marked increase in the amount of experimentation. In 1937 Rhine estimated that there were at least a score of institutions in the USA carrying out parapsychological researches; and of these he reported only three as having failed to confirm the Duke findings. With all this research going on it became necessary to have a new outlet for the results, and in 1937 the *Journal of Parapsychology* was founded under the editorship of William McDougall. We have already seen how this event, which is an important milestone in the history of psychical research, drew the wrath of Professor Kellogg. Across the Atlantic there was also an increase in experimental effort, although Rhine's results were at first treated with considerable scepticism in Britain. One of the chief sceptics was S. G. Soal, a lecturer in mathematics at Queen Mary College, London, who carried out hundreds of card-guessing experiments without a glimmer of success. However, in the autumn of 1939 Soal's scepticism received a rude shock when he discovered that two of his own subjects had produced strong evidence of ESP. During the next decade he worked hard with these two subjects, testing them under a variety of conditions with every safeguard he could think of to prevent error and fraud. The success of this mammoth piece of work did more than anything else to make parapsychology acceptable in Britain, and in 1945 London University awarded Soal a Doctorate of Science for his efforts.

For six years the *Journal of Parapsychology* continued to report successful experiments on telepathy, clairvoyance and precognition. Then in March 1943 reports of a new and even more surprising phenomenon began to appear in its pages. The experimenters claimed to have obtained evidence that human thought can directly affect a physical object—a 'mind-over-matter' effect. To describe this phenomenon the term *psycho-kinesis* (PK) was adopted. The research into PK had been initiated nine years before, when a young gambler called in at J. B. Rhine's office and offered to give him a demonstration of dice-willing. Crouched in a corner of the office, the boy threw his dice along the floor, willing them to land with various faces uppermost. Although this was a very informal test and could in no way be regarded as a scientific experiment, Rhine was sufficiently impressed with the results to begin dice-willing experiments in earnest with his students. Following the same procedure as with the ESP tests, the conditions were gradually made more and more rigorous until eventually the experimenters considered that they had conclusive proof of the reality of psycho-kinesis. From then onwards, PK took its place in the Duke repertoire as the complementary phenomenon to ESP. In fact, Rhine considered the existence of PK to be a logical corollary of the existence of clairvoyance. He reasoned that, since in clairvoyant perception the mind becomes aware of a physical object, it must exert some force upon it, however slight. If matter can affect mind, then mind must also affect matter. Therefore, to those parapsychologists who follow the rationale of the 'Rhine school', ESP and PK are twin phenomena, corresponding to the sensory and motor aspects of the ordinary nervous system. Because of the wave of hostile criticism which was then being directed against the ESP experiments, Rhine decided not to publish the results of the PK tests immediately. Publication was held back for eight years, until the researchers felt that all conceivable criticisms had been met, and the opposition to ESP had begun to die away.

William McDougall died in 1938, five years before the publication of the first PK report, but he had seen enough of the Duke experiments to know that strong evidence for the mind-over-matter effect had been obtained. In his Clark University lecture of 1926, McDougall had pleaded for the acceptance of psychical research as a university study: before he died he had the satisfaction of seeing his wishes at least partly fulfilled. The Duke laboratory had been established on firm foundations, with an enthusiastic team of researchers led by the indefatigable J. B. Rhine; a great increase in research was taking place across America and around the world; and the evidence for the four basic phenomena of psychical research— telepathy, clairvoyance, precognition and psychokinesis—had been markedly strengthened. Considering that all this was achieved in the teeth of almost savage opposition during one of the most strongly mechanistic phases in the history of science, it represents no mean achievement.

6. Beyond Space and Time

In the early days of the psychical research societies a great deal of attention was paid to the topic of telepathy, the alleged direct contact of mind with mind. This was because those early workers were primarily concerned with the problem of survival after death, and the chief evidence for such survival existed in the form of statements made by spiritualist mediums during seances. If the medium produced information about a deceased person which could not have been obtained from any normal source, then that information must have come either from the mind of one of the sitters (by telepathy), or from the deceased person himself. Telepathy was thus seen as an alternative to the survival hypothesis; and a convincing demonstration that telepathy did *not* occur under seance conditions would have strengthened considerably the spiritualist position. In fact, many of the early experiments suggested very strongly that telepathy *did* occur, not only during seances but spontaneously in everyday life. We now know that there are other forms of ESP which might also assist the medium (clairvoyance, for example), and there is no known way of preventing the operation of any of these extrasensory faculties. Because of this difficulty it has never been possible to devise a conclusive test of the survival hypothesis, although there is some very suggestive evidence in favour of it. However, those who wish to avoid the spiritualistic interpretation of seance-room phenomena can always invoke some form of ESP to explain away the data.

One of Rhine's great contributions to parapsychology was to steer it away from the early telepathy-oriented research. Most of his first experiments were concerned with clairvoyance, a faculty which the British researchers considered hardly worth bothering about, although the French had devoted some attention to it. For his clairvoyance tests Rhine employed randomised packs of cards, each card bearing one of five geometrical shapes: star, circle, square, cross, and wavy lines. His subjects had to guess the order of the cards when they were concealed from view, no other person having any knowledge of the order. Sometimes an experimenter lifted each card off the pack and placed it face downwards as the subject made his guess (BT technique); sometimes the subject simply guessed straight down through the undisturbed pack (DT technique). In addition to these two methods, a variety of other techniques, some involving card matching as distinct from card calling, were developed by the Duke University team. In all the better controlled experiments the utmost care was taken to ensure that the subject could not pick up any clues from slight marks on the backs of the cards, or in any other way obtain sensory information about the card order.

Some psychical researchers have criticised Rhine's methods on the grounds that card guessing is a boring procedure, bearing little or no resemblance to the emotionally-rich situations of everyday life in which spontaneous ESP seems to occur. This is true enough, but it misses the essential purpose of Rhine's work, which was to obtain indisputable evidence for the reality of the phenomenon. The vast collections of spontaneous cases built up by the psychical research societies had signally failed to impress the scientific world. Such cases could always be dismissed as mere coincidences, however remarkable they might seem to be. Experiments with 'free' material, such as drawings, were subject to the same difficulty; for how could one judge whether the degree of resemblance between two drawings was too great to be attributed to chance? Rhine's introduction of card-guessing and dice-throwing tests made it possible to specify *exactly* how unlikely the resemblances were. The enormously high anti-chance odds* obtained in Rhine's clairvoyance experiments made it impossible for the sceptics to cry 'coincidence' any longer : they were compelled to turn to other forms of criticism.

Not only did the new techniques provide fresh evidence for

---

* The author is aware that the mathematically sophisticated will justifiably criticise the use of this inexact term. It is employed here as a popular, if crude, substitute for phrases such as 'the probability of a deviation from mean chance expectation as large as, or larger than, this is extremely small on the assumption of the null hypothesis.'

the reality of ESP, they soon began to yield a rich harvest of information about the conditions under which it operates. The most startling finding of all was the discovery that ESP seems to be almost totally independent of the physical circumstances of the experiment. Most subjects scored equally well with card calling and card matching techniques, and there seemed to be no systematic differences between the use of the BT and DT methods. The interposition of physical obstacles—screens, walls, even buildings—between the subject and the cards apparently made no difference, once the initial psychological effect (caused by the subject *believing* the task to be more difficult) had been overcome. Hubert Pearce, who averaged about 8 hits per run of 25 when sitting about a yard away from the cards, actually increased his scoring rate to 8.8 hits per run when he was moved into another building 100 yards away. When the distance was further increased to 250 yards the scoring rate fell to 6.7 hits per run; even so, it was statistically highly significant at all three distances. Since a run consisted of 25 guesses, and there were five different symbols, the average number of hits per run expected by chance was five.

Several experimenters carried out research projects aimed specifically at investigating the effects of distance and various obstacles upon ESP scoring. Table 1 shows the results of some

Table 1 : Distance tests in telepathy, with Miss Ownbey as agent.

Percipient	Same room		Wall between		Two walls between		250 miles distance	
	No. of trials	Average per 25	No. of trials	Average per 25	No. of trials	Average per 25	No. of trials	Average per 25
T. C. Cooper	1,800	9.2	300	5.8	–	–	–	–
June Bailey	275	11.4	450	9.7	150	12.0	–	–
George Zirkle	950	14.0	750	14.6	250	16.0	–	–
May Frances Turner	275	7.7	–	–	–	–	200	10.1

(after Rhine, *Extra-Sensory Perception*, 1935, p. 143)

trials carried out by Miss Sara Ownbey, one of Rhine's graduate assistants, in the early 1930s. Miss Ownbey acted as the agent (sender) in these tests, which were tests of 'pure telepathy'. She visualised the ESP symbols in her mind without having any actual cards present, thereby eliminating the possibility of clairvoyance. With two of her percipients, Mr Cooper and Miss Bailey, increasing the distance led to a reduction in the scoring rate, as might be expected if telepathy were due to some kind of radiation. However, the other two subjects actually obtained *higher* scores at the greater distances. The most staggering result of all was an average of 10.1 hits per run obtained over a distance of 250 miles in July 1933. The percipient, Miss May Frances Turner, was at Lake Junaluska, North Carolina, and there were several mountain ranges between her and the agent at Durham.

Viewed in retrospect, there are several objections which can be brought against the Ownbey experiments. It is a well-known fact that if a person is asked to make up a series of numbers or symbols in his head (as Miss Ownbey did) he will seldom produce a random series. Usually his choices will fall into certain stereotyped patterns. If these patterns happened to coincide with the guessing-habits of the percipient, an above-chance score would arise, giving a false impression that telepathy had occurred. Fortunately Miss Ownbey was aware of this possibility, and took care to vary her symbol choices in as nearly-random a manner as possible. Subsequent statistical analysis of the record sheets showed that she was remarkably successful in randomising her targets, and a cross-check (that is, scoring the percipient's guesses against target runs for which they were not originally intended) produced no evidence of coinciding patterns. It therefore seems reasonable to accept the Ownbey work as evidence for the operation of ESP over large distances.

While the Americans were busy exploring the physical limitations of ESP, a new development was taking place in England. This originated with the work of W. Whately Carington, a somewhat eccentric psychologist with a brilliantly inventive mind. He served as an airman in the First World War, and later carried out research for the Air Ministry. He was one of the first psychologists to experiment with what was then known as the 'psycho-galvanic reflex' (PGR), the name given to the change in the electrical resistance of the skin under the influence of emotion, and he published a book on this subject in

1922. Later, he used the PGR, and also Jung's word-association test, to investigate the nature of the entities which purport to communicate through spiritualist mediums during seances. Following the publication of Rhine's work, Carington decided to turn his attention to ESP, and in 1935 he made a largely abortive attempt to demonstrate precognition by getting forty subjects to predict the fall of a die. By 1939 he had come to the conclusion that it would be better to use free response material, rather than the ESP symbols employed by Rhine. He therefore devised an ingenious experiment with drawings, which has since become a classic in the literature of parapsychology.

Carington's procedure was as follows: on the day of each test he selected at random a three- or four-digit number from a set of mathematical tables, and used it to determine a page in Webster's dictionary. His wife then made a sketch of the first drawable object named on that page. The sketch was hung up in a locked and heavily curtained room in the Caringtons' house, where it remained from 7 p.m. until 9.30 a.m. the following day. Hundreds of guessers in Britain, Holland, and the USA, many of them connected with university psychology departments, tried to reproduce the drawings, sending their efforts to Carington by post. After randomising the percipients' drawings, Carington handed them to a 'blind' judge (that is, one who did not know which drawing was intended for which target), and he attempted to match them. A statistical formula was used to determine whether there were significantly more successful matchings than would be expected by chance. Carington's technique thus combined the precision of a mathematical analysis with all the interest and spontaneity derived from using free-response material.

The results of the Carington experiments are of considerable importance, for several reasons. Not only were they statistically significant, showing that ESP had indeed been operating during the tests, but the percipients at Duke University, over 3,000 miles from the targets, did significantly better than the 105 subjects in Britain and Holland. In those halcyon days just before the Second World War, Duke seems to have assembled a unique galaxy of psychically gifted persons, perhaps as a result of the enthusiastic climate of belief created by J. B. Rhine. To have performed a successful ESP experiment over a distance of 3,000 miles was remarkable enough; but Carington discovered something else which was even more startling. Not only were his subjects producing significant scoring on the target pictures, they were also tending to reproduce drawings from the days preceding and following the targets. In other words, ESP appeared to be *not too sharply focussed in time*. This time-displacement effect, together with the enormous distances involved, virtually rules out any physical theory of ESP, at least within the present meaning of the word 'physical'.

Dr Soal, whose conversion to a belief in ESP was mentioned in the previous chapter, also found evidence of time displacement. In fact, the discovery of his first high-scoring subject came as a result of a discussion with Carington on this very subject. By the autumn of 1939, after several years of unsuccessful card-guessing experiments, Soal had more or less abandoned any hope of demonstrating ESP in England. Then Carington drew his attention to the remarkable displacement effects found in the picture-drawing experiments, and suggested that he might try comparing each guess with the cards immediately preceding and immediately following the card for which the guess was intended. Without very much hope, Soal set about the task of re-examining his records for a possible displacement effect. He decided to look first at 2,000 guesses made by Mrs Gloria Stewart, a London housewife who had shown some slight promise in previous experiments. Almost at once he realised that he had made a striking discovery; for when he matched Mrs Stewart's guesses against the cards in front of, and behind, the target card the scores were statistically highly significant. In the terminology of modern parapsychology, a subject who repeatedly guesses the card before it has been concentrated upon by the agent is said to show *forward* or *precognitive* displacement. Similarly, a subject who successfully guesses the card after the agent has changed his attention to the next one is said to show *backward* or *postcognitive* displacement. In addition to these rather clumsy terms, a shorter symbolism is also used : thus, a hit on the card one place ahead of the target is described as a $(+1)$-*hit*, whereas a hit on the card one place behind the target is described as a (-1)-*hit*. By the same symbolism, a direct hit on the target can be described as a *(o)-hit*, and hits two places ahead or behind can be represented as (+2), (−2), and so on. Mrs Stewart's results showed both (+1) and (−1) displacement, with odds against chance of just over 1,000 to one in the backward direction, and about 63,000 to one in the forward direction. Her score on the intended card (i.e., the target), was also significant, but here the odds against chance were only about 117 to one. To put these figures in perspective for the non-statistician, it is worth remarking that in ordinary biological or psychological work, odds of 20 to one are usually taken as 'probably significant'. Odds of 100 to one are regarded as 'significant' (that is, almost certainly *not* due to chance alone), and odds of 1,000 to one as 'highly significant'.

After discovering the displacement effect in Mrs Stewart's data, Soal pressed on with his examination of the results of his other subjects, without at first finding anything remarkable. Then, after Christmas 1939, he came upon a set of 800 guesses which had been made by a young photographer, Basil Shackleton. When checked against the target card Shackleton's guesses had been totally insignificant, the final score being only five hits more than the average expected by chance. However, examination for forward and backward displacement showed a very different picture. Both (+1) and (−1) scores were far above anything that could reasonably be attributed to chance, with odds of 9,000 to one in the backward direction, and 3,000 to one in the forward direction. The following year Soal sought out Shackleton again, and invited him to take part in some further experiments. At this time Shackleton had just been invalided out of the Army, and was operating his photographer's business from a basement in Shaftesbury Avenue. He willingly agreed to take part in some more experiments, and Soal thereupon embarked upon one of the most brilliantly conceived and executed pieces of research in the history of parapsychology. For several years while the bombs were falling upon London, Soal and his helpers tested the extrasensory ability of Basil Shackleton under a wide range of experimental conditions. The results more than justified the effort; not only was the displacement effect amply confirmed, but a number of new effects were discovered in the course of this work, some of them of considerable theoretical interest. In December 1943 the SPR published the 'Soal-Goldney' report on the Shackleton experiments, which quickly became famous. Meanwhile Mrs Stewart, whose displacement scoring had been the first to be discovered by Soal, was living in Worcestershire. However, she returned to London in the summer of 1945, and on August 3rd Soal began a further series of experiments with her. Once again the ESP effect was confirmed, Mrs Stewart obtaining highly significant scoring on the target card (odds of 10^{70} to one!). The displacement scoring, however, assumed a different pattern from the earlier work, for this time there was a significant number of *misses* on the $(+1)$ and (-1) cards. In an attempt to explain this puzzling variation parapsychologists have made very detailed statistical analyses of Mrs Stewart's results, which show that she was responding in a rather complex way to the extrasensorially-perceived card patterns. At any rate, there can be little doubt that Gloria Stewart and Basil Shackleton must be ranked among the most gifted ESP subjects ever to be discovered by scientists.

We cannot pursue the intricacies of the Shackleton and Stewart experiments much further here, since it would lead us into some highly technical matters. Readers who are interested should consult the text by Soal and Bateman (132), which gives a full account of all the experiments. However, Shackleton's demonstration of forward displacement does raise the important question of the relationship between ESP and time, which we must consider because of its philosophical importance. On first consideration it seems as though Shackleton's mind was somehow able to go into the future and perceive an event which had not yet happened, namely the appearance of the next card in the series, but this is not necessarily the correct interpretation. Soal determined the target sequence in advance, using random numbers. An experimenter displayed each number in turn at a small aperture in a screen, and the agent then concentrated on the ESP card corresponding to that number. If we assume that Shackleton's unconscious mind could become aware of the next random number in the sequence by clairvoyance, and also the order of the five target cards in front of the agent, it is possible to explain forward displacement without invoking the paradoxical idea of precognition. To test this hypothesis, Soal arranged for some of

Shackleton's targets to be determined *immediately* before the subject made his guess. This was done by giving the agent a bag of coloured counters, which were carefully shaken up before each trial. The agent then drew out a counter, which indicated to him which of the five target cards to concentrate upon. Under these conditions the card one place ahead had not been determined at the moment the subject made his guess. Nevertheless, Shackleton continued to score on the (+ 1) targets, giving odds against chance of about a hundred thousand million to one. It seems impossible to account for these results by clairvoyance; the only alternative to the acceptance of precognition is to assume that Shackleton's mind somehow influenced the agent in his selection of the counters.

An important fact discovered by Soal was that Shackleton's ability to go ahead in time seemed to be focussed at a more or less constant point in the future. When the average time between guesses was 2.80 seconds Shackleton tended to hit the (+ 1) card, but when the rate of guessing was approximately doubled, giving a trial interval of 1.44 seconds, he obtained highly significant scores on the card *two* places ahead (i.e., the (+ 2)-card). It thus appears as though Shackleton's ability to 'see' into the future was limited to a point in time about 2.8 to 3.0 seconds ahead of the present moment. This is hardly of great practical importance, but the implications for our understanding of the nature of reality are immense.

Soal's initial discovery of a precognitive effect in his data was accidental; but in America, Rhine had been deliberately looking for evidence of precognition since 1933. His star subject, Hubert Pearce, was asked to guess the order of a pack of cards *before* they were put into a mechanical shuffler. When they emerged from the machine, the card order was checked against the prediction. Although this procedure produced undoubtedly significant results, Rhine was not entirely happy with it. He had already obtained evidence that some human beings can influence the fall of dice in an electrically driven wire-gauze cage; could it not be that the subject was influencing the fall of the cards in the mechanical shuffler to make them coincide with his predictions? Strange as such a PK effect may be, it is nothing like as damaging to our commonsense view of the universe as precognition, which seems to imply that an event which has not yet happened can influence our behaviour here and now. In order to eliminate PK as an alternative to precognition, Rhine devised a number of ingenious experiments in which the final target order was determined by methods thought to be beyond the reach of mental influence. Sometimes the point at which the pack was cut before the check-up was decided by the daily temperature readings in the local newspaper, so that in order to influence the target sequence the subject would have to exert a PK effect upon the weather (or its recording instrument). In other experiments a number of dice were thrown and a highly complicated calculation performed on the resulting digits in order to determine an entry point in a set of random number tables. The random numbers then determined the card sequence. In order to affect the outcome of this operation the subject would have to use his PK with almost 100% efficiency, as well as carrying out subconsciously a calculation which would tax his conscious mind to the utmost. A single slip anywhere along the line would lead to a wrong entry point in the random number tables, and thus give the wrong target sequence. Using methods such as these, the Duke laboratory eventually produced some highly significant evidence for precognition in which the counter-hypothesis of PK was virtually ruled out.

Just as the long-distance studies showed no clear signs of a decline in ESP scoring with increasing distance, so attempts to conduct precognition experiments over varying intervals of time revealed no obvious relationship between temporal separation and ESP. It would be rash to assert that ESP is wholly independent of time, for the volume of research done on this aspect of the problem is relatively small. However, Margaret Anderson's precognition experiment of 1959 showed *higher* scoring over a time interval of one year than over a time interval of a few days (1). Dr Karlis Osis also conducted successful precognition experiments with varying time intervals (96), and reported no significant differences between the results of tests scored after 30 days and the results of tests scored within 7 days. Lois Hutchinson in 1940 *did* find a difference between ten-day and one-day precognition, the shorter time-interval giving significantly higher scores; however, she attributed this difference to the psychological effect of having to wait longer to see one's results. One of the serious difficulties facing any experimenter wishing to investigate the physical relationships of ESP is the problem of separating effects due to psychological factors from those due to the physical conditions of the experiment.

As stated earlier, some people who are interested in ESP, yet have no particular love for the scientific approach to knowledge, complain about the aridity of these experiments. They question whether the guessing of hundreds of card sequences and the performing of complex mathematical calculations can really tell us anything important about the operations of the human mind. It is instructive, therefore, to compare the accumulated results of the past 40 years of laboratory experimentation with the collections of spontaneous cases made by the psychical research societies. The resemblances are often quite striking. For example, we have seen that card-guessing was found to operate over very great distances, and how it was found to have a rather unclear focus in time, sometimes spreading to targets in the immediate past or future. If the reader will now turn to the two spontaneous cases summarised in the previous chapter, he will find the same characteristics there. James Wilson's telepathy-type experience occurred over a distance of approximately 100 miles, and the Rev. Andrew Dukes' experience spanned the Atlantic Ocean. Furthermore, the Dukes' experience was slightly ahead of time, in much the same way as Shackleton's card guessing. These examples could be matched many times from the vast literature of psychical research, leaving little doubt that the laboratory parapsychologist, in spite of his totally different techniques, is dealing with essentially the same phenomena as the collector of spontaneous cases. The laboratory experiments and the spontaneous cases are complementary; each confirms and reinforces the other. Both are essential to the future progress of parapsychology, although it is inevitable that some researchers will prefer to devote their time to one rather than the other.

For those who prefer to approach ESP through the spontaneous cases, there are some exceptionally fine examples of precognition which have been recorded during the past half century or so. Great national disasters, of which this century has had more than its fair share, seem to be extremely effective in evoking precognitive dreaming. In her valuable little book

Some Cases of Prediction, Dame Edith Lyttleton records her investigation of two dreams in which the dreamers apparently foresaw the great airship disaster of October 5th 1930, when the R101 crashed in France with heavy loss of life. The first of these dreams, by a Mr J. S. Wright of Liverpool, was so disturbing and carried such a strong sense of conviction that the dreamer discussed it many times with his friend, Mr G. Coxon, and the two men wondered whether they ought to inform the War Office. 'Knowing however, from past experience, how futile it has been to attempt to make any impression on this Governmental Department,' wrote Mr Coxon, 'we refrained from pressing the matter' (86, p. 127). Mr Wright's dream occurred twice, with an interval of about a week between, several months before the actual disaster. Another dreamer, Mr R. W. Boyd of Enfield, had a much more detailed dream of the disaster only two days before it occurred. He recounted his dream to his fiancée, Miss Catharine Hare, who supplied Dame Edith with written confirmation of the story.

At approximately 9.15 a.m. on October 21st 1966, there occurred what is probably the most horrible disaster ever to take place in peace-time Britain. A massive coal-tip slid down a Welsh mountainside on to the little village of Aberfan, killing 144 people. The horror of the event was enhanced by the fact that 128 of the victims were children attending the local Junior School, which was partially destroyed by the avalanche. Dr J. C. Barker, a consultant psychiatrist of the Shelton Hospital, Shrewsbury, was on the scene the next day, and was appalled by the suffering and devastation he saw everywhere. Since the disaster was such an unusual one, he thought it might provide an opportunity to investigate precognition. Therefore he immediately put out a request through the mass media, asking people who thought they had experienced some forewarning of the disaster to come forward. Altogether about 200 persons replied, and among the mass of information collected by Dr Barker are some of the most striking examples of apparent precognition ever recorded. Since they provide such excellent examples of spontaneous ESP, we will describe two of Dr Barker's cases here.

The first case involves one of the child victims of the disaster, a 10-year-old girl who was a pupil at the village Junior School.

A fortnight before the disaster she said to her mother 'Mummy, I'm not afraid to die.' Her mother replied, 'Why do you talk of dying, and you so young; do you want a lollipop?' 'No,' she said, 'but I shall be with Peter and June' (schoolmates). The day before the disaster she said to her mother, 'Mummy, let me tell you about my dream last night.' Her mother answered gently, 'Darling, I've no time now. Tell me again later.' The child replied, 'No, Mummy, you *must* listen. I dreamt I went to school and there was no school there. Something black had come down all over it!' The next day she went off to school as happy as ever. In the communal grave she was buried with Peter on one side and June on the other.

The second case concerns Mrs C. M., a 47-year-old Plymouth woman, who described a vision she had on the day before the tragedy:

'First, I "saw" an old school house nestling in a valley, then a Welsh miner, then an avalanche of coal hurtling down a mountainside. At the bottom of this mountain of hurtling coal was a little boy with a long fringe looking absolutely terrified to death. Then for a while I "saw" rescue operations taking place. I had an impression that the little boy was left behind and saved. He looked so grief-stricken. I could never forget him, and also with him was one of the rescue workers wearing an unusual peaked cap.'

She described her vision at a church meeting on October 20th, and her testimony was confirmed in writing by six witnesses. She also told her next-door neighbour about it at 8.30 a.m. on the morning of the tragedy. Later, when watching a television programme about the disaster, Mrs C. M. recognised both the little boy and the rescuer in the peaked cap, whom she had seen in her vision.

The accounts of these two cases are taken directly from Dr Barker's paper in the SPR *Journal* of 1967 (5). Apart from their obvious intrinsic interest, such cases serve to counter the accusation, sometimes put forward by sceptics, that psychical researchers are constantly quoting the same old cases, mostly dating from the nineteenth century. Dr Barker's Aberfan collection is quite as well documented and as evidentially impressive as anything from the age of Myers and Sidgwick. In spite of the sceptics, the phenomena which those two eminent scholars set out to investigate are still occurring, even in the second half of the twentieth century. Evidently the reality which they represent is no less real in this age of space travel, nuclear energy, and molecular biology than it was in the days of the ancient Greeks.

Since ESP can apparently operate in the time dimension, it is very unlikely that it would be stopped by any kind of physical barrier in the here-and-now. Nevertheless a number of studies have been made in which barriers of various kinds were erected between the percipient and the targets. Perhaps the most notable of these were the experiments conducted by Leonid Vasiliev, a pupil of Bechterev, during the 1930s (146). Vasiliev did not use card-guessing, but instead tried to put his subjects into a hypnotic trance by willing from a distance. Believing that some kind of electromagnetic radiation was passing from himself to the subject, he performed some of the experiments with the subject inside a Faraday cage, a metal box made so as to exclude most forms of radiation. In other tests the agent was placed inside a lead chamber sealed with mercury, and in some experiments the distance between agent and percipient was increased to 1,700 kilometres. None of these attempts to obstruct the passage of the telepathic impulse had any effect whatsoever, and Vasiliev reported that when he willed his subjects to fall asleep or waken, he was successful on 90% of the occasions. Owing to the ideological situation in Russia, these experiments were not published until 1962, some 25 years after they had been performed. Dr Soal was therefore unaware of the Russian researches when, in 1946, he tried the effect of confining Mrs Stewart to the X-ray chamber at the Royal Free Hospital, London. With a wall of lead 2mm thick between her and the agent, Mrs Stewart obtained some of her most significant scores. Later Soal tried interposing even greater thicknesses of lead (up to 1½ inches), again without any detectable effect on the scores.

The overwhelming mass of evidence, then, both from spontaneous happenings and from laboratory research, strongly suggests that ESP is independent of space, time and matter. Yet this cannot be the whole story. If ESP operated *entirely* outside our space-time world, it would never be able to provide us with any useful information about that world, nor would it be detectable by any kind of experiment performed on this earth. Somehow or other, it must be able to focus in on specific events in the space-time continuum. Whatever theory of ESP we adopt, this focussing remains the most puzzling aspect of the situation. In a 'down-through' (DT) clairvoyance experiment, for example, the subject guesses straight through an undisturbed pack of cards which lies in front of him on the table. Even if the cards were completely transparent, or every card was giving off some kind of radiation, it is difficult to see how the subject's ESP faculty could separate the impressions coming from targets which are in such close proximity. Or, to take a spontaneous case, it is hard to explain how the Rev. Andrew Dukes' mind could focus in on the sufferings of his brother thousands of miles away, and at the same time ignore the impressions coming from the millions of other suffering people all over the world.

In fact, it seems as though ESP really does belong to a different order of reality from the physical world revealed through our senses, and it is only with great difficulty that it can be focussed on specific events in this world. Even the best card-guessers come nowhere near achieving 100% success; usually they maintain their scoring only a little above the average expected by chance. Provided that it persists long enough, even a small above-chance scoring rate is sufficient to prove that something other than chance is operating; however, such low scoring rates are hardly of much *practical* value. In both spontaneous and experimental ESP we experience the greatest difficulty in getting the phenomenon to fulfil any useful function in the physical world. Of all the millions of people in Britain only a tiny minority focussed in on the Aberfan disaster, and their information was not specific enough to enable preventative action to be taken. Most of us experience an extra-sensory impression only once or twice in a lifetime. Apparently it requires very intense motivation (a disaster, or a strong desire to please an experimenter) to enable ESP to focus at all; and even then it may systematically miss its target, as happened with Shackleton. The problem for ESP researchers seems to be not so much to explain its independence of space-time, as to explain how it manages to 'come down to earth' at all.

In fairness, it is important to point out that there are a few parapsychologists who doubt whether ESP really is independent of distance. Apart from the short-range quantum forces of the atomic nucleus, most known physical influences obey an inverse square law : doubling the distance from the source reduces the intensity to one quarter of its former value. Dr Karlis Osis, after making a comprehensive survey of the experimental literature relating ESP to distance, came to the conclusion that ESP does show some decline as the distance is increased, though not as rapid as one would expect if it followed the inverse square law (99). In an appendix to Osis's article, M. E. Turner suggested that the facts could best be accommodated by assuming that ESP obeys an inverse 2/5ths law; this would mean that doubling the distance from the source would reduce the intensity to about three quarters of its former level, instead of one quarter. Thus we would expect a very slight fall off with increasing distance, but very much less than we observe with other forms of physical radiation. To support this hypothesis Osis and his co-workers have carried out a number of ingenious experiments at varying distances, using complicated statistical analyses to separate the distance effect, if any, from the effects of psychological factors (99, 100). The complexity of this work makes it impossible to discuss fully here, and interested readers must consult the original papers. However, it is probably true to say that most parapsychologists are not convinced that Osis has demonstrated a connection between ESP and distance, in spite of the ingenuity of his experiments. Rao, for example, has pointed out that in one of Osis's experiments there was actually a significant *increase* in the scoring rate when the target distance was increased, which is not at all what one would expect on the basis of a physical transmission theory (106, p. 69). However that may be, the existence of precognition is the big stumbling block for any physical theory of ESP; for a faculty which can receive information before it is transmitted cannot be operating on any of the known forms of physical energy.

During the early years of the Duke laboratory a great deal of attention was paid to the problem of establishing the reality of the different forms of ESP as separate types. Intricate experiments were devised to demonstrate telepathy under conditions which were supposed to rule out the operation of both clair-voyance and precognition. Precognition tests themselves had to be made secure against the possibility of PK, and vice-versa. Gradually, as it became evident that all these phenomena operate, at least to some extent, outside the normal space-time framework of our world, parapsychologists began to question whether the classical distinctions between telepathy, clairvoy-ance, precognition and PK had any validity in nature. Perhaps they were nothing more than man-made labels for describing the different conditions under which a single basic faculty of the mind displays itself. In 1947 a Cambridge psychologist, Dr R. H. Thouless, proposed that all the forms of ESP and PK phenomena should be described by the single term 'psi', which is the first letter of the Greek word *psyche*, meaning mind or soul. This has now been widely adopted, although the older terms are still in common use. Any kind of occurrence in which mind apparently interacts with matter without using either the sense organs or the musculature of the body is now known as a 'psi-effect' or a 'psi-phenomenon'. Parapsychology, therefore, may now be defined quite simply as the study of psi-phenomena.

7. The Confident Years

We have seen how, by the end of 1940, the wave of criticism directed against the discoveries of Rhine and his colleagues had more or less collapsed. American parapsychology then entered upon an extended period of quiet consolidation and steady, if unspectacular, progress. For the workers at Duke University the mere existence of psi ceased to be a live issue; from now on their research effort was to be concentrated upon the task of establishing the properties of this strange phenomenon. Since ESP seemed to operate without regard for physical barriers its limitations, if any, must lie within the province of psychology rather than physics. It seemed likely that some factor or factors connected with the mental state of the percipient determined whether or not he would be successful in the card-guessing tests. Since there was already available a vast battery of psychological tests for exploring mental characteristics, it seemed sensible to apply these tests to the study of ESP in the hope of discovering the best psychological conditions for its occurrence. Rorschach ink-blot tests, personality inventories, intelligence tests, questionnaires relating to the subject's interests and moods, were all pressed into service in an attempt to reduce the capriciousness of psi. Investigators travelled all over the globe and subjected every imaginable type of humanity to the card-guessing procedures, ranging from Dutch schoolchildren to Australian aborigines. Even schizophrenic and manic-depressive patients in mental hospitals were tested. While many of these groups showed evidence of psi, it did not appear to be exceptionally well developed in any one of them rather than the others. ESP effects were found to occur among both males and females, young and old, without any apparent regard for class, creed, or colour. Psi seemed to be a universal faculty of mankind.

In 1946 a young psychologist, Betty M. Humphrey, submitted to Duke University a PhD dissertation with the formidable title *Discrimination between High- and Low-scoring Subjects in ESP Tests on the Basis of the Form Quality of Their Drawings*. This work was based upon the idea of dividing a group of subjects into two according to some psychological criterion, and then comparing the ESP scores of the two categories. For her psychological criterion Dr Humphrey chose the 'expansion-compression' test, a projective technique developed by Dr Paula Elkisch for use with children. The subject is given a blank sheet of paper and asked to draw anything he likes: if he produces a bold, imaginative drawing which makes full use of the available space he is classified as an 'expansive' type; if he produces a faint, timid drawing, or one squashed into a corner of the page, he is classified as a 'compressive'. Expansives are said to be less inhibited than compressives, and therefore more easily able to form relationships with other people in their everyday life. Dr Humphrey carried out an analysis of twelve series of clairvoyance tests, and found that there was a consistent tendency for the expansives to produce positive scores (that is, scores higher than would be expected by chance), while the compressives tended to produce negative scores. This was a most remarkable finding; for of course *all* the subjects were consciously trying to score high. In spite of their conscious desire to succeed the compressives must have been using their ESP in order to *avoid* hitting the target, since they got significantly lower scores than would be expected if nothing but chance were operating. In a further series of nine experiments a human agent looked at each target in turn, so that significant scoring could have been due to either telepathy or clairvoyance. Under these conditions the scoring trends were reversed, with the expansives scoring below chance and the compressives above. Probably a subject's direction of scoring (above or below chance) is somehow linked with his ability to relate to the other persons involved in the experiment, such as the agent (if there is one), and the experimenter.

Humphrey's research with the expansion-compression ratings is an early example of a type of investigation which became increasingly common from about 1940 onwards. Unfortunately, later studies showed that the expansion-compression criterion is not very reliable as a means of separating high and low ESP scorers. Other experimenters have generally failed to reproduce Humphrey's results, and this is almost certainly because 'expansiveness' and 'compressiveness' are not fixed attributes of the human personality, but are more like fleeting moods. Smith and Humphrey, in a later piece of work (130), found that a subject who drew a compressive drawing in one session would sometimes draw an expansive one in the next. Therefore it is quite likely that a person's 'expansiveness' could change while the ESP test was actually in progress; it might even change in response to success or failure in the test itself. Under these circumstances we would not expect to obtain reliable correlations between expansiveness and ESP. Nevertheless, the expansion-compression work was an important first step, and Humphrey followed it up with a long series of personality studies in which she employed tests such as the Bernreuter Personality Inventory and the Stuart Interest Inventory. The results of some of these investigations were quite bizarre. For example, it was found that high-scoring ESP subjects generally like history, dramatics, bridge, formal occasions and salesmanship, are indifferent towards cowboys, stamps and birds, and dislike nature study. In contrast, the low-scorers like military drill, boxing, zoos and geography!

On the whole, the attempt to find psychological correlates of ESP was not a great success, in spite of the enormous amount of detailed and careful work that went into it. Although individual experimenters often obtained quite significant correlations, when others tried to repeat their work they were frequently unsuccessful. In some cases the replication even showed a complete reversal of the original trend. It soon became clear to the enthusiastic ESP researchers that they were dealing with one of the most elusive properties of the human mind, and one which would not easily submit to being captured in their statistical nets. Thirty years have elapsed since Dr Humphrey presented her dissertation, yet even today we are only a little further along the road towards an understanding of the psychology of psi. Modern researchers such as Kanthamani and Rao (75, 76) have achieved a rather higher degree of reliability by combining a number of psychological factors; even so, it is still not possible to guarantee that any particular experiment will be repeatable. However there do seem to be two broad principles which have emerged from all this work, and no account of twentieth-century parapsychology would be complete without at least a brief mention of them.

The first principle concerns the famous 'sheep-goat' dichotomy discovered by Dr Gertrude Schmeidler of the City College of New York. She noticed that people who disbelieved in ESP seemed to produce scores which were below the chance level, whereas the believers often scored above chance. She therefore divided a large group of students into believers ('sheep') and unbelievers ('goats'), and gave them all a clair-voyance test using the standard ESP cards. As expected, the sheep scored higher than the goats, and in some experiments the goats actually produced scores that were significantly *below* chance (see figure 2). In later studies using the Rorschach

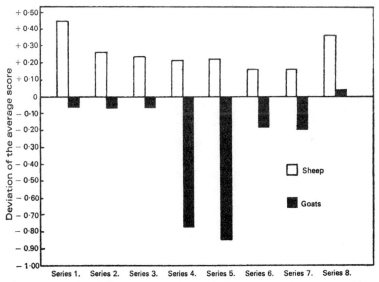

Fig. 2: Dr Schmeidler's comparison of the ESP scoring rates of be-lievers (sheep) and disbelievers (goats). (After Rhine, 108, p. 118)

test, Schmeidler showed that it was the well-adjusted sheep and goats who produced the biggest deviations from the chance level; poorly adjusted subjects, whether sheep or goats, achieved only insignificant scores. This interesting finding suggests that the *amount* of ESP ability possessed by an individual is related to his degree of social adjustment; whereas the *direction* in which it operates (positively or negatively) depends upon his beliefs.

Those sceptics who like to dwell upon the 'unrepeatability' of parapsychological experiments would do well to make a careful examination of the very extensive literature on the sheep-goat effect. Apart from the massive amount of research carried out by Schmeidler herself there have been many replications by other workers, not only in the USA but in countries as far apart as India and Argentina. Not all of these investigators used exactly the same criteria as Schmeidler for separating the sheep from the goats; nevertheless, most of them succeeded in confirming her general finding that believers score higher than unbelievers. In a recently published British study (Barrington, 8), the experimenter divided her subjects into four categories: moderate believers, uncertain but inclined to believe, unconvinced, and doubtful. Apparently there were no strongly convinced sheep in this sample. As expected, the ESP scores of the four groups were in descending order, with the moderate believers attaining a marginally significant positive score and the doubtful group producing a non-significant below-chance score. The odds against these results falling into the expected pattern purely by chance are about 24 to one. Considered in isolation this is not overwhelmingly significant; but it does provide yet another welcome confirmation of the sheep-goat effect. When we consider that Schmeidler's original experiment was carried out in a different country under very different conditions some thirty years ago, the repeatability of the sheep-goat effect looks very good indeed. True, some workers have failed to confirm it; but they represent only a small minority. Even in the physical sciences there are occasions when an experiment fails to work, for no apparent reason.

The second broad principle which has emerged from research into the psychological aspects of psi derives from personality investigations. For the past half-century or more psychologists have been trying to separate the personality characteristics of human beings into various 'factors'. The usual method of achieving this is by the application of rather difficult techniques of mathematical analysis to the answers to questionnaires. The questionnaires, the methods of analysis, and the names used for the various factors have differed so much from one psychologist to another that it has often been difficult to see the connections between them. However, Hans Eysenck has recently introduced a great simplification by showing that the personality factors of the various experimenters can be grouped along two broad dimensions of personality, which he calls *Extraversion* (E) and *Neuroticism* (N). Neither of these terms was new to psychology, but it was a considerable achievement to put them on a more precise footing, and to show how they could be related to the numerous personality traits and factors of earlier workers. Eysenck has gone even further, and suggested that the E and N dimensions of personality can be related to differences in the structure and functioning of the brain, particularly of the ascending reticular formation. His evidence suggests that introverts are usually in a state of greater cortical arousal than extraverts; or, to put it more crudely, the 'thinking' surface of their brain is more wide awake. For this reason, they are less dependent than extraverts upon external stimulation to keep them going. Whereas the extravert constantly seeks company and excitement, the introvert is perfectly content with his own inner thought-processes.

Since ESP is, by definition, *extra*-sensory, it is reasonable to expect that a high level of cortical arousal would be unfavourable to its occurrence. After all, if an organism is trying to tune in to some subtle influence from outside, it seems likely that noise from within its own nervous system would be a hindrance rather than a help. In practice, it is found that many spontaneous ESP-experiences occur during sleep, in trance, or in that peculiar half-way state between sleeping and waking which many people experience in the early morning. If this argument is correct, we might expect the less cortically active extraverts to perform better in ESP tests than the introverts, and this does indeed seem to be the case. Eysenck has pointed out that many of the individual high-scoring subjects were apparently extremely extraverted; for instance, Soal described Basil Shackleton as 'an expansive type .... talkative and sociable', and the eight major subjects studied by Rhine were all described as 'sociable, normal, intelligent, and artistic'. The numerous psychological tests used by the ESP experimenters varied a great deal in their reliability and in the traits they were intended to measure. Nevertheless, by carefully comparing the results of these researches, Eysenck was able to show that in most cases the high-scoring ESP subjects were also high in some factor related to the E-dimension of personality: that is, they tended to be extraverts rather than introverts (46). Since the publication of Eysenck's important paper on this topic, additional confirmation has come from the work of Kanthamani and Rao (76), who carried out ESP tests on groups of children studying in English schools at Waltair, India. As expected, the extraverts scored higher than the introverts in each of the four experiments conducted, with overall odds against the difference being due to chance of more than twenty thousand to one. In a rather different study with English grammar-school boys, the present writer also found evidence of greater ESP ability among extraverts, although in some cases this ability was employed negatively (i.e., to produce significantly *low* scores) (104). Although perhaps not quite as convincing as the sheep-goat dichotomy, there does seem to be a fairly strong body of evidence in support of the view that extraverts make better ESP subjects than introverts.

Group testing, as a basic research method, is essentially an American idea. In Britain group tests have been used chiefly as a means of discovering individual high-scoring subjects, who could then be subjected to intensive investigation of the kind described in the Soal-Goldney report. For several years after the publication of Rhine's first monograph, British attempts to obtain experimental evidence of ESP were abortive. Then came Soal's discovery of Basil Shackleton and Mrs Stewart, and the researchers' hopes began to rise, although most British workers were still very sceptical about Rhine's claim to have found evidence of ESP in approximately one person out of every five tested. However, British parapsychology at last got off the ground, and during the 1950s some very valuable experimentation was carried out by small groups of workers from the SPR. The driving force behind most of this experimentation was a young psychiatrist, Dr D. J. West, who was appointed Research Officer to the Society.

In January 1950 G. W. Fisk began a large-scale ESP experiment in Britain at the request of the Council of the SPR. He sent out packs of cards, instruction leaflets, and record sheets to volunteer experimenters who gave the ESP test to 236 subjects in their own homes. A grand total of 3,895 runs was completed. Of course, Fisk realised that such informal amateur testing could not in itself provide cast-iron proof of the reality of ESP; but he hoped that it would show up one or two good subjects who could then be tested more rigorously at the SPR headquarters. In fact, only one outstanding subject was found as a result of these tests, an electronics engineer who lived near Bournemouth. Out of 900 guesses he scored 88 more successes than would be expected by chance, an achievement which corresponds to odds of 150 million to one against the chance hypothesis. Further examination of his record sheets showed some tendency to displacement, particularly in the backward (postcognitive) direction, and a tendency to score better on the 'cross' symbol than on the other four. Unfortunately this subject left the district soon after, and it was not possible to continue experimenting with him. However, a subsequent examination of the record sheets of the other 235 subjects led to an even more remarkable discovery : while the combined score on the target card was totally insignificant, there was highly significant *negative* scoring on the ($+$ 1) and ($-$ 1) cards. The odds were about 100,000 to one for the forward score, and 10,000,000 to one for the backward score.

Careful examination of the Fisk data by D. J. West showed that the highly significant negative scores on the forward and backward cards were not due to exceptional scoring by one or two subjects, but were widely spread throughout the data (158). Could this, perhaps, be some kind of statistical artefact, due to inadequate randomisation of the cards by the amateur experimenters? To test this possibility Fisk carried out a cross-check on a large sample of the data, scoring each subject's guesses against the cards of runs for which they were not intended. If there were any statistical artefacts, they ought to show up equally well under these conditions. In fact, the cross-check gave totally insignificant scores, both on the 'target' cards and on the ($+$ 1) and ($-$ 1) cards. Therefore it does not seem possible to explain away this strange scoring pattern as a mere artefact. Why, then, should 236 subjects, all working under different conditions with different experimenters, use their ESP ability to avoid scoring on the cards in front of, and

behind, the one they were aiming at? Most of these subjects
had probably never even heard of displacement scoring, and
even if they had, they would expect it to be positive (like
Shackleton's) rather than negative. As West pointed out, the
subjects had only one thing in common: *their relationship
with the organiser of the project, G. W. Fisk*. This raises the
staggering possibility that the chief experimenter, even when
he is not present in person during the tests, may influence the
scoring of his subjects. Such a possibility could well explain
why some experimenters have been consistently successful
in obtaining evidence of ESP whereas others have not. In this
particular case, we may suppose that Fisk had an unconscious
desire to produce results that were in some way different from
Soal's results with Shackleton, and that this generated negative
scores in the $(+1)$ and (-1) positions.

A later piece of research provided even stronger evidence
for what we may call the 'experimenter effect'. Thirty-two
sealed packs of cards were sent, in sets of four packs at a time,
to each of twenty subjects. Sixteen of these packs had been
made up in random order by Fisk, and sixteen by West. All
packs were posted to the subjects by Fisk, and returned, un-
opened, to him, together with the records of the subjects'
guesses. The subjects did not know that half of the packs had
been made up by West, and even if they had known, they
would not have been able to tell which were which. Nevertheless, the scoring on Fisk's packs was highly significant (odds
of more than 6,000 to one against chance), whereas the scoring
on West's packs was only at the chance level. This particular
ESP test was one of clairvoyance, by the method known as
DTSP ('Down through sealed packs'), so there was no agent
looking at the cards; under these circumstances the determining factor seems to have been the experimenter who prepared
the cards. Out of the twenty subjects three produced scores
which were individually significant, and the best of these, SM,
scored significantly on both West's packs and Fisk's packs. We
may conclude, therefore, that the ESP abilities of most subjects
are quite strongly affected by the personality of the experimenter, even when they are not consciously aware of who he
is; but that there are also a few exceptional subjects who can

overcome this influence, and obtain significant scores in spite of the experimenter effect.

The discovery of the experimenter effect enables us to make sense out of many experimental results which previously seemed to be anomalous. It explains, for example, why Rhine was able to detect ESP activity in about one-fifth of his students, while Soal tested hundreds without success. Rhine, Pratt and Fisk seem to belong to a group of investigators who are able to evoke psi phenomena in a substantial proportion of their subjects; Soal, Beloff and West seem to belong to a group which is generally doomed to failure. Fortunately for Soal, he happened to come across two subjects with exceptional psi ability; others have not been so fortunate (or perhaps not so patient!), and some 'failed' experimenters have turned bitter, and accused their more successful colleagues of dishonesty or incompetence. Today the most distinguished British parapsychologist is Dr Beloff, who runs the parapsychology laboratory at Edinburgh University. ESP experiments conducted by him seldom yield significant results; nevertheless, he is a confirmed 'sheep', and has never descended to the level of attacking the integrity of others. In 1969 Beloff and his colleague David Bate carried out some guessing experiments with Edinburgh schoolchildren of the 12-13 age group, which again showed the experimenter effect at work. Preliminary experiments had led the researchers to expect negative scoring in this particular test; in fact, the children tested by Beloff produced a quite substantial *positive* score, whereas those tested by Bate produced the expected negative score. A follow-up series confirmed this trend, and statistical analysis showed that the odds against its being a chance effect were about 100 to one. In this instance it seems that Beloff's influence created a positive score, simply *because* he was aiming for a negative one! (14). Unfortunately we cannot tell at present what personality characteristics are important in a would-be parapsychologist: clearly it is not simply a matter of belief, for Beloff and West are both believers in ESP. There seems to be only one way to find out whether someone is a successful experimenter, and that is to get him to perform some experiments! Perhaps one day some enterprising psychologist will begin applying psychological tests to ESP-experimenters, as Schmeidler and Humphrey did to ESP-subjects. Until that is done we are not likely to solve the mystery of the experimenter effect.

One of the subjects who scored significantly in the Fisk-West dual ESP experiment was Jessie Blundun, a lady physician living in Devon. Not only was she gifted with ESP ability, she also became one of the best PK subjects to be discovered in Britain. At this time many British researchers, including a number who accepted the reality of ESP, were very doubtful about the American PK results. They suspected that some, if not all, of the high scores obtained in the dice-throwing tests were due to careless experimentation, recording errors, or bias in the dice. In 1951, Fisk and Mitchell embarked upon a series of PK experiments in which ten subjects, including Dr Blundun, took part. Each subject was provided with a 5/8ths inch die which had been carefully tested for bias, and was asked to throw it from a cup, working in his own home. The targets were chosen by Fisk using a random method so that each die face was made the target an approximately equal number of times. The subjects did not know what the targets were until after they had finished their series of throws, and sent the results off to Fisk. They therefore had a dual task : to determine the target by ESP and to influence the fall of the die by PK. It was hoped that by keeping the whole of the psi-process at the unconscious level of the mind, better results might be obtained than in the kind of test where the subject knows consciously what he is aiming for. The targets were displayed at Fisk's home in Long Ditton, Surrey, and the ten subjects were widely scattered : three in Devon, two in France, and one each in Birmingham, London, Kingston, Liverpool and Eire.

The overall results of the Fisk-Mitchell tests were clearly significant, with odds of more than 4,000 to one against the chance hypothesis (91). Of the ten subjects, six achieved individual scores with odds of twenty to one or more, but the outstanding subject was Dr Blundun, with odds of about 600 to one. In addition to counting the numbers of direct hits the experimenters also used a method of differential scoring which takes into account the numbers of 'near misses'. When evaluated by this method the odds against chance rose to 50,000 to one for the whole experiment, and over 7,000 to one for Dr Blundun's score. Here then, was very strong evidence in support of the American claim to have demonstrated PK with dice, and since the subjects could not have known consciously what the targets were, cheating was virtually ruled out. Over the next six years Dr Blundun continued to score significantly above chance in this type of experiment, thereby proving herself to be a persistent PK-subject in the same way that Shackleton proved himself to be a persistent ESP-subject (48).

It is a commonly held belief that ESP is more likely to occur when the target material is some object or event of great emotional significance to the percipient, such as a love affair or the death of a close relative. Evidence in support of this idea was obtained in a small, but interesting, experiment reported by Fisk in 1955. The subject was a young man, KG, who was in a state of conflict over sexual matters. He confessed to Fisk that he had recently taken to homosexual practices, which he found both more enjoyable and easier to obtain than intercourse with women. Nevertheless he was very unhappy about it, and was particularly concerned about its possible effect on his physical health, and whether eventually he would be able to marry. Fisk noticed that in ESP card-guessing tests, KG showed a preference for the circle and the cross, which he called more often than the other three symbols. The subject explained that the cross and circle carried a strong emotional content for him, symbolising the male and female genital organs respectively. This gave Fisk the idea of replacing the cross and circle symbols with erotic pictures cut from *La Vie Parisienne* and similar journals, in the hope that they would effectively stimulate the subject's ESP ability. This device proved astonishingly successful. The subject's overall score showed odds against chance of approximately 1,400 to one, but when this was broken down into the scores on the five separate symbols it was found that the high scoring had occurred entirely on the erotic targets, the three 'neutral' symbols apparently evoking no ESP response whatever. In view of KG's expressed sexual preference it is interesting to note that scoring on the male pictures was highest, with odds of more than 100,000 to one, the scoring on the female targets being at about the 100 to one level. A further interesting point concerns the 'wavy line' cards; at one point in the experiment the subject told Fisk that these also had an erotic significance for him, representing the pubic hair of either sex! Since they were neither specifically male nor specifically female, the wavy-line targets did not evoke the subject's ESP in the same way as the erotic targets. However, there was evidence that the subject often called 'male' or 'female' when the target was actually 'waves'. G. F. Dalton (31) has recently pointed out that the other two symbols—the square and the star—were not distinguished at all by the subject: his ESP ability seems to have operated only on targets which had sexual significance for him, and which therefore related to the emotional conflict uppermost in his mind (47).

In recent years it has become almost fashionable to belittle psychical research in Britain, and some critics have declared that it is a waste of time carrying out ESP and PK experiments on this side of the Atlantic as there are hardly any good subjects to be found. There has even been talk of an alleged 'trans-atlantic factor' which somehow produces a rich harvest of psychically gifted persons in the USA, whilst leaving Britain and much of Europe almost completely barren! Now it is true that a large number of high-scoring subjects have been found in America, and it is also true that the greater part of modern parapsychology stems from that country. Nevertheless, a careful examination of the publications of the SPR during the forties and fifties shows that there was a surprisingly large amount of successful research published during those years when parapsychology was forging confidently ahead. Most of this British research is unknown to the general public, which is why we have spent some time describing it here. Soal, Goldney, Bateman, West, Fisk and Mitchell all made important contributions which were complementary to the American work, and in no way inferior to it. Their efforts deserve to be more widely known than they are.

G. W. Fisk died in 1972 at the ripe old age of ninety. Among the papers he left behind was a short autobiographical sketch, in which he refers to his parapsychological discoveries in the following words:

Alas, that it should add up to so little. But then I am only like a man stroking the fur of a cat and wondering at the faint crackle of the tiny blue sparks occasionally produced. He must leave to others the understanding of what that phenomenon may mean and also the development and harnessing of that scarcely perceptible power into the dynamos and engines that will rock and illumine the world. Why should one believe that evolution on this planet has reached its peak with the appearance, within the last few seconds of geological time, of the mind of man? (64)

8. Critics' Reprise

By the mid 1950s it began to look as though the teething troubles of parapsychology were over. In 1952 Dr Lucien Warner repeated his survey of the members of the American Psychological Association and found that the percentage willing to accept ESP as 'an established fact' or 'a likely possibility' had risen from 8.8 (the 1938 figure) to 16.6, while the number of those who regarded ESP as 'an impossibility' had fallen from 14.5 to 10.3 per cent of the total. Although the majority of American psychologists were still very wary of the new science, Warner's figures did suggest that the rapidly accumulating mass of experimental data was beginning to have some effect upon psychological opinion (153). In Britain too, a number of eminent individuals and learned institutions were beginning to take ESP more seriously. In 1950 the Psychiatric Section of the Royal Society of Medicine sponsored an address by Dr Rhine, and the Royal Institution listened to a discourse by Dr Thouless, both on the topic of extrasensory phenomena. In 1953 the first chair in parapsychology was established, strangely enough not in Britain or America where so much of the experimental research had been carried out, but in Holland, at the University of Utrecht. Its first occupant was Dr W. H. C. Tenhaeff, a psychologist and member of the Dutch Society for Psychical Research. That same year an International Congress of Parapsychology was held at Utrecht, and four years later the Parapsychological Association was formed to meet the needs of the growing army of professional research workers all over the world. At long last parapsychology was becoming internationally organised as an autonomous, fully-grown branch of science, no longer dependent on the support, or even the goodwill, of its parent psychology.

In general British psychologists were inclined to look much more favourably than their American counterparts upon the subject-matter of parapsychology. This is probably because behaviourism never became quite as much a craze in Britain as it did in the USA, where it exercised a powerful restrictive influence upon psychological thinking for several decades. The English psychologist Sir Cyril Burt, described in *The Times* as 'for over forty years the leading figure in the applications of psychology to education and the development of children and to the assessment of mental qualities', was not only a believer in ESP but contributed a number of important papers to the parapsychological journals. Margaret Knight, another distinguished British psychologist, wrote rather reluctantly that 'the more recent experiments (in ESP) seem impervious to criticism,' and agreed with Thouless that 'it is a waste of time to conduct further laborious experiments merely to *demonstrate* the occurrence of ESP. This has now been established beyond reasonable doubt.' Mrs Knight did not *welcome* the new discoveries, however : to her they were too disturbing, too difficult to organise within the accepted scientific framework, and she admitted that they aroused in her a feeling of 'acute intellectual discomfort' (78). Yet perhaps the strangest of all the psychological converts to belief in ESP was Dr Hans Eysenck, whose work on personality variables was mentioned in the previous chapter. Known as a hard-headed thinker and an enthusiastic supporter of the behaviouristic approach to man, Dr Eysenck nevertheless found himself compelled to accept the evidence for the reality of ESP. In 1957 he wrote a passage which has been quoted many times by both believers and sceptics :

> Unless there is a gigantic conspiracy involving some thirty University departments all over the world, and several hundred highly respected scientists in various fields, many of them originally hostile to the claims of the psychical researchers, the only conclusion the unbiased observer can come to must be that there does exist a small number of people who obtain knowledge existing either in other people's minds, or in the outer world, by means yet unknown to science. (45)

With such a goodly company of supporters, the future of parapsychology might seem to have been assured. However, the sceptics had by no means disappeared, although the difficulty of finding loop-holes in the better kinds of ESP experiment had caused most of them to become silent after 1940. As the fifties gave way to the sixties the battle was joined yet again, and renewed critical attacks began to divert the energies of the parapsychologists from experiments to arguments. What was worse, this renewed critical activity coincided with what seemed to be a worldwide shortage of good ESP subjects : even the Americans found it increasingly difficult to obtain significantly high scoring in the card-guessing tests. Of course, this weakness did not pass unobserved by the critics, who used it as evidence for the non-existence of ESP. The earlier successes, they argued, were due entirely to faulty experimentation, fraud, or recording errors; now that conditions had been improved to the point where these things could no longer occur, the scoring had declined to the level expected by chance. What further proof was needed that ESP was nothing more than a mere chimera, a passing delusion in the minds of a few misguided scientists who found in it a substitute for the religious faith of their childhood ?

The first shots in this new battle were fired as early as 1955 when an American chemist, Dr George R. Price, launched a scathing attack on the ESP research in the pages of *Science*, the journal of the American Association for the Advancement of Science. He admitted at once that many of the experiments carried out by Rhine and Soal were performed under such rigorous conditions that they effectively ruled out all the usual counter-hypotheses, such as sensory cues, recording errors, unconscious whispering, statistical artefacts and the like. In fact, the latest experiments left the scientific world with a clear choice between only two alternatives : either ESP is real, in which case the mechanistic theory which underlies modern science is false; or the experimenters who claim to have obtained evidence for ESP are dishonest. Price went on to demonstrate that even the famous Soal-Goldney experiment, so widely acclaimed for the rigour of its experimental design, *could* have been faked if we are willing to assume that Soal was in collusion with some of the other persons who participated in the experiment. Admittedly it is highly unlikely that scientists of the calibre of Rhine and Soal would be dishonest; but is it *more* unlikely than that the whole of our scientific world-picture should be false ? David Hume, the

Edinburgh philosopher, had written two hundred years ago: 'No testimony is sufficient to establish a miracle unless the testimony be of such a kind that its falsehood would be more marvellous than the fact which it endeavours to establish.' Applying this principle, Price argued that, since we know that some people *do* commit deceptions and frauds of various kinds, the fraud hypothesis is more probable than the hypothesis that ESP exists:

> When we consider the possibility of fraud, almost invari- ably we think of particular individuals and ask ourselves whether it is possible that this particular man, this Professor X, could be dishonest. The probability seems small, but the procedure is incorrect. The correct procedure is to consider that we very likely would not have heard of Professor X at all except for his psychic findings. Accordingly, the prob- ability of interest to us is the probability of there having been anywhere in the world, among its more than 2 billion inhabitants, a few people with the desire and ability to pro- duce false evidence for the supernatural. (102)

Parapsychologists everywhere were staggered by the out- spokenness of this attack; it was a new experience to find them- selves openly accused of faking their own experiments. The Price article was extensively quoted in books, journals and lectures, and several of the leading parapsychologists replied in understandably heated language. In the SPR's *Journal*, Dr Soal expressed his 'amazement' at the article, and added:

> ... Dr Price makes these suggestions without being able to produce the least fragment of factual evidence that any such fraudulent malpractice ever took place. It is, I think, safe to say that no English scientific journal would have published such a diatribe of unsupported conjecture. (131)

But not all the believers in ESP were as amazed as Dr Soal; some were even quite pleased with the Price critique, in a back-handed sort of way. They recalled the words of Henry Sidgwick, who in his first Presidential Address to the SPR in 1882 had said:

> We must drive the objector into the position of being

forced either to admit the phenomena as inexplicable, at least by him, or to accuse the investigators either of lying or cheating or of a blindness or forgetfulness incompatible with any intellectual condition except absolute idiocy.

George Price had admitted, in effect, that the ESP experiments were now so perfect that there was no alternative left to the sceptic except to accuse the researchers of deliberate dishonesty. That, at any rate, was a kind of victory for the protagonists of psi. But the Price attack turned out to be only a small skirmish compared with the battle which was now beginning, as critic after critic assaulted the accumulated evidence of psychical research from every conceivable angle. Even the basic statistical procedures, considered inviolable ever since the pronouncement of the American Institute of Mathematical Statistics in 1937, came under renewed attack from Mr George Spencer-Brown of Oxford (133), though few of his fellow statisticians agreed with his arguments. Although some parapsychologists found themselves spending more time writing long and detailed answers to criticisms than doing experiments, they rightly considered that it was vitally important that no critic should be able to claim that his criticism had been ignored. In fact, the psychical journals were extremely generous in their allocation of space to the opponents of parapsychology.

The critical attacks were by no means confined to the statistical evidence for psi. Almost at the same time as George Price's article appeared in America, a detailed analysis of one of the most famous of the spontaneous cases was being prepared in Britain. Borley Rectory, situated on the boundary between Essex and Suffolk, had been the focus of an extraordinary variety of apparently paranormal phenomena almost from the time of its construction in 1862. From 1929 onwards it became the subject of a number of investigations, the most striking being those of Mr Harry Price, a rather flamboyant free-lance psychical researcher who ran a private laboratory for the study of paranormal phenomena. During his life-time he clashed with leading members of the SPR on several occasions, but the laws of libel and slander seem to have protected him to some extent from any overt attacks on his integrity. Harry Price died in 1948, and in 1956 the SPR published The Haunting of Borley

Rectory: A Critical Survey of the Evidence, by E. J. Dingwall, K. M. Goldney and T. H. Hall. Although the SPR does not officially express corporate views on the reality of any paranormal phenomenon, it could not escape public notice that this report was prepared at the request of the Society's Council, and printed in the Society's Proceedings. Rightly or wrongly, therefore, it came to be regarded as an official verdict on the Borley case. The report quite openly accused the now deceased Harry Price of having deliberately faked many of the happenings at Borley in order to obtain material for his books. Again the cry of 'fraud' was raised against a psychical researcher, but this time one who could not be present to defend himself. Printed in book form by Duckworth's, the Borley report achieved a circulation far beyond the membership of the psychical research societies, and was widely acclaimed as having disposed of Borley (and Harry Price) once and for all. Thirteen years later the SPR published a second report on Borley, this time written by R. J. Hastings (63), which did much to redress the balance and restore the good name of Harry Price. The second report was also published in Proceedings, but it received nothing like as much attention from the press and the public as the first one. To this day, many people believe that Harry Price was proved to have been an unprincipled fraud, and that there is nothing worth considering in the Borley records.

The Haunting of Borley Rectory made psychic history, since it was the first publication by a respectable psychical research society to openly accuse a fellow researcher of fraud. In its train came a stream of similar writings, mostly by Trevor H. Hall, one of the signatories of the Borley report. In these writings various distinguished figures from the early history of psychical research were accused of carelessness, incompetence or fraud, and naturalistic explanations were offered of the phenomena they had reported. Thus the famous British chemist Sir William Crookes was said to have connived at the fraudulent activities of the medium Florence Cook, in order to cover up a sexual liaison between them (57). Whatever the truth of such matters, Hall and his fellow debunkers were on fairly safe ground since all the accused persons had been dead for many years, and it was highly unlikely that anyone would be in a position to contradict the sceptic's version of the events. This did not prevent some indignant psychical researchers from rising to the bait, however, and page after page of the SPR's *Journal* and *Proceedings* was devoted to lengthy discussions of cases which were over fifty years old. New experimental reports became less frequent, and at one time it began to look as though the SPR was turning into a society for the study of the *history* of psychical research. Certainly little new material was appearing in the pages of its publications.

On February 26th 1959 yet another critic appeared on the horizon. *New Scientist* magazine carried an article by Dr C. E. M. Hansel, then a Senior Lecturer in the Department of Psychology at Manchester University. Hansel took up the attack where George Price had left off, and for several years he maintained a vigorous assault on the work of all the major ESP experimenters, culminating in the publication of a full-length book in 1966. This volume, entitled *ESP—A Scientific Evaluation*, carried a foreword by the distinguished historian of psychology Edwin G. Boring, and was described in the publisher's note as 'an authoritative and exhaustive work'. Such powerful backing, coupled with the use of the prestige word 'scientific' in the title, led many people to believe that Hansel had disposed of the case for the reality of psi for ever. In fact, the Hansel critique was a very mixed assortment. When dealing with some topics (PK, for example) Dr Hansel presented a very incomplete and sometimes factually inaccurate picture. Thus, the Schmeidler sheep-goat studies were dismissed in a single eight-line paragraph with the misleading remark '... repetition of the test by other investigators did not confirm the original result.' However, when we come to the great classic experiments which were regarded as providing the basic evidence for the reality of ESP, it must be admitted that Hansel presented a formidable challenge. After a detailed examination of the procedures used in the Pearce-Pratt, Pratt-Woodruff, Soal-Goldney and other experimental series of the past, Hansel claimed to have shown that in every case fraud *could* have been perpetrated, either by one of the subjects, or by collusion between subjects and experimenters:

It cannot be stated categorically that trickery was responsible for the results of these experiments, but so long as the possibility is present, the experiments cannot be regarded as satisfying the aims of their originators or as supplying conclusive evidence for ESP. (58, p. 241)

Hansel did not even grant the subjects and the experimenters the benefit of assuming that they cheated from idealistic motives only :

> In the early 1930s at Duke University, during the depression, students who acted as subjects in ESP experiments were paid an hourly wage for their services. If Pearce was paid to act as a subject, he had every incentive to continue in that capacity. The Pratt-Woodruff experiment was a continuation of work started by Woodruff constituting part of the requirement for a higher degree. The Soal-Goldney experiment gained Soal his Doctorate of Science at London University. Would that degree have been given for a series of negative experiments? Mrs Stewart was paid for her services. The Jones boys earned large rewards for high scores. (58, p. 235)

There were many who felt that the case for ESP must be strong indeed if a sceptic was forced to resort to insinuations of this kind in order to avoid the force of the evidence. The parapsychologist Dr K. Ramakrishna Rao described the fraud hypothesis as 'the disgraceful argument of the dogmatic goat ... (it) has no merit as scientific criticism' (106, p. 18). Reacting to the implied charge against Dr Soal, Dr R. H. Thouless, who had been one of the examiners responsible for awarding Soal his D.Sc., issued the following statement with the permission of the Academic Registrar of London University :

> The implication .... that a degree would not have been awarded for negative results is absurd. The business of the examiners is to examine the quality of the work submitted including the logic of its conclusions, not to ask themselves whether they agree with the conclusions. (141)

Referring to the results of Soal's experiments with Basil Shackleton and Gloria Stewart, Dr Evelyn Hutchinson, a professor of biology at Yale University, wrote that any fraud hypothesis would 'imply a conspiracy involving at least two percipients and five agents in 1936-1938 which arranged some extremely odd but hardly noticeable results and then went underground until Whately Carington induced Soal to re-examine his records, and finally involved a number of further people including perhaps Soal himself' (quoted by Rao, 106, p. 20). Viewed in these terms, it seems extremely unlikely, to put it mildly, that Soal's results can be explained as the outcome of such an extensive conspiracy.

It would take a sizeable book to discuss in detail all the arguments and counter-arguments generated by the Hansel critique. Ten years after the publication of Hansel's 'scientific evaluation' his disciples are still continuing the battle. In 1973 *Nature* carried a paper by C. Scott and P. Haskell, who claimed to have found evidence in support of a theory that Soal cheated by altering certain figures on the record sheets during the Shackleton experiments (126). The 'evidence' consisted of a minor statistical anomaly which *could* be interpreted in terms of a fraud hypothesis; it was found in only three of the forty sittings which constituted the Soal-Goldney experiment. A similar kind of paper, this time by Medhurst and Scott (89), appeared in the *Journal of Parapsychology* in 1974. On this occasion the experiment under attack was the Pratt-Woodruff series of 1938-9, carried out at Duke University. Once again, rather obscure statistical evidence was invoked in support of a hypothesis that Woodruff, either consciously or unconsciously, altered the positions of certain cards to create a bogus ESP effect. Whether the reader is impressed by such arguments depends to a large extent upon his philosophical presuppositions. If he is the sort of man whose philosophy excludes the possibility of psi, he has no option but to adopt a naturalistic explanation, however far-fetched it may seem to be; for to accept the validity of a single successful ESP experiment would be to undermine everything else he believes in. The demand for a 'fraud-proof' experiment is something of a red-herring; for no matter how carefully an experiment is designed, or how many eminent observers are inveigled into taking part, it is always possible for the hardened sceptic to claim that the results are due to some sort of collective fraud. Eysenck recognised that, in the final analysis, the sceptic can always postulate a 'gigantic conspiracy' involving people all over the world. However, as the years go by, and the number of successful experiments increases, the fraud hypothesis becomes more and more difficult to sustain with any degree of plausibility.

In an address to the Parapsychological Association delivered in September 1959, Dr Thouless pointed out that there is at least one class of person who is in a position to know the truth about the existence of psi with complete certainty, namely the person who has had direct experience of it. Others may be willing to speculate about whether Soal cheated or not: Soal himself must *know* whether he did. If we agree with Dr George Price that the Soal-Goldney experiment was so designed that it leaves us with a clear choice between the hypothesis of ESP and the hypothesis of the fraudulent experimenter, then Dr Soal must know whether ESP exists. The best possible answer to a sceptic such as Dr Hansel would be to provide him with a good ESP subject, and let him see for himself that the phenomenon is real. Unfortunately, as we have seen, psi effects are extremely sensitive to the personality of the experimenter, so that in the present state of our knowledge we cannot guarantee that the good ESP subject would be able to perform under such conditions. Nevertheless, there have been a number of sceptics who have become 'converted' as a result of their own experiences. On the other side are a number of investigators who were initially favourable towards the ESP hypothesis, but who have become sceptics as a result of their own failure to obtain significant results.

Perhaps this is as good a place as any to explain the attitude adopted by the author of this book. Having studied the experimental literature over a number of years, he came to agree with Margaret Knight that the reality of psi phenomena had been proved beyond all *reasonable* doubt. Not being particularly enamoured of the mechanistic philosophy, he had no *a priori* reasons for rejecting the evidence of Rhine, Pratt, Soal, Fisk and the others, and therefore no reason to suspect them of fraud. Until a few years ago, the author's belief in psi rested *entirely* on his reading of the work of others. Today, he is in the happy position described by Thouless: he has been fortunate enough to witness significant ESP scoring under conditions where only he could have cheated; and he *knows* that he did not. In the author's own laboratory a schoolboy subject, Colin Norris, obtained statistically significant scores in three different types of ESP tests: clairvoyance using the 'BT' technique; clairvoyance using the 'DT' technique; and a test of 'general ESP' with an agent looking at the cards (105). The overall odds against the chance hypothesis were more than 50,000 to one. While it is *just* possible that some alternative hypothesis, such as unconscious whispering, might account for the results of the general ESP tests, there is no possibility of any such explanation being applicable to the BT and DT tests, which were independently significant. The subject was given no opportunity to examine the cards beforehand: they were made up in the author's own home and taken to the laboratory in sealed envelopes. For the DT tests (which alone produced odds of over 100 to one) the cards were taken straight from the author's pocket and placed face downward under a sheet of thick black paper, which was not disturbed until the end of the run. The subject was under careful observation throughout, and at no time did he touch or examine the pack. Only the experimenter could have faked the results of this experiment; and he knows that he did not. Of course, such an argument cannot be convincing to the Hanselian sceptics, who will presumably simply consign the author to the rogues gallery, along with Rhine, Pratt, Woodruff and Soal. It is indeed a goodly company!

Parapsychology undoubtedly went through a bad time during the 1960s, with the rise of the Price-Hansel school of criticism and the shortage of good ESP subjects. Only one star appeared on the horizon during that time: the remarkable Czech psychic Stepanek, who was extensively studied by scientists from several countries for more than a decade (cf Pratt, 13, pp. 95-121). Unfortunately even Stepanek could not make up for the dearth of subjects elsewhere. It began to appear as though the sceptics were right, and parapsychology would soon be on its death bed. In 1965 Dr Rhine reached retirement age, and Duke University decided it could no longer sponsor the work of the famous Parapsychology Laboratory. Fortunately the Foundation for Research on the Nature of Man (FRNM), a body which had been established three years earlier, was able to take over the sponsorship of the laboratory and its staff, and the whole organisation moved to a site outside the University campus. However, the expulsion of the parapsychologists from Duke seemed an ominous sign: it looked as though the Rhine revolution had failed since, after some thirty-five years of research, parapsychology was still not considered important enough to justify the continued support of the University. Although research was still going on in a number of widely scattered institutions around the world, few of these were supported by official academic bodies. Psi phenomena seemed as elusive as ever, and parapsychologists wondered ruefully whether they would ever reach that breakthrough point which occurs in the history of most sciences, when suddenly some new discovery triggers off a rapid acceleration of research progress. Many critics felt that the fact that no such rapid expansion had occurred in parapsychology after so many years of research was a sign that they were dealing with a pseudo-science, based only on mal-observation and fraud.

In a *New Scientist* article in 1969, Dr Christopher Evans painted a picture of parapsychology as a dying subject, 'a relic of the past with an aura of faded pre-war newspapers, the Graf Zeppelin and the Entente Cordiale' (42). Yet even while he was writing these words, an extraordinarily brilliant piece of work was being performed in the USA which was to lift parapsychology out of the doldrums and raise it to a position of respectability never before achieved. This new research will be described in the next chapter. It would be an exaggeration to present it as the much looked-for breakthrough, yet it certainly gave a badly needed boost to the morale of the parapsychologists, and confronted the critics with the most powerful challenge they had had to face so far. Parapsychology, conceived in the seance-rooms of Victorian England and brought to birth in the psychological laboratories of Duke University, was now about to enter the Space Age.

9. Psi in the Space Age

In the final chapter of his critical book on ESP, Professor Hansel wrote as follows:

> A great deal of time, effort, and money has been expended but an acceptable demonstration of the existence of extra-sensory perception has not been given.... An acceptable model for future research with which the argument could rapidly be settled one way or the other has now been made available by the investigators at the United States Air Force Research Laboratories. If 12 months' research on VERITAC can establish the existence of ESP, the past research will not have been in vain. If ESP is not established, much further effort could be spared and the energies of many young scientists could be directed to more worthwhile research. (58, p. 241)

The reader will recall that Hansel dismissed the results of all the major ESP experiments as unacceptable on the grounds that they could have been produced by error or fraud on the part of one or more of the subjects or experimenters taking part. In the passage quoted above, he indicated clearly the kind of evidence he *would* regard as acceptable. VERITAC was a machine which automatically generated randomised targets, recorded the subject's guesses, and computed the scores. Human error, along with the possibility of fraud, was virtually eliminated. At the time Hansel wrote, VERITAC had already been tried out on 37 subjects without revealing any evidence for ESP, which is perhaps why he felt himself to be on safe ground in referring to it.

The notion of using machines to test for the presence of ESP was not entirely new. Before the Second World War the English experimenter G. N. M. Tyrrell carried out a series of clairvoyance and precognition experiments using a machine, and obtained some apparently significant results. In 1952 a young Harvard student, David Kahn, published a report on some studies carried out with an IBM machine, again with results that indicated the operation of ESP (74). Over the years there had been various other suggestions for automating the psi-test procedures, but none were put into practice in anything more than a desultory fashion. Probably the main reason for this lay in the major difficulties encountered in designing and constructing such machines. It is by no means easy, even today, to build a machine which will ensure a *truly* random series of targets; ordinary computers only hold a store of what are usually known as 'pseudo-random numbers'. If the delicate methods of statistical analysis are to be applied to ESP results, it is important that the target sequences should conform as closely as possible to the mathematician's theoretical concept of randomness, and a great deal of attention has been given to this problem in the parapsychological literature. However, with the coming of the 'space-race', and the consequent boom in the electronics industry, there became available those wonderfully compact devices known as integrated circuits, in which quite complex circuitry is built on to silicon chips only a few millimetres across. With the use of these devices, it became possible to build very sophisticated randomisers which could be fitted into a very small space.

The first ESP machine to make use of the new technology was built by Dr Helmut Schmidt, a Senior Research Scientist at the Boeing Research Laboratories in Seattle. His great innovation was to use a radioactive source, a piece of strontium-90, to provide randomness. According to modern physics the radioactive decay of atomic nuclei is entirely random, and therefore unpredictable. We can calculate the approximate number of atoms that will have decayed after a certain time, just as we can estimate, within certain limits, the number of people who will be knocked down by motor vehicles in a certain month of next year. What we *cannot* predict is the exact moment when any particular atom will decay. Now when a strontium-90 atom decays it fires out a high-speed electron which can be registered with a Geiger-Muller tube. These electrons are emitted from a piece of the strontium-90 at random time intervals, and it is these random intervals which determine the targets generated by the Schmidt machine.

Inside the machine is a high-speed oscillator built from inverters, which drives a modulo-4 counter constructed out of gates and flip-flops. All the while the machine is switched on, this internal counter is advancing through its four positions in the sequence: 1, 2, 3, 4, 1, 2 ... etc, passing through each position about a million times per second. The human subject sits in front of a panel on which are four coloured lamps, with a push-button corresponding to each lamp. As long as the subject takes no action the lamps remain unlit, although the internal counter continues to run through its four-position sequence. Now suppose the subject presses one of the buttons; the circuitry is so arranged that the next electron which arrives in the Geiger-Muller tube stops the modulo-4 counter in whatever position it happens to have reached at that moment. At the same time, various output gates are opened so that the corresponding lamp on the panel lights up. If the subject has correctly predicted which lamp will light, the machine automatically registers a 'hit'; otherwise the subject's pressing of the button will be registered as a 'miss'. Since there are four lamps, the number of hits expected by chance is one quarter of the total number of trials. The Schmidt machine has various built-in safeguards which prevent the subject from cheating by pressing two buttons simultaneously, or by using any other kind of manual dexterity. The numbers of hits and misses are registered by electro-mechanical counters built into the machine, and also recorded externally by a punch-tape machine, so that any attempt to cheat by re-setting the electromechanical counters is prevented.

The Schmidt machine is undoubtedly the most advanced piece of equipment ever used in parapsychology. By employing integrated circuits Schmidt was able to make it no larger than a fairly large book, yet it satisfies all the requirements laid down by Hansel. Automatic recording of both targets and guesses effectively eliminates human errors, and the fact that the whole device is enclosed in a sealed box disposes of the problem of fraud. Even if the subject had the equipment entirely to himself (which he usually does not) it is difficult to see how he could fake a significant score. The security thus provided by the electronics leaves the experimenter free to concentrate on the important human task of coaxing his subjects into the best mood to achieve a good ESP score. He no longer needs to adopt the role of a watch-dog, constantly regarding his subjects with a suspicious eye lest they try to cheat; he can relax and try to create a warm and friendly atmosphere which may encourage the emergence of ESP. Since the machine is readily portable, tests can be conducted in the subject's own home without any loss of experimental rigour.

Having constructed his machine, Schmidt carried out some exploratory trials with about 100 subjects. Most of these obtained only chance scores, but there were a few striking exceptions. Among the more promising subjects was Dr DW, a physicist with an active interest in music, who told Schmidt that he frequently experienced precognitive dreams. In several short sessions DW made a total of 7,600 trials and scored 2,065 hits, which is 165 hits more than the number expected by chance. The odds against such a score occurring fortuitously are about 100,000 to one. Unfortunately DW moved away to another city shortly afterwards, and it was not possible to continue experimenting with him at that time. Schmidt therefore continued his search for subjects who could obtain significant scores with the machine, at first with very little success. His great breakthrough came when he decided to lay aside his prejudices against professional mediums, and approach a spiritualist group in Seattle. Among these people he found several good subjects, including a male medium (KMR), a teacher of 'psychic development' (Mrs JB), and a truck driver who was also an amateur psychic (OC). Having carried out a few informal tests to discover the best working conditions for these subjects, Schmidt embarked upon a carefully controlled and lengthy series of experiments.

In the first main series the three subjects made a total of 63,066 trials with the machine, scoring at a rate 4.4% higher than would be expected by chance. To those unfamiliar with probability theory this may not seem very much; it involves only 4 or 5 extra hits in every hundred trials. Nevertheless, the maintenance of such a scoring rate over such a large number of trials is staggeringly significant: the odds against it happening by chance are more than 500,000,000 to one. In order to check that there was nothing wrong with either the machine or the theory of probability, Schmidt arranged for a 'control' run to be performed. For this, the buttons on the machine were activated automatically in the same sequence in which the subject OC had pressed them, and the numbers of hits and misses recorded as before. The results were well within the range predicted by the theory of probability.

For the second series of experiments SC, the sixteen-year-old daughter of the subject OC, joined the group of subjects in place of KMR, who had become unavailable. In this series the subjects were allowed to choose whether they would aim for a high score or a low score. In aiming for a low score the subject has to select a lamp which will *not* light, and press the corresponding button. The decision whether to aim high or low was made at the beginning of each session, and recorded on the tape in code so that the evaluating computer could make the appropriate assessment. Altogether a predetermined total of 20,000 trials were made during 21 sessions held during the months September-November 1967. The results turned out to be among the most significant in the whole history of parapsychology, giving odds against chance of more than ten thousand million to one. A summary of them is given in Table 2, for the reader's inspection.

Table 2: Results of Schmidt's second precognition experiment

Subject	Goal	No. of trials	Deviation from chance	Odds (approx)
OC	High Score	5,000	+66	30 to 1
JB	High Score	5,672	+123	6,200 to 1
JB	Low Score	4,328	−126	120,000 to 1
SC	Low Score	5,000	−86	200 to 1

(adapted from Schmidt, 116, p. 107)

A remarkable feature of this experiment was the subjects' ability to score above chance (positive deviation) or below chance (negative deviation) at will. Many years ago, a critic suggested to Dr Rhine that perhaps the remarkable scoring of Hubert Pearce in card-guessing experiments was just a matter of chance: Rhine pointed to the fact that Pearce was able to obtain either a positive or a negative score at the request of the experimenter, and added 'if this is a matter of chance performance, then the rise and fall of that steam shovel I see out of the window is a chance performance.' There are still many critics who like to emphasise the unpredictability and unreliability of psi phenomena: here we are confronted with definite evidence of *lawfulness*. ESP may be difficult to control, but it is by no means entirely chaotic or purposeless in its operation, either in the laboratory or in real-life situations.

The high scores of Schmidt's subjects might be attributable to the operation of either precognition or psychokinesis. The precognition hypothesis implies that the subject somehow *foresaw* which lamp would light next, whereas the PK hypothesis implies that he influenced the machine to make his prediction come true. In the preliminary tests the medium KMR tried out both approaches to his task. In some tests he waited for an intuition concerning the next target, and then pressed the corresponding button; in other tests he concentrated on only one of the lamps, pressed only the button corresponding to this lamp, and tried to force it to light with increased frequency by PK. Both approaches were successful in producing statistically significant above-chance scoring. Unfortunately we cannot conclude from this that both precognition and PK were operating. Psi phenomena operate at the level of the unconscious mind, and merely because a subject *thinks* he is using a particular form of psi we cannot assume that he is actually doing so. KMR might have been using precognition when he thought he was using PK, and vice-versa. With this particular experimental set-up there does not seem to be any way of distinguishing between the two. However, Schmidt's third experiment used a different arrangement which definitely excluded the possibility of PK. This time the targets were not determined by a radioactive source, but by a paper tape containing over 100,000 random numbers which had been taken from tables and punched on the tape in advance. Before the subject pressed his button, the target was already in existence in the form of a hole in a certain position on the paper tape, which was inside the tape-reading machine. As soon as the button was pressed the subject's guess was registered by the recording apparatus, and one tenth of a second later a voltage was applied to the reading contacts of the tape-reader. The random number on the tape was then recorded and displayed to the subject by the lighting of a lamp. Since the sequence of random numbers was already in existence before the experiment began, it would seem to be impossible to influence it by PK. Success in this form of the experiment might be due to precognition (foreseeing which lamp would light next) or clairvoyance (seeing the number on the tape inside the machine). In fact, Schmidt described it as a clairvoyance experiment (117), although it would probably be better to call it an experiment in 'general ESP'. Six subjects took part, including OC and JB who had performed successfully in the previous tests. The other subjects were two housewives (VH and MK) who had both reported occasional psychic experiences, a married woman who had taken part in classes for 'psychic development' (RL), and Dr DW, the physicist who had assisted in the preliminary testing of the machine. Altogether these six completed 15,000 trials, of which 7,091 were high-aim and 7,909 were low-aim. The high-aim trials produced 108 hits more than the average expected by chance, and the low-aim trials 152 hits less. This is a highly significant result, for the odds against it occurring by chance are about three million to one.

Having demonstrated yet again the reality of ESP, Schmidt next set his electronic expertise to work on the problem of PK. Here he was on well trodden ground, for PK machines of one kind or another had been in use in parapsychology ever since the motor-driven die tumblers of the early days at Duke University. Indeed, Schmidt was not even the first to use radioactive materials in this context: the credit for this goes to Beloff and Evans, who reported an unsuccessful attempt to exert a psychokinetic influence upon the emission of alpha particles from plutonium and uranium in 1961 (16). Seven years later two Cambridge researchers, Wadhams and Farrelly, also reported the failure of a similar kind of experiment, this time using beta particles (high-speed electrons) from a strontium-90 source (151). However, two French experimenters had in the meantime achieved a certain measure of success with this type of experiment. Dr Remy Chauvin and Jean-Pierre Genthon used seven children as subjects in their experiments, asking them to try to speed up or slow down the counting rate of a Geiger counter which was registering particles from a piece of uranium nitrate (24). Two of the subjects, 13-year-old boys,

Plate 1   Dr. J. B. Rhine, the founder of modern experimental
parapsychology.

Plate 2 A clairvoyance test, using the 'down-through' (DT) procedure. The subject calls out his guesses while the pack remains undisturbed under a piece of opaque black paper. The subject here is Colin Norris (*see* p. 120).

Plate 3 A clairvoyance test, by the BT method. The experimenter lifts off (but does not look at) each card as it is called. Here the author is taking the record.

Plate 4   A PK experiment with dice in a rotating wire-gauze cage. The subject tries to influence the dice as they roll from one end of the cage to the other. Tests with such cages provided a large part of the evidence for PK during the early period of research at Duke University. Today they have been largely superseded by electronic testing machines.

Plate 5   Testing for precognition with a Schmidt four-channel random number generator. By pressing one of the four buttons the subject registers her prediction of which of the four lamps will light next (*see* page 123). The subject here is Dr. Schmidt's daughter, Karen.

Plates 6 and 7   PK-testing with a Schmidt two-channel machine. In plate 6 the subject is trying to influence the moving light on the panel so that it moves in a clockwise direction. In plate 7 the subject is trying to make one lamp flash more often than the other.

Plate 8   PK on living targets : in the author's laboratory a schoolboy subject tries to influence the movements of a woodlouse on a board divided into sectors (*see* page 181). A perspex screen prevents the subject's breath from affecting the animal.

Plate 9   A similar experiment to No 8. Here the subject, suitably screened from view, attempts to make a gerbil run to the left or right, according to a randomly-determined target order.

Plate 10 Precognition testing with gerbils. Enclosed in the testing cage, the animal can avoid receiving an electric shock by being in the 'correct' half of the cage. A binary random number generator determines which is to be the target side for any particular trial (*see* page 149). This photo was taken at the Institute for Parapsychology, N. Carolina, in 1970.

11   12

13

Plates 11, 12 and 13   *Experiments in paranormal healing*
These three pictures show an ingenious kind of experiment devised by Graham
and Anita Watkins (*see* page 169). Pairs of mice are anaesthetised in identical
etherisers (plate 11). Later, a human subject tries to make one mouse recover
from the anaesthetic more rapidly than the other. Here, the human subject is
shown attached to monitoring devices which register her brain rhythms,
heart-rate, respiration, skin resistance, and other variables while the experiment
is in progress (plate 12). Photocells connected to automatic recording equipment enable an objective record to be kept of the exact time at which each
mouse awakens (plate 13).

achieved highly significant scores, with odds against chance of about 300,000,000,000 to 1 and 30,000,000,000 to 1 respectively. Even so, the French experimenters regarded their work as merely exploratory: it certainly did not seem at this stage as though PK-testing with radioactive isotopes would be any more successful than any of the older methods.

For his PK tests Schmidt built a simpler version of his precognition machine, this time with only two outputs (a binary random number generator). This was coupled to a visual display panel on which were mounted nine lamps arranged in a circle. The coupling was so arranged that one, and only one, of the lamps was lit at any particular time. When the generator produced the number $+1$, the light jumped one step in the clockwise direction; when it produced the number -1, the light jumped one step in the anticlockwise direction. Assuming that the binary RNG was producing a purely random distribution of $+1$'s and -1's, the light would be expected to perform a random walk among the nine lamps of the circle. For a standard test run the light was started at the top of the circle, and the RNG was set to produce a sequence of 128 numbers, which took about two minutes. The subject sat in front of the panel and tried to will the light to move in a clockwise direction, which was equivalent to willing the machine to produce more $+1$'s than -1's. In between runs the machine was left running in order to check that, in the absence of deliberate human influence, it did indeed behave randomly. Also, as a further safeguard against possible bias in the machine, the two outputs from the RNG to the display panel were frequently reversed, so that an excess of hits could not be due to any tendency for the machine to favour one number rather than the other.

Schmidt's preliminary tests with the PK machine involved eighteen subjects and showed, rather surprisingly, a general tendency to score *negatively*, that is, for the light to move in the opposite direction to that intended. Only three of these first subjects scored positively. Since the negative scoring seemed so consistent, Schmidt decided to concentrate on trying to produce it deliberately. Choosing nine of the best negative scorers from the preliminary tests, he later added a further six to produce a new team of fifteen subjects. He decided in advance that this team was to perform 64 sessions of four runs each—a grand total of 32,768 trials, with the expectation that the scoring would be significantly below chance. Although the subjects were told to *aim* for a high positive score, Schmidt set out to create conditions which would be as discouraging as possible, in the hope of obtaining a negative one. He avoided praising subjects when their scores rose above chance, and generally did everything he could to produce feelings of failure and pessimism about the experiment. The result was a deviation from chance of −302 hits, corresponding to odds of more than 1,000 to one. Later Schmidt discovered two star subjects

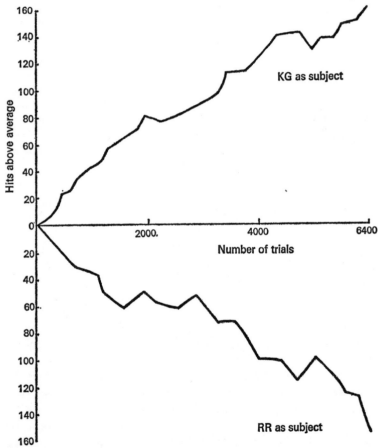

Fig. 3: Result of a machine PK experiment with two preselected subjects. (After Schmidt, 13, p. 27)

who were able to produce consistent scoring with the PK machine: an 'aggressively outgoing American girl' (KG) who produced positive scores, and a 'reserved, methodical researcher in parapsychology from South America' (RR), who produced negative scores (see figure 3). Each of these subjects completed 6,400 trials with the machine, obtaining odds against chance of about 30,000 to 1 and 6,000 to 1 respectively. The odds against the *difference* in their scores arising fortuitously are more than ten million to one (118).

In so far as it is humanly possible to prove anything in this uncertain world, the Schmidt experiments provide us with the final proof of the reality of both ESP and PK. There is now only one possible escape for the sceptic who wishes to avoid accepting the reality of psi, and that is to believe that Schmidt deliberately falsified the whole series of experiments. Even that is becoming less and less feasible, since other researchers have used Schmidt's machines and obtained similar results. Between October 1969 and January 1970 Erlendur Haraldsson, an Icelandic psychologist who was staying at the Institute for Parapsychology in North Carolina, repeated the original Schmidt precognition experiment using ordinary subjects instead of professional psychics. The subjects were drawn from several sources: some were students at Duke University, some were casual visitors to the Institute, and some were ambulatory patients at the Duke hospital. After preliminary trials with 74 subjects Haraldsson selected the eleven best scorers for his main experiment, which produced odds against chance of 2,000 to one (59). Later a young Australian worker, Eve André, obtained significant results with a Schmidt PK machine using only three subjects. She found, however, that above-chance scoring was obtained only in the morning sessions (2). Encouraging as these supporting studies are, it would be unfair to leave the reader with the naïve belief that anyone can obtain evidence of psi, merely by using an electronic testing machine. In 1971 Dr Robert Thouless reported a failed attempt to obtain significant scores with a Schmidt machine (142), and Beloff and Bate reported a similar failure with a machine of rather different design (15). However, neither of these experiments was really comparable with Schmidt's: Thouless used only himself as a subject, and Beloff and Bate used only five subjects drawn from a local spiritualist society, none of whom was a professional medium. It will be recalled that Schmidt screened a very large number of subjects before selecting the teams for his major experiments, and most of his subjects had obtained previous evidence of their own psi capacities. This careful subject selection was undoubtedly part of the reason for his success. There is also the complication of the experimenter effect, described in chapter 7: it could hardly be expected that the use of electronics would somehow confer success upon experimenters who had been unable to obtain it by other methods. None of these limitations can detract from the immense significance of Schmidt's work, which has provided the complete answer to Professor Hansel's challenge. On the basis of his own words, Hansel ought now to accept the reality of psi, and admit that the past research has not been in vain.

At the time when he produced his first papers on precognition Schmidt was still at the Boeing laboratories. In 1969 he moved to the Institute for Parapsychology, which had been set up to replace the old Duke University Parapsychology Laboratory. Since then Schmidt has been a full-time parapsychologist, and has conducted a number of important researches with both human and animal subjects. The animal experiments will be described in a later chapter; here we shall describe some of the more sophisticated researches which he has recently completed with human subjects.

The first of these was an attempt to settle the question of whether the scoring in the original 'precognition' experiment was really due to precognition, or whether it was a manifestation of PK. To clarify this problem, Schmidt cleverly modified the circuitry of the original machine so that extra-chance scoring could *only* be produced psychokinetically. To understand how this was achieved, imagine the four numbers of the RNG arranged in a circle, thus:

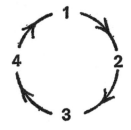

Let us suppose the subject presses the button representing Lamp No. 1, and immediately afterwards the RNG produces the number 3. Instead of this causing Lamp No. 3 to light up (as happened in the original machine), a logic circuit causes the lamp *three places ahead of the one chosen by the subject* to light instead. This is Lamp No. 4, so our subject has scored a miss. Suppose he now presses the button representing Lamp No. 2, and the machine then generates the number 2; examination of the circular arrangement above shows that Lamp No. 4 will light, so the subject has failed again! On reflection, it is easy to see that the subject can only score a hit when the RNG generates the number 4; for whatever button he presses, only the generation of a 4 will cause the lamp corresponding to that button to light. Therefore, in a machine connected in this manner, significant above-chance scoring can *only* be produced by forcing the machine to generate an excess of 4's, in other words, by the exercise of PK ability. The beauty of the experiment lies in the fact that, as far as the subject is concerned everything is exactly the same as it was in the original precognition experiment. The panel with its four lamps and four buttons appears to be exactly the same, and unless the subject is told about the altered circuitry there is no normal way in which he can become aware of the change in experimental conditions.

Schmidt carried out two experiments using this arrangement. For the first he used miscellaneous groups of subjects (mainly schoolchildren, students, and teachers), whereas for the second he used a single high-scoring subject, Lee Pantas. Trials with the machine connected in the manner described above ('PK-oriented trials') were alternated with trials in which the machine was connected in the same way as in the original experiment ('precognition-oriented trials'). The results were statistically highly significant under both conditions. In the first experiment the PK arrangement gave slightly better scores, whereas in the second experiment the precognition arrangement produced the highest score. However, the differences between the scores under the two conditions were not statistically significant; that is, they were well within the fluctuations which might easily be produced by chance. There was therefore no evidence to suggest that one arrangement was really more successful than the other (121).

In a later experiment Schmidt compared the effect of PK upon two internally different binary random number generators. One of these was a 'simple' RNG of the type already described. The other produced its binary output by taking the 'majority vote' of 100 random numbers produced by a high-speed randomiser inside the machine. Thus, if the randomiser produced fifty-one $+1$'s and forty-nine -1's, the machine gave an output of $+1$. Once again, the display actually seen by the subject was the same, whichever machine was in use. In fact, a random selector determined which of the two machines (simple or complex) was to be used for any particular trial, so that neither the subject nor the experimenter knew which was in use on any particular occasion. Two experiments, of about 1,000 trials and 3,000 trials respectively, were performed with this apparatus: both gave highly significant evidence of PK. The first experiment suggested that the PK effect had worked rather better when the simple RNG was in the circuit; however, the second experiment showed no significant differences between the scoring with the two machines. Once again, it seemed as though the psi-effect was totally indifferent to the kind of machine used (120).

In 1887 two American physicists, Michelson and Morley, performed what seemed to be an essentially simple experiment to measure the velocity of the earth. The answer they received was quite astonishing. The experiment gave the clear result: $v=0$; the earth is stationary! Such an answer seemed to be in flat contradiction to the central tenet of the Copernican theory, which had been accepted by astronomers for over 300 years. Yet the Copernican theory was not wrong: rather, Michelson and Morley had asked a nonsensical question, for we now realise that there is no such thing as absolute velocity. The Newtonian concepts of space and time led the nineteenth-century physicists to create divisions in their picture of reality which had no basis in fact.

One cannot help wondering whether a Michelson-Morley situation exists in relation to our present-day attempts to distinguish between precognition and PK. Schmidt's subjects seemed to perform equally well whether the circuitry was arranged for a PK experiment or a precognition experiment: they were usually quite unaware of the difference. Could it be, then, that there really *is* no difference; that the distinction between the two phenomena exists only in our own minds? Suppose that one night a person dreams of an event which occurs the following day, and let us assume that the circumstances are such that we can rule out all normal counter-hypotheses such as faulty memory and chance coincidence. We seem to be left with two possible interpretations of this occurrence:

(1) The future event somehow caused the subject's dream (precognition), or

(2) The subject's dream somehow caused the future event (PK).

Both interpretations are exceedingly strange in terms of our present world-view: the first involves reversed causality (the future affecting the present), while the second implies a magical power of mind over matter. Furthermore, there does not seem to be any clear way of distinguishing between the two. Perhaps, then, it would be better if we stopped thinking in terms of PK and precognition, and merely regarded the two events as psychically linked occurrences in the four-dimensional space-time continuum. Something similar to this was suggested by the Swiss psychiatrist C. G. Jung, who proposed the term 'synchronicity' to denote the paranormal coupling of events. Some years ago W. G. Roll put forward the hypothesis that *all* instances of precognition can be understood in terms of a PK mechanism, thus avoiding the bewildering concept of reversed causality. This drew the following dry comment from G. F. Dalton (30):

Applied to spontaneous cases ... (Roll's hypothesis) gives alarming results. A rough check through a few recorded sources suggests that, on this theory, ostensible precognitionists have been responsible for at least

100 deaths
8 railway accidents
5 fires
2 shipwrecks

1 explosion

1 stroke of lightning

1 volcanic eruption

2 world wars.

If PK is really operating on this scale, no one is safe.

The criticism is both apt and entertaining. The suggestion put forward here, however, is not that precognition can be explained in terms of PK, or vice-versa, but that, viewed from a standpoint outside the space-time world of everyday events the distinction between the two would be seen to be meaningless. This universe may be only a thin cross-section of a much larger reality in which past, present and future (and therefore cause and effect) have no meaning. If psi-phenomena are intrusions from this timeless reality, it is not surprising that they show no respect for our attempts to make fine experimental distinctions between precognition and PK. Such attempts depend for their meaningfulness upon the Newtonian concept of a unidirectional time-flow. If we are ever to understand psi at all, it will have to be in terms of a greatly expanded concept of reality which will go far beyond what is recognised by our present-day science.

While Helmut Schmidt was busily applying the fruits of space-age technology to the study of psi, a team of investigators at the Maimonides Medical Centre in Brooklyn, New York, was also attacking the problems of parapsychology with the help of modern electronics. The work began in 1960 when a New York psychiatrist, Dr Montague Ullman, conceived the idea of using sleep-monitoring techniques to investigate the occurrence of telepathy in dreams. He realised that the setting up of a dream laboratory would be a highly expensive project, so he approached Mrs Eileen Garrett, then president of the Parapsychology Foundation. Having experienced many psychic occurrences in her own life, Mrs Garrett was keen to see the whole subject developed on a scientific basis, and she readily agreed to provide rooms, equipment and research personnel at the Foundation's headquarters. Before long exploratory experiments were underway, with Mrs Garrett herself acting as the experimental subject. After two years of this preliminary research, Ullman considered he had sufficient evidence to justify the establishment of a full-scale dream laboratory. With the help of a grant from the Menninger Foundation he transferred the whole project to the Maimonides hospital, where he held a post as director of the Community Mental Health Centre.

Modern dream research takes its origin from the work of two scientists at the University of Chicago, Dr Nathaniel Kleitman and Dr Eugene Aserinsky. In the early 1950s these researchers noticed that when a person is dreaming, certain clearly identifiable changes occur in the pattern of electrical activity in the brain. These changes can be monitored with an electroencephalograph (EEG), a sensitive machine for measuring and recording electrical brain activity. In addition, the dreaming subject shows rapid movements of the eyes which are not present in the non-dreaming stages of sleep. These rapid eye movements (REMs) can also be monitored electrically. The discovery of these phenomena was something of a breakthrough for dream psychologists: for the first time it was possible to know exactly when a person was dreaming from purely physiological observations. By watching the recording instruments, it was possible to wake the subject immediately after he had had a dream, and make him recount his dream into a tape recorder. In this way many dreams were recorded which would have been completely forgotten by the following morning. Dreaming turned out to be much more frequent than most people had realised, amounting to about 25% of the total time spent in sleep. Almost everyone has at least four dreams every night, although the vast majority of these are forgotten on waking.

In Ullman's Dream Laboratory the set-up for a typical telepathy experiment is as follows: the subject who is to act as the telepathic percipient goes to sleep with electrodes attached to his head in several places. Wires run from the electrodes to the monitoring equipment in an adjacent room, where the experimenter keeps watch upon the subject's sleep patterns. As soon as he sees that the subject is beginning to dream, the experimenter presses a button which sends a one-way signal to the agent, who is situated in a room some distance away. The agent then concentrates on a randomly selected target picture, and tries telepathically to influence the sleeping percipient's dream. At the end of each dream period the subject is awakened and asked to describe what he has dreamt into a tape-recorder. In the morning an interview is conducted in which the subject is asked to give additional information, and to describe any associations that occur to him when he thinks about his dream. At the end of each experimental series transcripts of the dreams and their associations, together with copies of the target pictures, are sent to a group of judges who are not told which dream was supposed to correspond to which picture (that is, they judge 'blindly'). Each judge independently matches the dreams against the pictures to produce what he considers to be the best match. Statistical calculations are then applied to determine whether there are more correct matchings than could reasonably be expected to occur by chance.

The first major experiment to be conducted along these lines took place in 1964. Dr Sol Feldstein and Miss Joyce Plosky, both members of the laboratory staff, alternated as experimenter and agent for a series of twelve nights. Seven men and five women, all paid volunteers, acted as the subjects. Each subject participated for one night only, and a different target picture was used on each occasion. The results of this first study were only marginally significant (odds of about 20 to one against chance), but it served as a useful 'screening' study. Feldstein turned out to be the better of the two agents, and the best of the twelve subjects was a young psychotherapist, Dr William Erwin. These two were therefore paired up for a second experiment, extending over seven nights. This time the results were much more clearly significant, the judges' ratings producing odds of more than 100 to one against the chance hypothesis. Some of the individual dreams were quite striking. For example, on the third night of the experiment the target picture was Salvador Dali's *The Sacrament of the Last Supper*, which shows Christ seated at a table surrounded by his disciples. On the table is a loaf of bread and a cup of wine, and in the background can be seen the sea with a fishing boat upon it. While Feldstein concentrated on this picture, Erwin dreamed of 'an ocean ... It had a strange beauty about it ... boats come to mind. Fishing boats. Small-size fishing boats.... There was a picture in the Sea Fare Restaurant that came to mind.... It shows, oh, I'd say about a dozen or so men pulling a fishing boat ashore right after having returned from a catch.' In the morning, when giving his associations to the dream and before having seen the target, Erwin added: 'The fisherman dream makes me think of the Mediterranean area, perhaps even some sort of Biblical time. Right now my associations are of the fish and the loaf, or even the feeding of the multitudes.... Once again I think of Christmas.... Having to do with the ocean—water, fishermen, something in this area....' (144, p. 113). It is interesting to note that Feldstein's religious background was that of an orthodox Jew, whereas Erwin's was that of a Protestant Christian (Disciples of Christ). On some occasions this difference seems to have affected the manifest content of the dreams. For example, when Feldstein concentrated on a picture of an elderly Rabbi, Erwin's subconscious seems to have converted it into a picture of 'Saint Paul', or 'An Anglican minister or priest'.

More than a dozen lengthy dream studies have now been completed by the Maimonides team. Not all have been successful, but the ones that have are so striking that they leave little doubt of the reality of telepathic dreaming. For the benefit of the sceptic we should point out that in all cases the dreamer was enclosed in a soundproof room, and the agent was in a room not less than sixty feet away. In some experiments the distance was considerably greater. For example, in one experiment the targets were slides shown to an audience of about 2,000 at a 'pop' concert in Port Chester, New York, while the dreaming subject was in the Maimonides laboratory in Brooklyn, a distance of about 45 miles. This experiment gave odds against chance of about 100 to one. In another long distance study the agent was subjected to a procedure known as 'sensory bombardment' in a laboratory 14 miles away from the sleeping subject; the results were significant, with odds of about 250 to one.

Sensory bombardment is a technique invented by Dr R. E. L. Masters and Dr Jean Houston in the course of their researches into altered states of consciousness (ASCs), a term which includes trance states, hypnosis, sleep, psychedelic 'trips', and the conditions brought on by various methods of meditation. The subject is placed in an 'audio-visual environment' in which slides are projected on to an eight-foot screen which curves around him, while his ears are bombarded with sound from a pair of stereo loudspeakers. The effect of this combined visual and auditory bombardment is so overwhelming that the subject may enter into an ASC in which he experiences profound emotional changes, or enters into a mystical or religious state of awareness. Dr Stanley Krippner of the Maimonides team felt that it was worth inflicting this treatment upon the agent in order to try to improve the quality of the telepathic 'transmission'. Although the results were statistically significant, they do not seem to have been any more so than in other experiments where sensory bombardment was not used. In fact, it is likely that the simple agent-to-percipient transmission model of telepathy is a vast oversimplification of what actually occurs in these Maimonides experiments. We cannot even be sure that *telepathy*, rather than *clairvoyance*, is the appropriate term to use, if indeed there is any difference between the two.

Among the many recorded examples of spontaneous ESP, by far the greatest number of those occurring during dreams can be classified as precognitive, and we have already given some examples of these in Chapter 6. One of the earliest investigators of the precognitive dream was J. W. Dunne (1875-1949), an English aeroplane designer who was responsible for building the first British military aircraft in 1906-7. When in his early twenties Dunne began to notice instances of apparent precognition occurring in his dreams, and he started to keep a careful record of them. After many years of dream-recording he published *An Experiment with Time*, a book which quickly became a best seller. In this he set out the accumulated results of his investigations, and propounded a new theory of the nature of time which he called 'Serialism' (37). Although philosophers have severely criticised Dunne's theory of time, there can be no question about the value of his work in drawing attention to the precognitive dream. However, the lack of an easily repeatable experimental technique deterred most parapsychologists from following the example of Dunne, at least until 1969 when the Maimonides workers re-opened the whole question. They set out to see whether, under the strict conditions of the Dream Laboratory, a subject could be made to dream about an experience which would be contrived for him on the *following* morning. The subject chosen was Malcolm Bessent, a young English psychic who had previously participated in other dream projects at the Laboratory. There was some prior reason to suppose that he had precognitive ability, for he had on occasions reported a number of predictions to the Central Premonitions Registry in New York, and some of these had been fulfilled. For example, he seems to have predicted the wrecking of an oil tanker, the death of General de Gaulle, and the result of the British general election of 1970 (144, p. 179). The sceptic would certainly attribute most of these hits to lucky coincidence or shrewd guesswork, but examination of Bessent's predictions suggests that there is rather more detailed information in them than can be entirely accounted for in this manner. At any rate, they provided the Maimonides researchers with a good enough *prima facie* case to justify further investigation. More evidence of Bessent's psi ability came from the results of 15,360 trials with a binary RNG, which yielded an above-chance deviation of 179, corresponding to odds of about 550 to one. It was therefore of considerable interest to see whether this remarkable young man could demonstrate his psychic faculty in yet another kind of situation, an artificially-contrived precognitive dream experiment.

In the event, the experimenters were not disappointed. For eight nights Malcolm Bessent went to sleep with the intention of dreaming about the things which would happen to him the following day. Every morning following a dream session, the experimenters selected, by a complicated random procedure, an 'experience' which was deliberately staged for the subject. The usual blind-matching procedures showed too many coincidences to be attributed to chance; the odds were more than 5,500 to one. For the first time in the history of psychical research a precognitive dream had been deliberately produced under laboratory conditions! In the summer of 1970 a confirmatory series was performed with the same percipient, again with significant results (odds of 800 to one). This series involved sixteen nights of dreaming in the laboratory: on the odd-numbered nights (1, 3, 5 ... 15) Bessent tried to dream about the target program he would be shown the following evening, whereas on the even-numbered nights he tried to dream about the program he had just seen. Thus on half the nights he was aiming to dream about the future, and on the other half he was aiming to dream about the past. In fact, only on the eight precognitive nights did the dreams correspond significantly with the targets: evidently this extraordinary subject was unable to produce anything so commonplace as a dream about something he had already seen!

By now it should be clear that the attempts of Evans and others to arraign parapsychology on a charge of being out of date are peculiarly absurd and unjust. In fact, parapsychologists were among the first scientists to make use of the new statistical procedures which became available during the twenties and thirties of this century, and today there are few modern techniques which are capable of being used for the study of psi which have not been employed for that purpose. Modern parapsychologists use double-blind experimentation, factor analysis, ranking methods and analysis of variance; among their equipment can be found plethysmographs, EEG machines, computers and random number generators. It is a striking fact that, throughout all the years of testing, whether by means of simple experiments with cards, pictures and dice, or by means of RNGs and sleep-monitoring apparatus, under an amazingly wide range of conditions and a great variety of different experimenters, *psi phenomena have continued to occur.* One cannot help wondering whether the 'aura of faded newspapers, the Graf Zeppelin and the Entente Cordiale' so graphically described by Dr Evans may not be found, not around the heads of the parapsychologists, but rather around those dogmatic sceptics who go on making the same criticisms long after they have been adequately answered, and years after new experimental techniques have rendered them pointless.

10. Breaking the Species Barrier

In the year 1940 the twelve-year-old son of the county sheriff at Summersville, West Virginia, was scheduled to have an operation. He was sent to the Myers Memorial Hospital at Phillipi, about 70 miles away as the crow flies. About a week after his arrival, on a dark, snowy night, he heard a fluttering at the window of his hospital room. Calling the nurse, he asked her to open the window, saying that there was a pigeon outside, and just to humour the lad, she did so. The pigeon came into the room, and the boy recognised it as his pet. He told the nurse to look for an identification tag numbered 167 on its leg, and when she did so she found the number as stated. The boy's parents arrived at the hospital a few days later and were surprised to find the pigeon, which the hospital authorities had allowed the boy to keep in a box in his room. How had the bird managed to find its young master? Not only had it traversed a distance of 70 miles to do so, it had even located the correct window of the building, at night and in a snowstorm. The possibility that the bird had merely followed the car which transported the boy was ruled out by the fact that the pigeon had been seen around the home after the boy had left.

The case of pigeon 167 is typical of a large number of cases of animal behaviour known to parapsychologists as 'psi-trailing' cases. It is important to distinguish psi-trailing from ordinary *homing* behaviour, such as a pigeon finding its way back to the loft. In normal homing there are a number of factors in the environment which might serve to guide the animal: the movements of the sun and stars, the earth's magnetic field, landmarks such as trees, buildings, etc. Careful experimental studies have shown that some of these factors are indeed important in homing, although they may not explain it altogether. The case of pigeon 167, however, is quite different. The bird had no way of telling in which direction its master had been taken, or how far. Even if it was familiar with the landmarks around the hospital at Phillipi (which is unlikely), it could not know that that was the place to which the boy had been taken, nor could it employ environmental clues to locate the exact room in the building. In short, there is no conceivable way in which the creature could have carried out this feat using only the ordinary sensory mechanisms. Either the story is untrue or exaggerated, or it seems we must postulate something equivalent to ESP in the pigeon.

During the years 1940-1960 the researchers at Duke University sifted through several hundred cases of apparent ESP in animals, seeking to obtain accurate verification wherever possible. Sometimes the reports were too vague to be of any value, or important witnesses could not be traced. However, after rejecting all such unsatisfactory cases, they were left with a hard core of 54 well authenticated examples of psi-trailing: 28 with dogs, 22 with cats, and 4 with birds. They included the remarkable case of Sugar, a cream-coloured Persian cat, who in 1951 psi-trailed its owners about 1,500 miles across the mountainous country between California and Oklahoma. Sugar had been raised from kittenhood in the family of Mr W, a school principal in Anderson, California. When Mr and Mrs W and their ten-year-old daughter set out for their new home in Oklahoma, they intended to take Sugar with them. However, the cat leaped from the car window, and could not be caught: his terror of cars was well known to the family. In the end, Sugar had to be left behind with the neighbours, who also had his litter-mate. Fourteen months later Mrs W was standing in the cow barn at their new home in Gage, Oklahoma, with her back to an open window, when a cat landed on her shoulder. Startled, she brushed him off, but then recognised the animal as Sugar. He had a peculiar deformity of the left hip joint which served as proof of his identity. Later, their former neighbours in California admitted that Sugar had disappeared about 16-18 days after being left in their care, but they had not had the heart to inform the W family (110).

Such cases are obviously of great interest from the parapsychological point of view, but there is another aspect of them which is sometimes overlooked, namely the question of motivation. Why should an animal undertake such a long and gruelling journey? According to the behaviouristically-orientated science of the twentieth century, animals are to be regarded as mere automata, responding to external stimuli in ways determined by their conditioned behaviour patterns, and in accordance with their biological needs. Any attempt to attribute motives such as loyalty and affection to an animal invariably brings the charge of being naïvely anthropomorphic. We leave it to the behaviourist, therefore, to suggest why Sugar undertook his hazardous fourteen-month ordeal, or why a pigeon should risk death in a snowstorm to reach the bedside of its youthful owner.

Strangely enough, it was one of the pioneers of behaviourism who carried out the first systematic experiments to test for the existence of telepathy between humans and animals. Just before the First World War, when Vladimir Bechterev was President of the Psychoneurological Academy and Director of the Institute for the Investigation of the Brain in St Petersburg, he performed some intriguing experiments with a pair of circus dogs. The dogs, a St Bernard and a fox terrier, belonged to the famous circus trainer Durov. Their act was performed in the following manner: two or three figures to be added up were written on a piece of paper or a slate, and then shown to Durov, who had his back to the dog. Immediately after Durov's verbal command, the dog gave the sum of the numbers by barking. The only restriction on this performance was that the sum should not exceed nine, since the dog was not supposed to be able to count any higher. In his own experiments with these animals Bechterev found that they seemed to respond to his unspoken thoughts, even when the trainer was not present. He would take the dog's muzzle into his hands and, holding the animal's head still, gaze into its eyes while mentally willing it to carry out a certain action. He would then release the dog, which would usually go at once and carry out the required action. Bechterev was fully aware of the possibility of the animal being guided by slight bodily or facial movements, and in his later experiments he took steps to exclude such sensory cues. In some tests he interposed wax and metal screens between the human agent and the animal, and took precautions to ensure that no other person present knew the task required of the dog. Not only were the results strikingly successful, but Bechterev later obtained similar results with his own dog, which unlike Durov's dogs had not been specially trained for circus work. Bechterev's report on the experiments appeared in the *Zeitschrift für Psychotherapie* in 1924, but was completely ignored by the scientific world (9).

In 1929 came a further report of apparent telepathy in an animal, this time from the Rhines (111, 112). It concerned a 'mind-reading' horse, Lady, who had been trained by her owner to answer questions of spelling or arithmetic by touching her nose on a series of lettered or numbered blocks laid out on a table. Careful experiments with Lady showed that she could only give the correct answer when one or other of the humans present knew it, which strongly suggested that she was reacting to the unconscious bodily movements of her interrogators. However, screening soon eliminated this possibility, for it was found that Lady's successes continued even when she could not see the body of her owner. The experimenters noticed an unusual aspect of the horse's behaviour: when she was doing her most successful work she appeared to be in a sleepy, sluggish state. Her head drooped, her eyes were half open, and she scarcely moved. This suggested that she may have been in a dissociated, trance-like state similar to that of some of the high-scoring human ESP subjects. Later, when Lady lost her mind-reading ability, she no longer fell into this dreamy state, but appeared active, alert and watchful. Under these conditions she failed to score correctly except when she was given quite obvious bodily cues by her owner. Nevertheless, the experimenters were satisfied that initially she had shown evidence of ESP ability.

During the 1950s the Duke Laboratory launched its 'Anpsi' project (short for 'Animal Psi'), in a deliberate attempt to find more evidence of ESP in animals. It was at this time that Dr Pratt carried out his important, although inconclusive, researches into pigeon homing, and Dr Karlis Osis conducted some laboratory experiments with cats. The cats were placed one at a time in a T-shaped maze, and a human agent willed them to turn either to the left or the right, according to a randomised target sequence. The agent was enclosed in a cubicle with a one-way window, so that he was completely invisible and inaudible to the animal. Some, though not all, of the cats produced highly significant scores, although after a time the scoring rate began to decline (97). Later, Osis modified the experimental design to test for clairvoyance rather than telepathy. On this occasion none of the humans present in the laboratory was told which was the target direction. Food rewards were used to provide the cats with an incentive to success, and mild electric shocks were given as 'punishments' for failure (98). Under these conditions the results were not as strikingly successful as in the earlier 'telepathic' experiments, but they were sufficiently significant to justify a tentative conclusion that some of the animals were using some kind of extrasensory faculty.

In 1958 came another animal report, this time concerning a mongrel dog called Chris. This animal had been taught to answer numerical questions by pawing at his master's sleeve the requisite number of times. The owner of the dog, Mr George Wood, decided to use the standard ESP cards to test his pet's ability, converting the five symbols into numbers by means of a predetermined code. Later the Wood family was visited by Dr Cadoret of the Duke Laboratory, who conducted some extensive tests with the animal (164). It was found that Chris could 'guess' the cards correctly even when they were sealed in black envelopes and stacked in decks, no humans present having any normal knowledge of the card order. This was clearly a clairvoyance test, corresponding to the DT method used with human subjects (cf page 52). On the face of it, it seems to eliminate all possibility of sensory leakage. Chris's results were highly significant, with odds against chance of millions to one: we must therefore conclude that either the animal was demonstrating a remarkable level of ESP ability, or his master was the real ESP subject, and the dog was simply responding to slight unconscious cues from the man's body. An interesting secondary feature of these experiments was that the dog produced significant *negative* scores when working in the presence of Dr Cadoret, and significant *positive* scores when working with Mr Wood alone, or with Wood in the presence of other observers. This seems to be yet another example of the ubiquitous experimenter effect.

In June 1952, just a year before Chris began his public career, two other dogs were being tested for their ESP ability on a beach north of San Francisco. They were a pair of German Shepherds known as Binnie and Tessie, who had been trained to locate underground objects. The experiments were conducted by J. B. Rhine under contract to the Engineer Research and Development Laboratories (ERDL) of Fort Belvoir, Virginia. The object of the research was to test the efficiency of the dogs in detecting land mines, presumably with a view to using them for military purposes. ERDL was, of course, mainly interested in whether the dogs could detect the mines at all, irrespective of whether they did so by using their ordinary senses or by ESP. However, Rhine was determined to make the test into a valid test of ESP by carefully excluding all known sensory clues. Small wooden boxes were used to simulate land mines, and they were planted in straight target lines along the beach. The lines were marked by lengths of white tape knotted at every yard, with a special marker to indicate each five-yard section. A single 'mine' was planted within each five-yard section, and the dogs had to indicate which of the one-yard spans of that section contained it. Since there were five one-yard spans within each section, the dogs should have had approximately one fifth of their attempts correct by chance alone. In fact, the proportion of successes varied from about one third to over a half, with odds against chance somewhere in the region of a thousand million to one. In terms of scoring rate, this was probably the most successful animal psi experiment ever conducted (109).

In considering such remarkable scores, the first point to be decided is whether the successes were really due to ESP, or whether the dogs were using some normal sense, such as smell. Most of the experiments were conducted with the boxes planted about four inches under the sand in shallow pools (containing six to twelve inches of water). There was generally a strong wind blowing and often light rain, with the surface of the water so rippled that it was difficult to see through it. The positioning of the boxes was carefully carried out in the absence of the dogs and their handler, using a set of random number tables to determine the positions. After planting each box the experimenter raked over the lines, not only where the boxes were planted but in all the other positions as well, making it impossible to locate the 'mines' by observing the disturbance of the sand. Under these conditions it is difficult to imagine any normal sensory means by which the boxes could have been located. In discussing the results of these experiments Dr Rhine suggested that some kind of ESP involving both the dogs and their handler may have been involved.

A rather different approach to the problem of animal psi comes from the work of Dr Robert Morris of the American Psychical Research Foundation. He placed nineteen rats one by one in an open field maze, and measured the activity of each rat by counting the number of floor squares traversed by the animal during a two-minute time interval. After this, a second experimenter either killed the rat or spared it, according to whether an odd or even number had been assigned to the rat by a random number table. Morris expected that rats about to die would anticipate their destiny by precognition, and show less activity than those which were to live. (It is well known in animal psychology that rats undergoing emotional stress show less activity than those which are not.) The results of this somewhat gruesome experiment were only marginally significant. In a second experiment, Morris measured the activity of goldfish before subjecting some of them to the emotional shock of being held aloft in a net. Here he had rather better success than with the rats: the goldfish about to be stressed showed significantly more activity than the others. This is in keeping with what is known about the behaviour of goldfish: whereas rats freeze when threatened, goldfish become more active in an effort to escape (94).

Morris's experiments were performed in 1967. The following year two French scientists reported one of the most ingenious animal psi experiments ever performed, and one which has placed the study of animal psi on an entirely new footing. A mouse was placed in a cage, the floor of which was divided into two equal parts by a low barrier. At intervals either the left or the right half of the floor became electrified, in a sequence determined by a binary random number generator. If the mouse happened to be in the 'wrong' half of the cage at the time, he received a small but unpleasant shock through the feet. There was thus an incentive for the animals to use precognition to find out which side would receive the electric current next, and avoid it by being in the opposite side. The whole experiment was automated; a light beam falling on a photoelectric cell detected each jump of the barrier, and the whole sequence of events was recorded on punched tape. In analysing their results the researchers considered only those trials where the animal jumped the barrier for no apparent reason. Thus, they excluded trials where the mouse jumped immediately after receiving a shock on the previous trial ('mechanical behaviour'), and also trials where the mouse merely remained passive ('static behaviour'). The remaining trials they called 'random behaviour trials', and it was among these that they looked for evidence of precognition. Examination showed that the mice had indeed managed to avoid the shock more often than would be expected by chance, with odds of more than 1,000 to one. Because of the possible reaction from the scientific 'establishment', the two French scientists who performed this ingenious experiment wrote their paper under pseudonyms ('Duval' and 'Montredon') (38), but the secret has since been leaked that the senior author was in fact Professor Remy Chauvin, a distinguished zoologist at the Sorbonne who is famous for his work on animal behaviour.

Parapsychologists all over the world were excited by the 'Duval-Montredon' report: here at last, it seemed, was the perfect animal psi experiment. Completely automated, it left no scope for human error or human influence—in fact it could be run without any humans present at all. Also, the fact that the random number generator had not yet determined the next number at the moment when the mouse made his choice entirely eliminated the possibility of any physical clues leaking through to the animal. There remained only one crucial question: would the experiment prove to be repeatable? Within a few months of the publication of the Duval-Montredon paper a team of young researchers at the Institute for Parapsychology in America had begun work on a similar series of tests. Before long they were also reporting significant evidence for precognition, not only in mice but in gerbils and hamsters as well. Between 1971 and 1973 the American teams published some eight papers reporting successful ESP experiments under fully automated conditions with various species of rodents.

Then, in the summer of 1974 came a near-tragic *dénouement* to the animal work at the Institute for Parapsychology. The principal experimenter involved in it was caught in the act of faking one of his experiments, and resigned from his post. Although there was no evidence to suggest that his previous experiments had been faked (the experimenter concerned insisted that they had not), the discovery of fraud in one instance inevitably placed a large question mark over all of his previous work. All experiments in which the fraudulent researcher had had a part now had to be regarded as suspect; and the largest number of these experiments were the ones which supported the French work on rodent precognition. The critics of parapsychology were not slow to take advantage of the situation. Popular and semi-popular scientific periodicals which would normally never soil their pages with a discussion of a successful ESP experiment quickly paraded the news of the exposure before the public. Sceptics who for years had been asserting that successful ESP experiments were mainly due to fraud now seized the opportunity to launch a general accusation of dishonesty against the whole field. In view of all this, it is perhaps important to point out that this one example at the Institute for Parapsychology is the *only* case in the history of parapsychology where a leading experimenter is known to have faked his results. It is quite unjustifiable to use it as an excuse for accusations of fraud against parapsychologists in general, just as it would be unjustifiable to condemn the whole science of paleontology because of the Piltdown fraud. In fact, the prompt way in which the fraud was dealt with at the Institute, and the absence of any attempt to suppress the facts gives some idea of the standards of honesty normally existing in this field. A report of the exposé was published immediately in the *Journal of Parapsychology* (June 1974), together with a warning against accepting the reports of the fraudulent experimenter.

What, then, of the rodent precognition experiments? Since the bulk of the supporting evidence for the Duval-Montredon effect came from the now suspect American work, the case for the reality of rodent psi is inevitably weakened. However, there remains a considerable body of evidence which has not been affected by the fraud disclosure. Thus, the French researchers have themselves performed two further replications of the experiment, both of which were successful with odds of more than 1,000 to one. Also, J. F. M. Extra, an Assistant Professor of Psychology at Leiden State University, Holland, published the results of a semi-automated ESP experiment with rats (44): they were only marginally significant (odds of 20 to one) but they serve to add to the general body of evidence in favour of animal ESP. At the time of writing there are further replications in progress, at the Institute for Parapsychology and elsewhere. One such replication, using gerbils in an automated testing cage, has been reported as moderately successful, with odds against chance of about 30 to one (Artley, 3).

Ever since the publication of the original Duval-Montredon report, there have been strong protests from antivivisectionists and others against the use of electric shocks in animal psi research. Understandably, the protesters feel that parapsychologists, of all people, should know better than to treat animals as though they were merely unfeeling automata. Whether one agrees with this view or not, it is gratifying to be able to report that alternative methods of testing have recently been developed. In the Psychology Department at the University of Utrecht, Sybo A. Schouten performed an automated ESP experiment with mice which used positive incentives (that is, rewards) rather than electric shocks. He began by training the mice to press a lever in whichever half of their cage an indicator lamp was lit. If the mouse pressed the lever on the side corresponding to the lighted lamp he received a drop of water as a reward; if he pressed the lever on the side corresponding to the unlighted lamp he received nothing. When the mice were thus fully trained, Schouten placed one of them in a cage containing lamps but no levers: a second mouse was placed in a cage several rooms away with levers but no lamps. When a lamp lit in the cage of the first mouse he had to transmit the information telepathically to the second mouse, who could then press the appropriate lever. Success in this operation resulted in both mice receiving the water-drop reward, so both were sufficiently motivated to use their ESP faculties, if any. Furthermore, the experiment could easily be adapted to test for clairvoyance rather than telepathy, simply by leaving the cage of the first mouse (the sender) empty. A binary random selector was used to determine the switching sequence of the two lamps, and the results of the whole experiment were recorded automatically on punched tape (122).

Ten mice were used in Schouten's experiment, each mouse performing 75 trials under clairvoyance conditions and 75 trials as the telepathic percipient. The overall results were marginally significant, with odds against chance of about 30 to one. However, when Schouten applied a similar criterion to that of Duval and Montredon, selecting out the 'random behaviour trials', he found a much higher level of statistical significance (odds of 200 to one). It is very satisfying to reflect that this experiment, so different in its basic design from that of the French workers, nevertheless confirmed their major findings quite neatly. An interesting additional discovery was that those mice which did well under telepathic conditions seemed to score badly under clairvoyance conditions, and vice-versa. It seems that, as with humans, individual animals differ in their psi abilities, a fact which was also observed by Osis during his cat experiments.

Since the Schouten experiments there have been several other attempts to demonstrate ESP in small animals using positive reinforcement methods. Susan Harris of Mt. Holyoke College and James Terry of the Maimonides Dream Laboratory used a female Wistar rat of about 130 days old in a two-choice Skinner-box experiment. The rat had to predict which of two bars would deliver a water drop reward when pressed. Using the random behaviour criterion, the results were significant with odds of 5,000 to one (62). At the Edinburgh University Parapsychology Laboratory Adrian Parker used three gerbils in an experiment in which a sunflower seed was automatically delivered as a reward for pressing the correct one of two keys (101). Two of the three animals scored significantly, the overall results giving odds of 250 to one against chance. As expected, a higher rate of scoring was found for the random behaviour trials. Later, Richard Broughton and Brian Millar, also at Edinburgh, tried to repeat Parker's experiment, this time without success (20). Of five animals tested during preliminary trials only one scored significantly, and this one unfortunately died before the main experiment was begun. Broughton and Millar point out that their gerbils were several years old, which may possibly account for their failure to score significantly in this kind of experiment.

In the *Journal of Parapsychology* for 1970 a brief account was given of an interesting and original animal psi experiment which perhaps deserves to be better known than it is. James Janik and Roger Klocek placed rats in a T-shaped maze, so arranged that by choosing the correct turn the animals could reach a food reward. The direction which would lead to the reward was randomly chosen for each trial. The experimental design was thus very similar to that used by Osis and Foster in their earlier work with cats. However, the originality of the Janik-Klocek experiment lies in the prior treatment of the rats; for some had been injected with adrenalin, some with nor-adrenalin, some with thyroxin, some with saline solution, and some had not been injected at all. Both adrenalin and nor-adrenalin are natural hormones produced by the central part of the adrenal gland in response to anger or fright: their function is to prepare the body for attack or defence by dilating the blood vessels in the skeletal muscles and raising the level of sugar in the blood. Thyroxin is produced by the thyroid gland in the neck, and its output is also increased under conditions of stress. It serves to regulate the basal metabolic rate, that is, the rate at which the body cells use up their fuel supplies. Janik and Klocek found that *all* their injected rats scored significantly in the ESP test, including those which had received only the saline solution, whereas the un-injected rats produced only chance scores. In their report (69) the experimenters point out that the very act of injecting a rat, even with saline, is sufficient to provoke the rat's body into producing more adrenalin and nor-adrenalin, and this could well account for the significant scores of the saline-injected rats. The highest ESP scoring of all was obtained from rats which had been given a moderate dose (0.5 mg) of nor-adrenalin. Parapsychologists have always wanted to find a drug capable of improving ESP performance: the Janik-Klocek experiment might provide a pointer in that direction.

All of the animal experiments described so far have been concerned with what we may loosely term 'animal ESP'. In some cases (such as Bechterev's work), ESP-interaction seems to have occurred between man and animal. In others, particularly the automated experiments of the Duval-Montredon type, the psi-effect seems to be centred in the animal alone. At the Institute for Parapsychology there have been a number of investigations which seem to indicate the existence of a form of animal PK. Unfortunately, many of these must now be regarded as of dubious value because of the involvement of the fraudulent experimenter mentioned earlier. However, there remains the interesting work of Dr Helmut Schmidt, who found that a domestic cat was apparently able to influence the output of a binary random number generator in order to keep warm (119). The animal was confined in an unheated garden shed during cold weather; also in the shed was a 200-watt lamp coupled to one of the outputs of the RNG, which was situated some distance away in the house. Schmidt found that when the cat was in the shed the machine turned on the lamp more frequently than would be expected according to probability theory; but when the cat was removed from the shed the machine showed no tendency to generate unusual sequences. Since then, Schmidt and others have carried out similar PK tests with a variety of species including cockroaches, locusts, lizards, chickens, goldfish and brine-shrimp. Even plants have been tested to see whether they are capable of influencing a random number generator in order to obtain light for their photosynthetic processes! Some, though not all, of these experiments have yielded statistically significant results, but in almost every case they are single efforts by one experimenter or group of experimenters. With claims as extraordinary as these, and particularly in view of the possibility of fraud, it is essential that all results should be replicated by several independent researchers before they are accepted as genuine. In spite of a great deal of suggestive material, therefore, we must proclaim the case for animal PK 'not proven'.

At this point it is necessary to mention a rather unusual type of psi experiment which has received an exceptional amount of publicity in the popular press. In 1968 an American polygraph expert, Cleve Backster, announced that he had obtained evidence for the existence of what he called 'primary perception' in plants. His experiments involved attaching a pair of electrodes to a plant leaf, and then connecting the electrodes to a polygraph pen-recorder. The pen produced a continuous trace, its movements indicating slight changes in the electrical resistance of the leaf. This was essentially the same procedure as that used for measuring the galvanic skin response of humans. Backster claimed that when he deliberately thought of inflicting harm upon the plant, the pen made a sudden movement, corresponding to that produced by an emotional reaction in a human being. He came to the conclusion that the plant was reading his thoughts, and exhibiting emotions analogous to that of fear in an animal. As a result of some further experiments, he concluded that the plants also displayed emotional reactions when other organisms were killed in their vicinity; for this purpose he set up a device which automatically dropped live brine shrimp into boiling water, and observed apparently synchronous changes in the polygraph tracings (4).

There can be no doubt about the originality and ingenuity of the Backster research. Unfortunately, attempts to replicate it elsewhere have generally not been successful, and there is good reason to think that Backster was mistaken in the interpretation of his results. In June 1970, following some extended tests, the Southern California Society for Psychical Research issued a critical report on Backster's work, pointing out a number of deficiencies in his experimental procedures (162). These included a lack of adequate screening on the leads to the leaf electrodes, the use of an unsuitable power source, an insufficient number of runs, and the rejection of an excessive number of charts for technical reasons. In their own laboratory the Californian researchers not only replicated Backster's brine shrimp experiment, but also tried the effects of putting salt on slugs and dropping rats into water. None of these rather repulsive activities provoked anything that could be called an emotional response in their plants. Another replication attempt, this one carried out by Rex V. Johnson at the University of Washington, also failed to confirm Backster's claims. Johnson found that when he took steps to control the temperature and humidity of the air in the laboratory, all unexplained fluctuations in the polygraph tracings disappeared. However, he could easily get them to return again merely by varying the temperature by one or two degrees centigrade, or by allowing the humidity to change by ten to fifteen percent. Such changes presumably affect the polygraph by causing slight alterations in the electrical contact between the leaf and the electrodes. In an open room, such as that used by Backster, temperature and humidity can easily change to this extent merely as a result of drafts or people moving about, not to mention such activities as dumping brine shrimp into boiling water. It seems very likely, therefore, that this is the true explanation of the Backster effect (71).

In spite of set-backs, frauds, and false trails, the study of psi phenomena in non-human species has had some notable triumphs. Looking back, we can see that animal parapsychology has followed much the same pattern of development as its human counterpart. Beginning with the collection and examination of spontaneous cases and a few relatively simple experiments with specially gifted individuals, it has now progressed to the stage of using elaborate statistical techniques and fully automated testing equipment. During these years of development a substantial body of evidence has accumulated, pointing strongly to the existence of psi effects in animals other than man. Since modern biology emphasises the essential unity of all living things, this is not surprising: indeed, it is what one would expect. However, it does lead to a change of perspective within parapsychology itself. The early psychical researchers regarded ESP phenomena as evidence of the reality of a spiritual component, a soul, which was unique to man: the discovery of animal ESP makes that viewpoint no longer tenable. If ESP is to be regarded as evidence for spirituality, then it must be a spirituality which permeates the whole of the living world. Man cannot use his psychic faculties as an excuse to set himself apart from the rest of the biosphere.

11. Body and Mind

Out of 103 men who sailed with Jacques Cartier on his second voyage to Newfoundland in 1535, all but three soon became desperately ill with scurvy, and twenty-five of them died. In their fear and distress, the sailors 'set up an image of Christ upon the shore and prostrated themselves before it in the deep snow, chanting litanies and penitential psalms. The pestilence continued unabated, however.'*

There could hardly be a clearer illustration of the power of Matter over Mind than this grim story. Despite the claims of religious propagandists, it is a commonplace experience that, in general, prayers for the healing of physical ailments are *not* answered, at least not in any direct and straightforward manner. Even the hard-headed atheist prays when he finds himself to be suffering from a painful and incurable disease, yet countless millions all over the world continue to suffer, in spite of the agonised entreaties of patients, relatives and friends. In the vast majority of cases the gods—if such there be—seem to turn a deaf ear. On the other hand, materialistically-based modern science often produces the most dramatic cures —a capsule of penicillin or an injection of insulin may do more for the patient's physical well-being than all the prayers in the world. Even Cartier's sailors discovered the effectiveness of a purely physical treatment, for one of them later learned from the Red Indians how to cure the scurvy with a decoction made from the needles of spruce trees. The effects of this medicine were highly dramatic : the disease disappeared almost immediately. Of course, it all seems so simple to us; for we have known for over half a century that scurvy is caused by a deficiency of vitamin C in the diet. To the sailors of Cartier's day, the contrast between the almost magical effects of the chemical treatment and the apparent futility of the religious rituals must have been striking.

* From *Vitamins in Theory and Practice*, by L. J. Harris.

If experiences such as those of Cartier's men were universal, there would be nothing more to be said. We should have to acknowledge, however reluctantly, the total impotence of spiritual factors when confronted with the harsh realities of the physical world. At the very least we should have to admit that the mechanist-reductionist view of man is the only one that works in practice. However, things are seldom as simple as they seem, and from the earliest times there have been numerous claims for the healing of apparently physical diseases by means of spiritual or mental techniques. To the westerner the best known examples are of course the healing miracles of Jesus and his disciples, as they are recorded in the Gospels and the Acts of the Apostles. Almost contemporary with Jesus was another 'wonder-worker', Apollonius of Tyana, who died about AD 98. His miracles were said to have paralleled those of the Galilean, much to the annoyance of the early Church. Throughout the long ages when the teaching of the Christian Church dominated almost the whole of the civilised world, belief in miracles was a part of everyday life. Countless numbers of pilgrims flocked to the shrines of the saints, seeking miraculous cures for every ailment under the sun. According to the contemporary accounts, they were not always disappointed.

Following the collapse of the unified structure of Christendom at the Reformation, belief in miracles began to decline sharply. By the eighteenth century the impact of modern science with its mechanistic outlook was beginning to be strongly felt. Most Protestant Christians had already rejected the mediaeval stories of miraculous cures, supposedly performed by one or other of the vast army of Catholic saints in answer to the prayers of the faithful. However, even Protestants continued for a time to believe in the biblical miracles, since they regarded the Bible as the directly inspired Word of God. Then, with the rise of the *Aufklärung* (Enlightenment) in Germany, even the Bible stories came under critical attack. By the end of the nineteenth century there was a widespread disbelief in miracles of all kinds. Psychology played a significant part in this growing scepticism, since it provided the would-be sceptic with possible rationalistic explanations of the miracle cures. It was known that under the influence of suggestion the human body sometimes became capable of quite remarkable feats; and it was also known that mentally induced illnesses could, on occasion, imitate physical diseases with remarkable fidelity, even to the extent of deceiving a trained physician. It seemed likely therefore that the healing miracles of Jesus were all examples of cure by suggestion. Thus the paralysed man described in Matthew's Gospel, Chapter 9, might have been suffering from *hysterical* paralysis, perhaps brought on by some traumatic experience of his early life. On hearing the authoritative words 'Son, be of good cheer, thy sins are forgiven,' his guilt feelings were discharged, and the hysterical symptoms therefore disappeared. During the First World War many cases of hysterical paralysis and blindness were successfully treated by psychological methods, and it soon became fashionable for theologians to explain away the miracles of Jesus in the language of the psychoanalyst's couch. Science—or so it seemed —had cast its bright light into yet another dark corner of the supernatural.

However there were some phenomena, and twentieth-century ones at that, which did not fit so neatly into this interpretative scheme. Probably the most startling were those which occurred at the Roman Catholic shrine of Lourdes, where diseases which could not by any stretch of the imagination be described as psychological were allegedly being healed. The percentage of such cures was not large, but the fact that they occurred at all was disturbing to those who accepted the orthodox mechanistic theory of man. Among the many medical men who investigated the Lourdes phenomena was one of France's most distinguished scientists, Dr Alexis Carrel (1873-1944). After obtaining degrees in both science and medicine, Carrel studied and taught for some years in Lyons. His scientific training soon led him to reject all forms of orthodox religious belief, but he was broad minded enough not to dismiss all inexplicable phenomena out of hand. In 1902 he became interested in paranormal healing, and in the following year he visited Lourdes in charge of certain patients with the National Pilgrimage. At that time he described himself as 'a tolerant sceptic, a positivist—*interested* in Lourdes cures but not *credulous* regarding them'. He seems to have accepted the common belief that all 'miraculous' cures could be attributed to suggestion. He stated openly that he was not prepared to believe in the miracles unless he witnessed the cure of a disease that was indisputably *organic*, such as the regrowth of a damaged bone or the disappearance of a cancer.

Accompanying Dr Carrel was a young patient of his, Marie Bailly, whose tragic history he knew well. All of her family had died of tuberculosis, and now she was in the final stages of tubercular peritonitis. The diagnosis had been confirmed by two independent medical men. There were tubercular lesions in her lungs, and tubercular sores on her body. Now the infection had spread to the lining of the body cavity, and Carrel expected her to die at any moment, certainly within a day or two. Yet when Marie was taken in front of the Grotto, he observed a most extraordinary change in her. Her pulse and respiration returned rapidly to normal, her distended abdomen began to shrink to its proper size, and the colour returned to her pale, emaciated features. That same evening Carrel gave the girl a thorough examination, in the presence of three other doctors—there could be no doubt about it: she was completely cured. From that moment onwards, Carrel was convinced that the Lourdes miracles could not be explained in terms of suggestion or any other purely psychological effect. In view of the hostility of the medical profession towards anything paranormal, Carrel showed considerable moral courage in openly declaring his belief in the miraculous healing of Marie Bailly. He was expelled from his position in the Lyons Medical Faculty, and in 1905 he left France to take up a post on the staff of the Rockefeller Institute in New York, where he remained for the rest of his active life. In 1912 he was awarded the Nobel Prize for his work on organ transplantation and the suturing of blood vessels, and his most famous book, *Man, the Unknown*, was published in 1935. Carrel never forgot his early experiences at Lourdes, and to the end of his life he remained a believer in the reality of paranormal phenomena (21).

Despite the conversion of Alexis Carrel and a number of other notable sceptics, there are still many medical men who are unconvinced by Lourdes. In 1956 a Protestant writer, Ruth Cranston, produced an enthusiastic account of the shrine and its healings (29) which was given a very cool reception in the pages of the SPR *Journal* (161). Two years later one of the

Society's own officers, Dr D. J. West, published the results of his own enquiries into eleven of the alleged miracles (159). He found that, when critically examined, the case histories were not as remarkable as they seemed to be. In some instances the medical investigations had been inadequate, or the tests employed had given conflicting results; in others there was evidence of suppression of some of the relevant data. On the basis of West's study, it seems that we must regard the Lourdes cures with the greatest caution. George Bernard Shaw once described Lourdes as the most blasphemous place on earth, because although it contained evidence of cures in the form of large numbers of crutches and wheel-chairs, it did not contain a single glass eye, wooden leg, or toupee. This, he said, implied a limitation of the power of God, and it was this that constituted the blasphemy. It is certainly true that none of the Lourdes miracles involve the regrowth of severed limbs or lost organs; yet Ruth Cranston records some cases which, if genuine, would seem to involve much the same kind of phenomenon. Thus, she reports two cases in which there seems to have been regeneration of the optic nerve (Madame Biré, p. 28, and Gerard Baillie, p. 182), and another in which nerves severed by a bullet eight years previously appear to have regrown with extraordinary rapidity (John Traynor, p. 118). Such claims cannot be lightly dismissed, and it is clear that there is a strong case for a thorough and impartial investigation of the phenomena of Lourdes.

Lourdes would be remarkable enough if it stood alone; but there have been many other claims of miraculous or paranormal healings in this century. On Sunday February 18th 1912, a twenty-three-year-old woman was dying in a house at Herne Hill, London. Miss Dorothy Kerin had suffered increasingly from ill health over a period of ten years. At the age of fifteen she contracted diphtheria, and later suffered attacks of pleurisy and pneumonia. Subsequent tests showed the widespread presence of tuberculosis bacilli in her body, and by December 1911 the two doctors who were attending her had come to the conclusion that hers was a hopeless case. The tuberculosis bacilli had invaded the membranes of the brain and the peritoneum; she was now blind, deaf, diabetic, and unable to move. On February 17th the doctor warned her mother that death might occur at any moment, and said that she was unlikely to survive another day. The following morning Dorothy received Holy Communion, and said that she saw a golden light radiating from the chalice and enveloping the priest. Later in the day she had a vision of angels, and in the evening she became aware of a great light surrounding her and a voice telling her to get up. She got out of bed, apparently completely cured, refused a cup of milk she was offered, and went down to the kitchen in search of solid food. The doctors were astonished by her rapid recovery, and the newspapers hailed the case as a modern miracle. Dorothy herself believed that she had been spared for some Divine purpose, and later she opened a healing home in Kent where many sick people are said to have been healed through her ministrations. She died in 1963.

Another example of a twentieth-century religious healer is Miss Kathryn Kuhlman. Born in Concordia, Missouri, the daughter of the local Mayor, she became ordained in the Baptist Church. During the 1940s when she was preaching in Franklin, Pennsylvania, members of her congregation began to report spontaneous healings occurring during the services. As the number of healings increased, she began to concentrate her preaching on the topic of healing through the power of God. Today she commands an enormous following in the USA, conducts large-scale healing services and broadcasts regularly on the radio networks. Like most religious healers Miss Kuhlman claims no unusual powers for herself, but insists that all healing is the work of God. Some of her cases match those of Lourdes in their dramatic quality. There is, for example, the strange case of James McCutcheon (83, p. 157-164) whose thigh-bone was badly damaged in a railroad accident. Five attempts to fasten the head of the femur back on to the shaft with metal pins failed, and X-rays showed progressive decalcification of the bone. However, while attending one of Kathryn Kuhlman's healing services McCutcheon suddenly experienced a sensation of warmth and an impulse to stand upright, which he did. He found that he could walk without crutches, and subsequent X-rays revealed that new bone had grown across the gap produced by the injury. McCutcheon's doctor described the cure as miraculous. Miss Kuhlman's writings contain descriptions of many similarly inexplicable cases, so that there would seem to be a rich field here for any medically qualified person who wishes to investigate the possibility of paranormal healing.

In view of its obvious potential importance for the health and happiness of mankind, paranormal healing has been surprisingly neglected by the medical profession, the Church and the parapsychologists. The SPR produced a non-committal report on Lourdes in 1894, and there were a few spasmodic investigations by individuals during the following half-century. However nothing of any substance was produced until the 1950s, when there was a minor revival of interest in the subject. In 1951 a Methodist minister, Dr Leslie Weatherhead, published the results of his own enquiries into the relationship between psychology, religion and healing (156). He came to the conclusion that while suggestion undoubtedly plays an important part in some miraculous healings, it does not entirely explain them. He argued that there may be *laws* of prayer, that is, certain specific conditions which must be fulfilled if healing is to take place. If this theory is correct, it would be worthwhile carrying out controlled experiments to compare the efficacy of different prayer techniques on various illnesses. In 1953 the Church of England also began to show signs of renewed interest in the subject, and the Archbishops set up a Commission to consider 'the theological, medical, psychological and pastoral aspects of Divine Healing'. This body consisted of twenty-eight members, the majority of whom were ordained clergymen: the results of its deliberations can only be described as a damp squib. After five years' work the Commission produced a slender booklet (25) in which it carefully evaded the one question which was of interest to most people, namely, do medically inexplicable healings occur as a result of prayer or other forms of spiritual activity? Instead, it timidly cited the testimony of a Committee of the British Medical Association to the effect that 'We can find no evidence that there is any type of illness cured by "spiritual healing" alone which could not have been cured by medical treatment.' In fact, an identical conclusion had been pronounced by a Committee of the Lambeth Conference set up in 1920, so at least the Church cannot be accused of inconsistency on this issue. However it is doubtful whether such *ex cathedra* pronouncements, either from the Church or the medical profession, really add very much to our knowledge of paranormal healing: what is needed is a prolonged period of careful, scientific research.

Among medical men who have investigated paranormal healings, pride of place must go to Dr Louis Rose. Over the years he has examined many alleged cures, and published the results of his enquiries in the *British Medical Journal* and the *Journal of the Society for Psychical Research*. In 1955 he published the results of a study involving 95 patients, the majority of whom were supposed to have been cured by the famous Spiritualist healer Harry Edwards.* Dr Rose found that in 58 cases it was not possible to obtain the patient's medical records, so that there was no way of confirming or disproving the alleged cure. The remaining 37 cases fell into the following categories:

(1) In 22 cases the records were so much at variance with the claims that it was considered useless to continue the investigation further;

(2) In 2 cases the evidence suggested that the healer may have contributed to the amelioration of an organic condition;

(3) In 1 case demonstrable organic disability was relieved or cured after intervention by the healer;

(4) 3 cases improved but relapsed;

(5) 4 cases showed a satisfactory degree of improvement although re-examination and comparison of medical records revealed no change in the organic state;

(6) In 4 cases there was improvement when healing was received concurrently with orthodox medical treatment;

(7) One case gained no benefit and continued to deteriorate.

From all this we may conclude that, *if* paranormal healings occur, they are probably rare events and are extremely difficult to substantiate. In this respect they are, of course, no different from any other kind of psi phenomenon. Before Rhine introduced his techniques of controlled laboratory testing the case for the reality of ESP and PK was just about as uncertain as the case for paranormal healing is today. Certainly there is very suggestive evidence that some people do benefit from unorthodox treatment; but the only way to be certain that we are dealing with a genuine phenomenon is to carry out a carefully planned experiment. It is very gratifying to be able to

* *Journal of the SPR*, 1955, 38, pp. 105-120.

report that, at long last, some parapsychologists are beginning to do just that.

The first fully controlled laboratory experiment with a psychic healer was carried out by Bernard Grad, Assistant Professor in the Department of Psychiatry at McGill University, Montreal. His experimental subject was Oskar Estebany, a Hungarian-born psychic who claims to be able to exert a healing effect on animals and plants as well as humans. Born in 1897, Estebany served as a lieutenant in the Hungarian army during the First World War. While he was a young cavalry officer he noticed that sick animals seemed to recover more quickly than usual when they were massaged by him : however, it was not until about 1940 that he began to apply his healing ability to the treatment of human sufferers. At that time psychic healing was forbidden in Hungary, but Estebany won the support of several Hungarian physicians who were willing to supervise his ministrations. Later he emigrated to Canada, where he has since become widely known for his healing abilities.

In order to provide a scientific test of Estebany's powers Grad inflicted small wounds on anaesthetised mice by surgically removing a piece of skin from their backs. The areas of the wounds were measured by placing a thin piece of transparent plastic over them, tracing the outline with a grease pencil, and measuring the area of the tracing with a planimeter. Starting on the sixth day after wounding, the wound areas were measured at two-day intervals until the 20th day, by which time healing was virtually complete. During that period, half of the mice were treated each day by Estebany, and half were left untreated, as 'controls'. Preliminary experiments extending over a two-year period showed that by Day 14 there was a statistically highly significant difference between the mean wound areas of the treated and untreated mice : those which had received the healing treatment from Estebany had healed noticeably more rapidly than the controls. Here, then, was clear-cut laboratory evidence for the existence of a paranormal healing effect associated with a particular individual.

However, there were complications. It has been known for some time that small animals grow faster and show greater resistance to stress if they are regularly stroked and fondled by humans (the 'gentling' effect). Could the rapid healing of the treated mice be due to something of this kind? It seemed unlikely, since Estebany had not actually *handled* the mice; his treatment had involved holding the cages between his hands for 20 minutes twice a day. Nevertheless, it seemed advisable to reduce the contact between healer and mice still further. Grad therefore planned a more elaborate experiment in which the cages were placed inside heavy paper bags. Some bags were fastened with staples and Estebany was permitted to touch only the outside of the bag, whereas others were left open so that he could hold the cage by putting his hands inside the bag. Under no circumstance was he allowed to handle the mice. To provide a further comparison, a second group of mice was treated in exactly the same manner by medical students who claimed no special paranormal abilities, and a third group was left untreated, as before. Elaborate precautions were taken to ensure that the staff concerned with the care of the animals and the measurement of the wounds were 'blind' as to which were the treated animals and which the controls (53).

Three hundred mice were used in this mammoth experiment, and the results satisfactorily confirmed the findings of the preliminary research. By Day 14 the mice treated by Estebany had, on the average, smaller wound areas than those treated by the medical students, or not treated at all. This was true for both the open-bag and closed-bag conditions, though only the open-bag results reached statistical significance (odds of more than 100 to one). Unfortunately this evidence is not sufficient to enable us to say whether the apparently greater success with the open bags was real or coincidental; more research is needed to investigate the effects, if any, of physical barriers. However, the results do strongly support Estebany's claim to possess some kind of healing power not found in ordinary people. The mice treated by the medical students recovered at almost exactly the same rate as the untreated mice.

The next stage in Grad's research involved examining Estebany's influence upon plants. Preliminary tests showed that barley seeds planted in peat pots grew faster when treated by the healer. Grad soon discovered that this phenomenon was most clearly marked when the plants were grown under conditions of water-deprivation, that is, when they had insufficient water to permit optimum growth. As with animals and humans, the 'healing' effect only became apparent when the plants were in a state of need. Eventually, Grad adopted the technique of deliberately inhibiting the growth of the plants by watering them with a 1% solution of sodium chloride, and then partially drying out the soil in an oven. Under these rather drastic conditions the healing effect of Estebany's treatment showed up remarkably well. Grad launched a full-scale experiment, using all the proper control procedures, and the results were statistically highly significant: by the ninth day of the experiment the odds against the difference in height between the treated and the untreated plants occurring by chance were more than 1,000 to one. Following this success the experiment was repeated a further four times, using proper 'double-blind' procedures and with additional restrictions: in each of the four replications the treated plants grew faster than the untreated, and in three of the four the difference was statistically significant. Such a level of consistency is remarkably good for a parapsychological experiment (54, 55).

A surprising feature of the Grad plant experiments is the nature of the treatment applied. Although in some of the preliminary trials Estebany treated the plants directly, in all the major experiments he merely treated the saline solution which was used to water the plants. Treatment consisted of holding a beaker containing the solution between his hands for 15 minutes, with his left hand supporting it from below and his right hand held three or four centimetres above the surface of the liquid. Grad realised that under these conditions there was a possibility that traces of some chemical substance or substances might pass from the healer's skin into the liquid, and perhaps act as a nutrient for the plants. In the later experiments, therefore, he enclosed the saline solution in tightly stoppered glass bottles, and only allowed the healer to place his hands on the *outside* of the bottle. The significant results obtained under these conditions left no doubt that whatever was passing from the healer into the liquid was not impeded by the glass. Later Grad carried out a detailed chemical and physical examination of the treated liquid, but failed to discover anything which might account for its growth-accelerating properties. Similar investigations have been conducted on the water from Lourdes, again without discovering anything out of the ordinary. Whatever lies behind the phenomenon of paranormal healing does not seem to be explicable in terms of present-day physics and chemistry.

Following Grad's example, other parapsychologists have begun to carry out experiments in healing, although so far the total output of research in this field is small. Sister Justa Smith, head of the departments of chemistry and biology at Rosary Hill College, Buffalo, carried out some tests with the long-suffering Estebany, using the enzyme tryspin. This is a substance which occurs in the digestive tract of man and other animals: its function is to bring about the break-down of proteins to polypeptides. Sister Smith showed that the 'influence' apparently emanating from Estebany's hands was able to bring about an acceleration in the activity of the enzyme, corresponding to a magnetic field of 13,000 gauss (128). At the Institute for Parapsychology in North Carolina, Graham and Anita Watkins performed some experiments which were not unlike those of the original Grad series. Instead of surgically wounding their mice, they inflicted a mild poisoning upon them by rendering them unconscious with ether. The mice were anaesthetised in pairs, using the same amount of ether for each, and one member of the pair was then randomly selected to be the recipient of the 'healing' process. A human subject concentrated on the chosen animal from behind a glass screen, willing it to recover quickly. The experimenters recorded the time taken for the treated and untreated mice to recover from the anaesthetic, and used statistical calculations to test the significance of the results. Of the thirteen human subjects used in these experiments, ten either claimed to have healing abilities, or else had performed successfully in other PK-type tests. Nine of these ten scored significantly above chance, thus showing that they were indeed able to influence the recovery rate of the mice. The overall results of the experiments were highly significant, with odds of about 100,000 to one against the chance hypothesis (154), and the experiment has since been successfully replicated by other researchers (157).

In view of the fact that a number of the Lourdes cures are said to have occurred in cancer patients, it is worth mentioning a pioneer study by Gita H. Elguin at the University of Chile (41). Ninety mice were inoculated subcutaneously with a suspension of tumour-producing cancer cells, and then divided randomly into three groups of thirty mice each. Group A was concentrated upon with the intention of increasing the tumour growth by PK; Group B was similarly concentrated upon with the intention of retarding the tumour growth; and Group C was left untreated, as a control. At the end of the experiment the Group B animals showed significantly less tumour growth than the controls (odds of more than 100 to one against chance); however, the Group A animals did *not* show any increase in tumour growth. The experimenter suggested that this was probably because she felt the task of willing an increase in the animal's suffering to be a highly distasteful one, and this may have prevented any possible PK effect on the tumours. It would indeed be an interesting discovery if it turned out that paranormal abilities can only be used for good, and never for evil!

From experimental studies, therefore, it appears that there are certain persons who can affect the progress of a disease in ways which are inexplicable in terms of present-day scientific knowledge. Harry Edwards, Kathryn Kuhlman and Oskar Estebany probably belong to this group. But what are we to make of the Lourdes phenomena, where healing seems to be associated with a particular place rather than a particular person? Even the thought-patterns associated with Lourdes seem to be occasionally effective in promoting healing, for cases have been reported where the healed person was nowhere near Lourdes at the time he was healed. If we accept such phenomena at their face value (and we must not forget the possibility of error or exaggeration), there would seem to be the following possibilities:

(1) The healing is a direct result of the activity of God, or some other supernatural being (an Angel, the Virgin Mary, etc);

(2) The healing is due to a powerful PK effect from the minds of the thousands of pilgrims at the shrine;

(3) The healing is due to a PK effect from the patient's own mind.

Of course, all these factors may be operating simultaneously, or there may be other possibilities which we cannot imagine with our present thought background. However there is some evidence that paranormal self-healing may occasionally operate in non-religious situations, and it is possible that PK plays a part in all recoveries from disease. In an interesting book on psychosomatic medicine (18) Dr Stephen Black has reported some of the surprising results he has obtained with the use of hypnosis. From Black's experiments, it seems clear that psychological factors can profoundly influence the course of diseases which a generation ago would have been regarded as purely physical. Most astonishing of all, a number of *congenital* conditions such as Brocq's congenital ichthyosis, linear naevus and pachyonychia are said to have been cured by hypnotherapy. Heredity disorders are supposed to be caused by mutated genes or chromosomes: the faulty information contained in these is mediated to the body structures by means of 'messenger' molecules. It is difficult to see how any kind of psychological influence could possibly affect such a mechanism, unless by direct PK action upon the genes themselves, or upon one of the biochemical systems which they control. In spite of appearances to the contrary, it seems that Mind *can* occasionally exert its mastery over Matter, even in the sacred hunting grounds of molecular biology!

We cannot leave the subject of paranormal healing without briefly examining a fascinating new theory put forward by an American psychologist, Lawrence LeShan (85). The starting point for this theory came from an examination of the concepts of reality presented by three different types of people: theoretical physicists, mediums or clairvoyants, and mystics. LeShan found that there was a considerable area of agreement between the three which led him to the conclusion that they were all describing essentially the same view of the world. This view he termed the *Clairvoyant Reality*, to distinguish it from the everyday, commonsense picture, which he called the *Sensory Reality*. A person experiencing the world in terms of the Clairvoyant Reality sees individual identity as mainly illusory; objects and events are observed as merely parts of a larger pattern. Since the knower and the known are one, there is no barrier to the transfer of information between them, so that psi phenomena are *normal* in this world-view. Past, present and future are also seen as illusory: time is a continuum in which all events coexist in an eternal 'now', and free-will has no meaning. Such, in very brief outline, is the picture of reality presented by mystics of all religions, by clairvoyants and by physicists who adopt the 'field-theory' approach. It is of course in flat contradiction to the picture presented by our biological senses, the picture we use in organising our everyday lives.

Which, then, gives us the more accurate account of the world: the Clairvoyant Reality or the Sensory Reality? Here LeShan takes the bold step of borrowing from physics an important idea, known as the Principle of Complementarity. Physicists have known for some time that it is impossible to construct a single, coherent account of certain kinds of phenomena: they have to settle for two apparently contra-dictory accounts, each of which is used in certain situations where the other is inapplicable. For example, in some experi-ments light is treated as though it were a stream of tiny par-ticles, or 'photons': in other experiments it is treated as though it were a train of waves. Both concepts are useful in their proper places, and we cannot say that one is more 'true' than the other. The principles of quantum mechanics make it quite clear to the physicist when it is appropriate to think in terms of particles, and when to think in terms of waves. Strange as it may seem to the non-physicist, this method has proved highly successful in elucidating the mysteries of the interior of the atom. LeShan suggests that we should adopt a similar 'complementarity' approach to the Sensory Reality and the Clairvoyant Reality: in spite of their apparently contradictory nature, both can give us useful information about reality, and there are occasions when it is appropriate to use one rather than the other.

All this is interesting enough; but what has it to do with paranormal healing? LeShan believes that there may be several different types of healing, but his theory is mainly applicable to what he calls 'Type 1'. In this type of healing the healer uses meditation or some similar method to enter the Clair-voyant Reality, in which he sees himself and the patient as one. The union thus psychically created enables the patient's self-repair systems to work at a much higher level of efficiency than normal:

> The healer does not 'do' or 'give' something to the healee; instead he helps him to come home to the All, to the One, to the way of 'unity' with the Universe, and in this 'meeting' the healee becomes more complete and this in itself is healing (85, p. 111).

According to LeShan there are no miracles, in the strict sense of the word: amputated limbs do not regrow, nor do destroyed tissues magically reappear. Spiritual or paranormal healing involves only the normal processes of cellular repair and recovery, accelerated many times because the sufferer has been restored to a state of harmony with the All. After formulating his theory, LeShan went on to put it to the test of practice. He began to attempt psychic healing by putting himself in contact with the Clairvoyant Reality through meditation, and also trained a number of other persons in the same technique. He believes that it is possible to develop the art of healing in ordinary people, just as it is possible to teach meditation techniques. Whatever one may think of LeShan's theory of the two Realities (and the present writer considers it to be a profound and important contribution to parapsychological theory), there can be no doubt that he has produced a fresh and original approach to the problem of healing.

Paranormal healing is undoubtedly the most complex of all the topics discussed in this book, and this probably accounts for the comparative neglect from which it has suffered until quite recently. In any particular healing, human or animal, there is certainly a variety of interlocking factors, some physical, some psychological, and some spiritual or parapsychological. Only very rarely is it possible to point to a single uncomplicated 'cause' for a healing: every doctor knows that the best drugs in the world are useless if the patient's own tissues have lost the ability of self-repair, or the patient has lost the will to live. Experimental parapsychology has so far merely touched upon this important field; but what has been achieved is not unimportant. The work of Grad, Smith, Elguin and others has at least disposed of one false theory, namely the notion that all paranormal healing can be written off as mere 'suggestion'. This ridiculous blanket word has been used for more than half a century as a means of avoiding the realities of a whole area of human experience, ranging from the phenomena of hypnosis to the healings of Lourdes and the Christian Scientists. It has served to prevent scientists from looking more closely at these phenomena, and thereby perhaps discovering something important about them. Now at last the suggestion theory can be quietly laid to rest; for surely no one will try to claim that the mice used by Grad, Elguin and the Watkins' were influenced by suggestion, or that Estebany's barley seeds grew faster because they had been listening to Catholic propaganda! We may hope that the work begun by this handful of pioneers will be taken up by others, so that parapsychology, like the other sciences, may begin to make a practical contribution to the relief of human suffering.

12. The Turning Tide

As the 1960s drew to a close parapsychology won a substantial victory in its ninety-year-old battle for scientific respectability. On December 30th 1969, the Parapsychological Association was officially accepted as an affiliate member of that most distinguished body of savants, the American Association for the Advancement of Science (AAAS). The decision to grant affiliation to the parapsychologists was taken by the AAAS Council, an organisation composed of delegates from about 300 other affiliated scientific, medical and engineering societies; so it represented the views of a considerable cross-section of American science. For the first time in its chequered history parapsychology had been recognised as a legitimate scientific pursuit; and from now on parapsychologists could present their papers at the bar of scientific opinion without feeling that they would be ridiculed or dismissed out of hand, merely on account of their subject-matter.

However, this particular victory was not won without a struggle. Three times previously, in 1963, 1967 and 1968, the parapsychologists had applied for affiliation and been rejected. Why, then, this sudden change of heart on the part of American orthodoxy? To some extent it may have been due to the many successes which were achieved towards the end of the sixties as parapsychologists began using increasingly sophisticated methods of experimentation. Thus Ullman's work with sleep-monitoring devices was published in a major psychiatric journal in 1966, the Duval-Montredon mouse experiments appeared in 1968, and the Schmidt research with electronic random number generators became fairly widely known during the summer of 1969. Each of these studies marked an important methodological breakthrough. But an even more important factor may have been the increasing awareness among scientists of the inherent limitations of their own work. A widespread tendency to reopen fundamental questions and to challenge accepted points of view became apparent during the sixties, especially among the young. In psychology, this took the form of a general dissatisfaction with the mechanistic concepts which had so powerfully dominated psychological thought during the first half of the century. Breaking through the old thought-patterns, the devotees of existentialist and humanistic psychologies set out to create a new emphasis on the character- istics of man, as distinct from the laboratory white rat. Once again, psychologists began to turn their attention to that inner world whose very existence had been roundly denied by the behaviourists. Kleitman's discovery of dream-monitoring methods, the rise to fame of the psychedelic drugs, and the arrival in the western world of oriental techniques of medita- tion, all served to stimulate a fresh interest in altered states of consciousness (the very term would have been anathema to the Watsonians!). In such a climate of opinion, psi phenomena no longer seemed quite so unimaginable.

In Britain the change of attitude was less obvious than in the USA, but even here the tide was beginning to turn. In 1972 Dr Christopher Evans, whose sceptical attitude to psi has already been described, received something of a shock when he examined the results of a questionnaire put out under the auspices of *New Scientist* magazine. Out of approximately 1,500 replies received, some 25% said that they regarded ESP as an established fact, and a further 42% thought it a likely possi- bility. Only a mere 3% of the sample regarded ESP as impossible. The figures appear even more remarkable when we realise that most of the respondents were qualified scientists with university degrees. Dr Evans concluded:

> ... the stated opinions of nearly 1,500 readers, the majority of whom are working scientists and technologists, on a topic as controversial as parapsychology cannot be lightly dismissed. Clearly, a large number of serious scientists con- sider it to be a highly interesting and potentially immensely significant branch of science (43).

Coming from such a dedicated opponent of parapsychology, this is indeed a handsome admission.

Of course, the growing acceptance of psi has not silenced the sceptics: as we pointed out in chapter 8, they are still very much on the move, although they now appear to be fighting for a lost cause. Almost without exception, their criticisms are directed against experiments which are *at least 30 years old*. Thus the two major attacks launched during 1974 were upon the Pratt-Woodruff experiment of 1939 (89) and the Soal-Goldney experiment of 1940-43. It is not difficult to see why this should be so: after a lapse of 30 years it is almost certain that most of the important eye-witnesses will either be dead, or too old to remember accurately what happened. If the critic puts forward some hypothetical method by which fraudulent results *might* have been obtained, he is unlikely to be contradicted by persons who were actually present at the experiments. By choosing to attack an old experiment, therefore, he is tilting the scales in his own favour. At this rate, we may expect criticisms of Dr Schmidt's experiments to start appearing in the literature around the year 2000!

The critic usually tries from the start to make the reader believe that the whole case for psi, or at least a major part of it, rests upon the experiment he is about to attack. Thus Scott and Haskell begin their criticism of the Soal-Goldney experiment by saying that 'for some writers at least (it) has stood as a mainstay of the evidence for ESP,' and Medhurst and Scott similarly describe the Pratt-Woodruff experiment as having been cited as 'one of the key experiments rigorously demonstrating the existence of ESP.' By such means, the reader is led to suppose that the whole of parapsychology rests upon a mere handful of experiments, and if these are shown to be fraudulent, the case for ESP collapses. In fairness to the critics, it must be added that some parapsychologists have encouraged this kind of criticism by focussing too much attention on the great classical experiments of the past. This is usually done with the plea that, since psi experiments are *unrepeatable*, we must needs put all our faith in a few successful experiments carried out under exceptionally rigorous conditions with a few gifted subjects. It may be said at once that the present writer regards this view as seriously mistaken; and he will therefore devote the remainder of this chapter to an examination of exactly where the strength of the evidence lies, so that the reader may be persuaded that parapsychology is indeed a genuine and legitimate branch of science.

In the first place, it is simply not true that psi experiments are unrepeatable. Every one of the major findings of parapsychology has been replicated many times. Successful ESP experiments have been reported in their hundreds from every civilised country in the world, as anyone can discover for himself if he is prepared to spend an hour or so browsing through the collected volumes of periodicals in the SPR library. Highly significant ESP scoring has been obtained from both human and animal subjects, and experimenters have used an enormous range of target materials: drawings, art prints, numerals, playing cards, ESP cards, cards with animal pictures, cards with clock faces, electronic machines. Successful tests have been conducted with the subjects awake, asleep, under the influence of drugs or hypnosis, and while practising meditation. In all these situations, and many others, the same basic phenomenon—the transfer of information without the use of the bodily senses—has been observed over and over again. In fact, there must be very few phenomena in the fields covered by the life sciences which have been replicated so many times. When to this is added the evidence from thousands of spontaneous cases, the case for the reality of psi seems well-nigh irresistible. To the present writer at least, it is the fact that psi phenomena have been repeatedly observed, both inside and outside the laboratory, under a great variety of conditions and by many different people, that constitutes the chief evidence for psi, *not* the results of a small group of allegedly crucial experiments.

Since psi effects have been repeatedly observed under laboratory conditions, why do the sceptics insist that they are unrepeatable? The reason is that psi experiments cannot be repeated *on demand*. To the sceptics, and to some believers also, 'repeatability' means being able to specify exactly what must be done in order to obtain a successful result every time. In spite of many years of research, we are still a very long way from that kind of repeatability in parapsychology. Some have argued that, because of this, parapsychology cannot be regarded as a science at all; they would claim that repeatability-at-will is a necessary condition for a phenomenon to be admitted to the ranks of accepted scientific knowledge. However, this is far too harsh a criterion: it would exclude a number of topics, such as earthquakes, comets, lightning flashes and meteorites, from scientific investigation altogether. A geneticist cannot make a particular specified mutation occur at will: he can only wait for it to turn up (although he can increase his chances by exposing the organisms to radiation). Furthermore, the 'non-repeatability' of parapsychological experiments is certainly no worse than in many other branches of the psychological sciences. A writer in the *American Psychologist* has pointed out that many psychological experiments are never replicated at all, and those that are sometimes lead to contradictory results (129). In the life sciences, it is virtually impossible to perform an exact repetition of an experiment: the mere fact that the experimenter now knows what to expect is likely to bias the results in various subtle ways. The very concept of the 'repeatable experiment' seems to be more applicable to the physical sciences than to the psychological, and psychology may well have to develop its own criteria rather than adopt those of the older sciences.

The fact that psi experiments are especially difficult to replicate is almost certainly a direct consequence of the space-time independence of psi, discussed in chapter 6. Theoretical physicists have long been aware that there is a sense in which every particle in the universe influences the behaviour of every other particle. Fortunately we do not have to worry about this too much when carrying out an ordinary physics experiment: the gravitational and electromagnetic forces which might disturb our apparatus fall off according to the inverse square law, so that we can ignore the effects of all but the nearest objects. However, with psi phenomena this is no longer true. We have seen that psi can operate across enormous distances, and in apparent defiance of the normal direction of time-flow; therefore it is quite possible that an idea passing through a parapsychologist's mind in London tomorrow might have a perturbing effect upon another parapsychologist's experiment in Edinburgh today! The usual 'double-blind' experimental controls are of course quite useless as a safeguard against this kind of extra-physical interaction. Researchers at Tel Aviv University have even found evidence that ESP may influence the outcome of ordinary psychological experiments, without either the experimenter or his subjects being aware of the fact. It would be ironic if, having been expelled from orthodox psychology, ESP were to take its revenge by injecting an element of 'unrepeatability' into the psychologist's own experiments!

Reading through the various critical articles which appear from time to time, the layman might be forgiven for thinking that, even if psi exists, it is so erratic and unpredictable that nothing definite can be said about it. This is not entirely true. There are a number of observed regularities in laboratory psi experiments which indicate that we are dealing with a lawful phenomenon, even though the laws underlying it are very imperfectly understood. Some of these we have already discussed: the sheep-goat effect, for example, and the fact that extraverts usually show more psi ability than introverts. There is also the frequently observed tendency for ESP to become displaced on to targets which are adjacent in space or time. This was first noticed by Dr C. G. Abbott, an American astrophysicist, in the course of some experiments with ESP cards in 1938; it occurred again in the picture experiments of Whately Carington, in Soal's researches with Basil Shackleton and Mrs Stewart, and in some of the Fisk home-testing experiments. More recently, it reappeared in rather different form during Pratt's experiments with the Czech psychic Stepanek, and again in some of the Maimonides dream experiments. It is clearly an important characteristic of psi phenomena, stemming from the fact that they operate outside the space-time continuum of everyday life, and are seldom susceptible to conscious control.

Salience is the name given to another characteristic frequently observed in both ESP and PK data. If a subject is instructed to perform a psi-task, such as guessing through a hundred cards, most of his hits tend to occur at the beginning and end of the sequence. The hit distribution thus follows a U-shaped curve, usually with the second arm of the U slightly lower than the first. Figures 4 and 5 show two such curves, deliberately chosen from experiments conducted under widely different circumstances. Figure 4 shows the distribution of hits obtained by Dr Rhine in his 'DT' experiments with Hubert Pearce during the early 1930s: the first point indicates the scoring rate on the first five cards in the pack, the second point the scoring rate on the second five, and so on. Figure 5 shows a

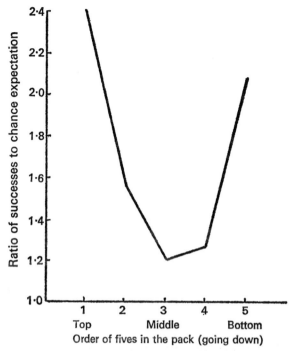

Fig. 4: Graph showing the distribution of hits throughout the pack in 1,500 DT trials with Hubert Pearce. (After Rhine, 107, p. 170)

curve obtained by the author during some experiments with PK on living targets, carried out in 1969 (103). Young male subjects sat behind a perspex screen and attempted to will a woodlouse to run into one of five equal sectors marked out on a circular board. Each subject completed four runs of 25 trials each, and the graph shows the hit distribution on each of the four runs. Calculation shows that the odds against the scores on these four runs varying so greatly by chance are more than 1,000 to one. That such similar curves should emerge from experiments conducted in two different countries, with different experimental designs, and with an interval of 40 years between them, is surely striking; but these are only a small sample of many salience curves obtained over the years. They have been found in clairvoyance, precognition and PK tests of many different kinds. As Dr Thouless pointed out in 1950:

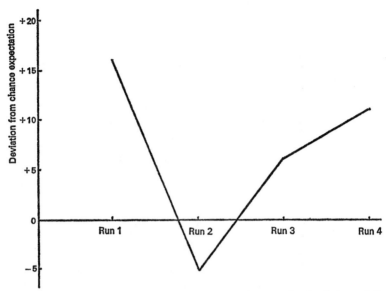

Fig. 5: Graph showing the distribution of hits obtained in a PK experiment, using woodlice as living targets. (Randall, 1969)

It is interesting that such odd effects should be found by different workers, experimenting independently of one another. They confirm the impression that we are travelling through a country that has features, even if we do not always understand them (140).

But perhaps the one consistent feature of the psi countryside which stands out more than any other is the *chronological decline.* Over a more or less lengthy period of systematic testing, every single psi subject has shown a steady downward trend in scoring until eventually he could no longer score above chance level. So consistent is this effect that it might almost be justifiable to regard it as the fully repeatable phenomenon demanded by the critics! It is of course depressing to the experimenter to see the scores of his best subjects steadily declining, but it seems to be an inevitable consequence of the testing procedure. A 'good' ESP subject may be able to score above chance for several months, or even years, but sooner or later the decline sets in, and the experimenter knows that it is useless to continue. Less gifted subjects may lose their psychic ability in a few weeks or even days. Dr Beloff has suggested that these declines may be due to a kind of habituation effect, similar to those produced when an organism strives to rid itself of an intruding stimulus. Clearly, we need *some* sort of defence against psi; for if ESP and PK phenomena were to occur continuously, ordinary biological existence would be impossible. It could be, therefore, that the human mind has a natural 'immunity', a sort of built-in defence mechanism against psychic intrusion. In some people this defence is rather weak, so that when they attempt a psi-task in the laboratory, a certain amount of information slips through the barrier, and we say that we have found a good ESP subject. However, the mind reacts to the intruding information in much the same way as the body reacts to an intruding virus, gradually building up immunity until the barrier is complete. From then onwards, the person will never suffer from an 'attack' of psi information again, and we say that he has lost his psychic ability. Of course, this is only a hypothesis; but it seems plausible, and it could be fruitful in suggesting new experimental approaches aimed at circumventing the 'immunological' effect.

It is probable that there will always be some dogmatic sceptics who refuse to believe in psi, no matter how much evidence is accumulated. After all, there are still some people who believe the earth is flat! However, all the signs are that parapsychology has now turned the corner, and the volume of research activity is steadily increasing, year by year. As might be expected, America leads the field: important parapsychological investigations are in progress at many centres throughout the USA, some of them officially connected with universities or colleges. In Europe the most active country seems to be Holland, and on April 1st 1974 Dr Martin Johnson, formerly a psychologist at the University of Lund in Sweden, took over the newly established permanent professorship in parapsychology at Utrecht University. Argentina, Israel, India, West Germany, Iceland, Canada, Switzerland, Denmark and Italy are among the many countries where parapsychological researches of one kind or another are in progress. Britain lags sadly behind in this field: only Edinburgh University sponsors a parapsychological laboratory, which in spite of its small size has produced a surprisingly large amount of very high quality work over the past few years. No other British universities have followed Edinburgh's example, and most British research remains in the hands of a small number of amateurs who, because of the fascination which the subject holds for them, are prepared to devote a large proportion of their spare time to it.

We have previously described how, with the exception of Stepanek, no first-class psychically gifted subjects appeared between about 1955 and 1968. Now, with the turning of the tide, the picture has begun to change. We have already mentioned the young English psychic Malcolm Bessent who worked for the Maimonides laboratory, and the several excellent subjects discovered by Helmut Schmidt. We may add to these the name of Lalsingh Harribance, a West Indian who has given evidence of his abilities in several reputable parapsychology laboratories. He produces highly significant scoring in an amazing variety of ESP and PK tests, and was one of the successful subjects in the mouse-resuscitation experiments described on page 169. Ingo Swann is another psychic who has recently made a name for himself in parapsychological circles. He has been tested by Dr Osis at the laboratories of the American Society for Psychical Research, by Drs Harold Puthoff and Russell Targ at the Stanford Research Institute (SRI), and by Dr Gertrude Schmeidler at the City College of New York. Swann seems to possess the ability to produce 'out of the body' experiences in himself at will, and to bring back information which could not have been obtained through the use of his ordinary senses. He also seems to have remarkable psychokinetic powers, for at the SRI he was able to influence a screened magnetometer, and in Schmeidler's experiments he apparently raised the temperature inside a sealed vacuum flask, merely by concentrating upon it. All these experiments are very recent (some have not been published at the time of writing), but they serve to indicate to the reader the kind of exciting work which is going on in parapsychology today. Furthermore, we have not exhausted the list of high-scoring subjects: other names, such as Bill Delmore, Pat Price and Matthew Manning, are already appearing on the horizon.

Surprisingly enough, there has even been a revival of interest in the *physical* phenomena of psychical research. During the nineteenth century and the first few decades of the twentieth, there were a number of famous physical mediums who claimed to produce table levitations and similar marvels. Perhaps the most famous was D. D. Home, who performed his extraordinary feats in broad daylight before some of the crowned heads of Europe. However, as the twentieth century drew on, the physical mediums gradually diminished in number. Sceptics said that this was because modern scientific devices (such as infra-red telescopes capable of seeing in the dark) made their fraudulent activities impossible to perform without detection. At any rate, most psychical researchers turned their attention to telepathy and other kinds of mental phenomena. Later, when Rhine demonstrated the existence of PK with his dice-throwing experiments, one or two psychical researchers began to wonder whether there might not be something in physical mediumship after all, but the dearth of good subjects made its investigation virtually impossible. Now, from Russia comes news of a housewife, Nelya Mikhailova (Nina Kulagina), who can apparently move small objects such as matches or cigarettes without touching them. She has been carefully studied by a number of Russian parapsychologists, notably Leonid Vasiliev and Edward Naumov, and has also impressed western visitors such as Dr Pratt. Whether she is genuine or not it is difficult to say, but there is certainly some impressive evidence in her favour. In the western world, physical phenomena have made something of a comeback in the achievements of the sensational Uri Geller, whose metal-bending and mind-reading feats have been described in the press and viewed by millions on television. Within a few months of his appearance in Britain, there grew up a vast literature on Geller, and the correspondence columns of journals such as *New Scientist* were literally jammed with lengthy arguments between sceptics and believers.

Mention of Geller brings us back again to the perennial temptation of the parapsychologist: that of placing too much reliance on a single piece of research or a single talented subject. After Geller's demonstrations in Britain, many scientists who had previously shown little interest in parapsychology began to wax enthusiastic over the phenomena. People who had apparently hardly heard of the painstaking experiments of Rhine,

Pratt, Schmeidler, Soal, Fisk, West, Ryzl, Ullman, Krippner, Schmidt, Grad and all the other serious parapsychologists suddenly became highly excited over this single wonder-worker. Now there is nothing wrong with a little excitement; but the danger comes when these enthusiasts begin writing and arguing as though the whole case for the reality of psi rests upon the honesty and integrity of Mr Uri Geller. In 1974 *Nature* published an account by Targ and Puthoff of their highly successful experiments with Geller at the SRI (135). As expected the report was strongly attacked by the sceptics. However, the attacks were entirely confined to that part of the report which dealt with Geller, although the Targ-Puthoff article also described some significant results obtained with another psychic, Pat Price. We must repeat, then, that the case for psi does not depend upon any one individual, no matter how dramatic his phenomena may be, nor how much publicity he receives in the mass media. The case for psi rests upon the fact that the same phenomena have been witnessed, over and over again, in many different subjects and by many different experimenters. Psi phenomena are occurring today in every country of the world, as they have done for many thousands of years.

What, then, does it all mean? Perhaps the implications were stated most clearly by H. H. Price, Wykeham Professor of Logic at Oxford University, when he wrote in the *Hibbert Journal* for 1949:

> We must conclude, I think, that there is no room for telepathy in a Materialistic universe. Telepathy is something which ought not to happen at all, if the Materialistic theory were true. But it does happen. So there must be something seriously wrong with the Materialistic theory, however numerous and imposing the *normal* facts which support it may be.

The continuing success of parapsychology has made a very large crack in the fabric of the materialistic philosophy. In the next section of this book we shall take a closer and more critical look at that philosophy, to see whether it is not time to loosen the stranglehold which it has maintained over human thought and human aspirations for the past hundred years, and in doing so, to free mankind from the grip of the existential neurosis.

Part III: Towards a new Synthesis

There is no absolute knowledge. And those who claim it, whether they are scientists or dogmatists, open the door to tragedy. All information is imperfect. We have to treat it with humility. That is the human condition.

JACOB BRONOWSKI, *The Ascent of Man.*

13. Mechanism Revisited

In his stimulating book *The Ghost in the Machine*, Arthur Koestler attacks what he calls the 'four pillars of unwisdom' which support the citadel of twentieth-century orthodoxy. They are the doctrines:

(a) that biological evolution is the result of random mutations preserved by natural selection;

(b) that mental evolution is the result of random tries preserved by 'reinforcement' (rewards);

(c) that all organisms, including man, are essentially passive automata controlled by the environment, whose sole purpose in life is the reduction of tensions by adaptive responses;

(d) that the only scientific method worth that name is quantitative measurement; and, consequently, that complex phenomena must be reduced to simple elements accessible to such treatment, without undue worry whether the specific characteristics of a complex phenomenon, for instance man, may be lost in the process (79, p. 3).

For many years now Koestler has carried on a kind of guerrilla warfare against what is usually known as *reductionism*, the practice of attempting to account for all the properties of highly complex systems in terms of their simplest components. Reductionism is not necessarily mechanistic, although in most instances the ultimate goal of the reductionist is to obtain an explanation in terms of the known laws of physics and chemistry. Freud's theory of human behaviour involves the postulation of non-physical entities (the Unconscious, the Ego, the Id), so that it cannot be strictly described as a mechanistic theory. Even so, it is clearly reductionist in that it denies the existence of any higher motives in man, ascribing all or most of his activities to the same sexual impulses which are found in the lower animals. In Freudian terms man is indeed nothing but a 'naked ape', and all those qualities which were once thought to make him only a little lower than the angels—altruism, heroic self-sacrifice, religion, artistic inspiration—are explained away as the results of repressed sexuality. In the behaviourist creed reductionism appears as the belief that all animal and human behaviour can be explained in terms of conditioned reflexes. It is not at all surprising that both Watson and Skinner provoke the wrath of Koestler who, as a creative writer, tries to see man as a complete being.

Yet despite the attacks of Koestler and others, there are two facts which cannot be denied : first, that western science has been almost entirely reductionist and mechanist for more than a hundred years; and second, that this approach has proved outstandingly successful. In Part I of this book we traced the triumphant advance of mechanism from the times of Descartes and La Mettrie to the present-day molecular biologists. A glance at any scientific periodical will confirm the fact that this advance is not only continuing, but accelerating, week by week. There can be no doubt whatever that mechanistic reductionism is a highly successful way of investigating the physical world. In contrast, those who have adopted a vitalistic or holistic position have seldom produced anything more than vague generalities. It certainly seems as though mechanistic assumptions are the only ones which lead to clear-cut, testable hypotheses, and are therefore the only ones which can further the progress of science as we know it. Different thinkers have attempted to come to terms with this situation in a variety of ways, some of which we must now consider.

Firstly, there are those who accept the mechanist picture in its entirety. This entails the belief that the physical world of atoms and energy is the only reality, and all metaphysical concepts are illusory. It is important to realise that the modern mechanist does not necessarily have to believe in a strict causality : he has studied the quantum theory, and knows full well that there is a fundamental indeterminacy about the behaviour of small particles of matter. He is also well aware that a highly complex system, such as the human brain, may contain randomising elements which will prevent us from ever making an exact prediction of its output. To him, such unpredictability provides no excuse for the introduction of non-material organisers such as entelechy, mind, or soul; it is merely an indication of the important part played by *chance* in the operations of the living organism:

> ... chance *alone* is at the source of every innovation, of all creation in the biosphere. Pure chance, absolutely free but blind, at the root of the stupendous edifice of evolution: this central concept of modern biology is no longer one among other possible or even conceivable hypotheses. It is today the *sole* conceivable hypothesis, the only one compatible with observed and tested fact. And nothing warrants the supposition (or the hope) that conceptions about this should, or ever could, be revised (Jacques Monod, 92, p. 110).

Koestler greets this with the acid comment that it reads more like a pronouncement of Moses from Mount Sinai than a statement from a geneticist of the Institut Pasteur (61, p. 236). However, it should be clear that those who wish to defend a non-mechanistic view of life are on unsafe ground if they try to do so by pointing to the *unpredictability* of living systems. The present-day mechanist does *not* claim that he could, given a detailed knowledge of chemical and physical conditions on the primitive earth, predict the whole future course of evolution. He does claim, however, that the development of life is entirely compatible with the laws of physics and chemistry, and requires no extra-physical principle to explain it. According to him, the exact direction it has taken is largely fortuitous:

> Let there be no misunderstanding. In saying that, as a class, living beings are not predictable upon the basis of first principles, I by no means intend to suggest that they are not *explicable* through these principles—that they transcend them in some way, and that other principles, applicable to living systems alone, must be invoked. In my view the biosphere is unpredictable for exactly the same reason —neither more nor less—that the particular configuration of atoms constituting this pebble I have in my hand is unpredictable. No one will blame a universal theory for not affirming and foreseeing the existence of this particular configuration of atoms; it is enough for us that this actual object, unique and real, be *compatible* with the theory (Monod, 92, p. 49).

This is a very plausible argument; and there is no doubt that those who adopt the fully mechanist viewpoint have all the big battalions on their side. The rapidly increasing successes in genetics, biochemistry and neurophysiology are all grist to their mill. Nevertheless, there are certain drawbacks to their theory. We have already seen how the existence of psi phenomena seems to be incompatible with a strictly materialistic approach; and in the next chapter we shall examine certain problems within the field of orthodox biology which should also give the mechanist reason to pause and reflect. But perhaps the most urgent reason for seeking an alternative to mechanism lies in the fact that it fails to satisfy the spirit of man: despite all its practical successes, it does not provide mankind with a satisfactory *Weltanschauung*. We have seen how, in many cases, the acceptance of the machine theory leads to the acute distress of the existential vacuum, the sense of the meaninglessness of life. Monod is indeed fully aware of this distress, which he regards as being due to the breaking of 'the ancient animist covenant between man and nature'. He seeks a possible solution through the acceptance of a socialist ideal based on what he calls the 'ethic of knowledge', by which he seems to mean the ethical standards of honesty and integrity which are taken for granted in most scientific work. Attractive as this ideal may be to some, we may doubt whether it is capable of evoking the same degree of self-sacrificing devotion and purposefulness among the majority of mankind as have the great religions which it is intended to replace. Monod's 'ethic of knowledge' seems even less likely to succeed than all the other, earlier attempts to create a 'Religion of Humanity' which we discussed in Chapter 4 (pp. 40-1).

Leaving aside the views of the full-blooded mechanists such as Monod, we turn next to a second group of thinkers. Those in our second category are fully aware of the colossal amount of evidence in favour of a mechanistic theory of the universe, yet they are reluctant to accept this as the only reality. They therefore adopt a kind of compromise, asserting that mechanism is correct as far as it goes, but that there is also a supernatural reality which lies entirely, and for ever, beyond the reach of science. By its very nature, they think, science *must* reveal a mechanistic world; it would be improper for scientists to frame any hypotheses which were not mechanistic. That other aspect of reality, the spiritual, is not a fit subject for scientific investigation: it can only be approached through the methods of religion. Therefore these thinkers spurn any attempt to find gaps or errors in the mechanistic world-picture, to make room for non-material entities such as God or the soul. Such attempts are, in their view, based on a misunderstanding of the relationship between the two realities. Furthermore, they are doomed to failure as science continually closes the remaining gaps. Science, then, is concerned with physical truth, which is mechanistic, whereas religion is concerned with spiritual truth.

At first sight this seems an attractive solution. It allows the mechanistic scientist to get on with his work without trespassing on the domain of the theologian, and it effectively protects religion from any conceivable advances which science might make in the future. Many Christians have, in fact, taken up positions similar to the one described here. The late Professor C. A. Coulson, for example, spent a great deal of his time valiantly defending the Christian faith against the advancing tide of scientific materialism; yet he resisted any attempt to find empirical evidence of the operation of spiritual factors in the physical world. Coulson believed that the discoveries of the parapsychologists would one day be incorporated into a revised scheme of *physical* laws:

> It is easy to see what will happen when these most interesting results are fitted into the general scheme of physics. They will become the basis on which we build a revised model of time and space.... Before we become too enthusiastic in 'thanking God' for this discovery in psychic behaviour, we should do well to ask ourselves whether it does really force us to believe in God in a manner different from all other experience (28, p. 27).

In common with the vast majority of twentieth-century thinkers, Coulson seems unable to conceive of the existence of *any* phenomena which cannot be 'fitted into the general scheme of physics'. In other words, he has accepted the mechanist-reductionist view of the world in its entirety, although he also believes in a supernatural God. Christians who think in this way are often quite vociferous in their condemnation of those who seek to find evidence of spiritual activity in the physical world, such as psychical researchers. Their God stands *behind* all the phenomena of the physical world; he is the 'Ground of all Being', but he does not interfere with the mechanistic laws which govern the operation of the universe. Any attempt to discover him by examination of natural phenomena must therefore be doomed to failure, so that a truly 'Natural Theology' becomes a contradiction in terms.

Despite the popularity of this view, the present writer finds it totally unsatisfactory. For one thing, it seems to achieve a kind of false reconciliation between religion and mechanistic science : the mechanists are left in full possession of the physical world provided they agree to make no intrusions into the spiritual realm. Ever since Darwin launched his revolution in 1859 theologians, aided by Christianly-minded scientists, have been trying desperately to place their God beyond the reach of advancing science. Arising out of an understandable, but wholly misguided, attempt to make the foundations of religion unshakeable by placing them outside the realm of empirical facts, the modern concept of God has been so emptied of content that it seems to have little, if any, relevance in the twentieth century. Gone is the dramatic figure of Yahweh, miraculously parting the waters of the Red Sea in order to deliver his people : in his place sits a 'demythologised' abstraction, a vague sort of cosmic mind which is supposed to lie behind all phenomena, but which is never permitted to exert any direct influence upon the observable world of science. Small wonder that some theologians have begun to talk of the 'death' of God!

Of course, it will not do. Statements such as 'there is a spiritual reality', or 'there is a God' are meaningless unless the entity thus named produces *some detectable effect* within our world. To hypothesise about the existence of something which lies forever beyond the reach of observation, or whose existence can never be inferred from any event or complex of events, is simply to talk nonsense. Our only justification for making the assertion 'God exists' must be that we believe that he has, at some time or other, revealed his existence by some kind of detectable effect within our world, whether that effect be upon physical objects or upon the minds (and therefore *brains*) of men. The moment this is admitted we have a 'God of the gaps', for there must be a discontinuity in the natural order at the point where divine intervention occurs. Similar arguments can be advanced in relation to the soul theory of man: if the soul is in any meaningful sense 'real', it must produce some detectable effects in the real world. If the soul theory is true, we would expect something similar to psi phenomena to occur, at least on occasions. It therefore seems futile to try to keep religion and mechanistic science away from each other's throats by confining each of them to a watertight compartment. There can be no compromise here, for if mechanism is true, religion (and the term is here taken to mean any view of life which assumes the existence of an extra-physical reality) must be false.

An interesting attempt to reconcile the mechanistic view of man with the existence of free-will, moral responsibility, and the religious outlook has been made by Donald MacKay, Professor of Communication at the University of Keele (88). Mac-Kay considers an imaginary situation sometime in the future when, as a result of enormous advances in neurophysiology, it has become possible to predict the course of action a man will take from a knowledge of his brain state. On the face of it, such a prediction would amount to a clear proof of the unreality of free-will. However, MacKay argues that the *real* truth about any situation must be valid for everyone; and in this case the truth of the prediction is valid only for those who are examining the man's brain *from the outside*. As soon as an attempt is made to convey the prediction to the subject himself, his brain state changes, and the prediction is no longer valid. There is thus a 'logical indeterminacy' about all such predictions, in that they cannot be valid for the person whose brain state is being described. Therefore the subject is perfectly in order in believing that he is free to make a decision for, from his point of view, that is exactly what he is:

> I want to suggest that he would be right to believe that he has a decision to make, that it will not be made unless he makes it, and that he will be responsible for the way it is

made. The validity for him of this belief is not challenged by the validity-for-the-observer of a different belief.... If, as I believe, this kind of 'gap' is wide enough for all that biblical religion requires here, there would seem to be no religious justification for any secret hope that science will come up against physical snags in explaining the physical brain (88, p. 66).

MacKay's argument is both ingenious and attractive; yet it is difficult not to feel that he has somehow side-stepped the problem. For one thing, it does not seem to be at all necessary to inform the subject about the observer's prediction. In order to prove that the subject's will is not free, it is only necessary to prove that his action was the inevitable outcome of a causal chain of events whose origin lay beyond the subject's control. Let us suppose that one afternoon, at precisely three o'clock, a young psychology student leaves his laboratory bench and performs a headstand in the corner of the room. Subsequently we learn the reason for his strange behaviour : on the previous day a distinguished professor had hypnotised him, and given him a post-hypnotic suggestion to carry out the action in question. We immediately realise that the student's action was not an act of free-will; for we have now traced it to a cause beyond the subject's control. Our belief that the action was not free is not in the least affected by the fact that the student himself is unaware of that cause; nor is it affected by the reflection that, if we had warned him in advance, he might have been able to resist the implanted suggestion. Surely, then, if it can be proved that a given action is the inevitable result of brain chemistry, childhood conditioning, a Freudian complex, or any other cause outside the subject's conscious control, then that action cannot be regarded as 'free'.

What, then, is meant by the expression 'free-will'? Clearly, it is not just a synonym for unpredictability. The output of a Schmidt random number generator is unpredictable (in the absence of ESP), both in practice and in principle, but we do not regard such machines as possessing free-will. There is undoubtedly a large element of unpredictability in the operation of the brain, partly due to the uncertainty inherent in the movements of electrons and other small particles (as described by the

Heisenberg principle), and partly due to MacKay's 'logical indeterminacy'. Some thinkers have seized upon the existence of quantum indeterminacy as though it provided a loop-hole through which free-will could operate in the brain. Yet the belief that one's actions are determined by some random process—a kind of cortical coin-flipper—is surely no more inspiring than the belief that they are determined by the inflexible laws of classical physics. Neither of these is what we mean when we say 'he acted of his own free will'.

Let us return to our eccentric student. Upon further investigation we discover that the story that he was hypnotised is totally untrue. Our puzzlement over his odd behaviour returns, and we decide to ask him directly why he stood on his head. He replies : 'Because I believe that Yoga is good for my health, and since I had a few minutes to spare I decided to put in a bit of practice.' At last the young man's action begins to make sense, and we realise that it *was* the result of a free decision after all. For if an act is to be regarded as free, it must have been *consciously* performed according to a clearly understood *purpose*. The existence of this conscious purpose, not the unpredictability of the act, is the criterion for deciding whether an action is free or not. We do not ascribe free-will to the actions of a sleep-walker, or a person under the influence of LSD, even though their behaviour may be unpredictable. Such persons are not in a normal state of consciousness, and are therefore not fully responsible for their actions. If it can be proved that a murderer was not fully aware of what he was doing at the moment he committed the crime, the jury are likely to take a more lenient view of his action. We thus see that the concept of free-will is inextricably bound up with the metaphysical concepts of *purpose* and *consciousness*, neither of which finds any place in the mechanistic view of man. These concepts may be illusory, as the behaviourists think, or they may be category mistakes. In that case, free-will is also an illusion or a category mistake. On the other hand, we must not rule out the possibility that consciousness, purpose, and free-will are fundamental realities of the world in which we live.

Many writers have sought to evade the more depressing implications of mechanism by taking refuge among the oddities of modern physics. Such persons point out that twentieth-century physics has completely abandoned the crudely mechanical picture of the universe which dominated scientific thinking during the eighteenth and nineteenth centuries. Relativity and quantum theory have shown that it is not possible to divide reality into observer and observed, and that such commonsense notions as time, space, mass, position, etc shift their values according to the particular reference-system used to describe them. From the standpoint of a theoretical biologist, Waddington sees in the confusion of fundamental particle physics a reason for denying the validity of the classical distinction between mechanism and vitalism in biology:

> It is very clear that (the physicists) do not yet know *the* fundamental constituents of matter and it is becoming more and more probable that there are no such things, but that the material universe is open-ended to investigation in both directions towards the very small (sub-nuclear) and towards the very large (cosmological). The recognition of this largely removes the point of trying to distinguish between vitalist and mechanist theories of biology, where vitalism is defined as the notion that the objectively observable behaviour of living systems demands the postulation of entities not contemplated by the laws of physics. Since we do not know in full what entities are demanded by the laws of physics, the distinction is more or less inapplicable (148, p. 1).

Arthur Koestler, in *The Roots of Coincidence*, described the concepts of modern physics as 'truly fantastic', and suggested that the seemingly fantastic propositions of parapsychology might appear to be less preposterous when seen against a background of quantum theory. David Bohm, a theoretical physicist of Birkbeck College, London, expresses surprise that the life sciences are tending to produce mechanistic explanations of their data, while physics is moving in the opposite direction:

> ... physics has really totally abandoned its earlier mechanical basis. Its subject matter already, in certain ways, is far more similar to that of biology than it is to that of Newtonian mechanics. It does seem odd, therefore, that

just when physics is thus moving away from mechanism, biology and psychology are moving closer to it. If this trend continues, it may well be that scientists will be regarding living and intelligent beings as mechanical, while they suppose that inanimate matter is too complex and subtle to fit into the limited categories of mechanism. But of course, in the long run, such a point of view cannot stand up to critical analysis. For since DNA and other molecules studied by the biologist are constituted of electrons, protons, neutrons etc, it follows that they too are capable of behaving in a far more complex and subtle way than can be described in terms of the mechanical concepts (148, p. 34).

Such reflections may well make us wonder whether mechanism is not merely a stage through which *all* sciences have to pass as part of the process of growing up. It is certainly noteworthy that the most recent sciences, such as molecular biology, tend to be the most aggressively mechanistic. Possibly in a hundred years from now biologists and psychologists will be looking back with some amusement at the crudely mechanistic ideas of their twentieth-century predecessors.

Yet in spite of all this, we may question whether these developments in modern physics *really* give us any cause to doubt the validity of the mechanistic theory of life. Certainly they show that our everyday notions of space, time and causality are inaccurate or inapplicable in the realms of the very large and the very small. Yet even if matter is not quite what we once believed it to be, is this really relevant to the problem of whether a living organism is 'nothing but' a complex arrangement of atoms? Can we really expect those who long to believe in the reality of the human soul as a distinct, non-physical, purposeful entity to be satisfied with the information that there is a fundamental uncertainty about the positions and momenta of electrons?

It seems that so far our attempts to come to terms with mechanism have achieved very little success. We may seek refuge in the complexities of modern physics: we may postulate a spiritual reality lying beyond the reach of science; or we may seek, with MacKay, for some kind of logical indeterminacy in the operations of the living world. Each of these various approaches has its value, but none provides a really satisfactory solution to the existential dilemma. Meanwhile, the mechanistic biologist stands confidently aloof from all such metaphysical speculations. He is fully convinced that he has solved the problem of the nature of life in all but detail, and that it has turned out to be fully explicable in mechanistic terms. He sees no point, therefore, in speculating about such non-entities as mind, purpose and consciousness. Have not the philosophers spent hundreds of years arguing about such things, all to no avail? Now that molecular biology has revealed the true basis of life, would it not be better to get on with the job of filling in the final details?

The physicists felt the same at the end of the nineteenth century. They too believed that their science was virtually complete, and that all that remained to be done was the final completion of the pattern. Few foresaw that the very foundations were about to be cut from under them. Yet in the twentieth century Planck, Einstein and others were to prove that the Newtonian laws, which had been experimentally validated over and over again for more than 200 years, were nevertheless based on entirely false assumptions about the nature of reality. The impressive edifice of Victorian physics provided a convincing model of the world *only so long as one did not look too closely at certain small, but awkward, facts.*

Something similar may be true of mechanistic biology today. In arriving at their apparently highly successful picture of the living world the mechanists may have ignored certain facts which cannot be fitted into that picture. Throughout this chapter we have discussed various attempts to deal with the serious problems created by the mechanistic philosophy; yet all those attempts started by assuming that mechanism is valid, at least within its own field of operation. It may be that we have been premature in conceding victory to the mechanists, even on their own ground. In part II we have already examined one set of facts—the findings of parapsychology—which do not fit into the mechanistic picture. In the following chapter we shall look at those areas where the mechanists claim their greatest successes to see whether here also there may not be certain awkward facts which have been quietly neglected.

14. Genesis

In the beginning God created the heavens and the earth: these familiar words form the opening sentence of that remarkable collection of writings which has probably exerted more influence on human history than any other single factor. For thousands of years, to Jew and Christian alike, it seemed self-evident that the cosmos could not have come into existence under its own steam. Some kind of Creative Mind was essential to account for the incredible beauty and complexity of the phenomenal world, and in contemplation of its wonders, man became overwhelmed with a sense of the numinous:

> For I will consider thy heavens, even the works of thy fingers: the moon and the stars, which thou hast ordained.
> What is man, that thou are mindful of him: and the son of man, that thou visitest him?
>
> (Psalm 8, Prayer-book version)

Today, all that is changed. The modern scientific materialist finds no use for the concept of a creator. How, then, does he solve the psalmist's problem of accounting for the wonders of the universe, and in particular, the origin and development of that amazingly complex phenomenon we call life? The answer is best expressed in the title of an article which appeared recently in *New Scientist* magazine: *In the beginning ... life assembled itself* (49). The resemblance of the wording to Genesis is both obvious and deliberate, for the evangelists of molecular biology are convinced that they have solved, once and for all, the problem of the origin of life. In the previous chapter we quoted Jacques Monod, one of the most forceful of the new hot-gospellers, as stating that chance alone is the source of all creation in the biosphere, and even more dogmatically asserting that this is the *only* conceivable hypothesis. The new mechanist-reductionist version of Genesis, then, runs something like this:

In the beginning there was nothing but gas dispersed through-

out empty space. Gradually stars and planets formed from this primordial nebula by a process of condensation. On the surface of one (perhaps more) of the planets lightning discharges, ultra-violet radiation and similar physical events caused certain chemical substances to combine together, thus producing giant molecules of proteins, nucleic acids etc. After millions of years some of these molecules, purely by accident, joined to-gether to form self-replicating units. Then Darwin's process of Natural Selection began to operate, picking out those which were best equipped to survive, and eliminating all the others. Over a long period of time this process led to the formation of the biosphere as we know it today, with its great variety of plants, animals, micro-organisms and men.

Such, in outline, is the modern theory, although there is still much disagreement between individual mechanists over the fine details. Since we are concerned with the nature of life, the first question we have to ask is : what is the likelihood that life formed itself spontaneously, in some such manner as that proposed by the modern theorists? In 1953 Stanley Miller, a young scientist at the University of Chicago, showed that some of the basic materials of life could have arisen through the action of lightning on the primeval atmosphere. He passed an electric discharge through a mixture of hydrogen, methane, ammonia and water-vapour (all of which are thought to have been present on the primitive earth), and obtained traces of 15 amino-acids, which are the building blocks of the proteins. Since then there have been many attempts to repeat Miller's experiment, with varying conditions. For example, Melvin Calvin used the same raw materials as Miller but exposed them to gamma radiation instead of an electric discharge. He obtained a mixture of amino-acids, sugars, and the purine and pyrimidine bases which enter into the composition of DNA and RNA. By heating and cooling some of these substances under various conditions of pressure and concentration, more com-plex substances such as polypeptides and nucleic acids can be obtained. It is assumed therefore that physical forces (heat, radiation, electricity) acting upon the mixture of gases present in the atmosphere of the primitive earth, led to the formation of a 'prebiotic soup' containing all the materials necessary for the first living organisms to assemble themselves.

So far so good; but we now come to the crucial step, for it is a very far cry indeed from the formation of giant molecules to the formation of self-replicating units upon which Darwinian selection can act. Even Monod has to admit that we are very far from understanding how this came about, although he does not regard the difficulty as insurmountable. Those biologists, chemists and physicists who are not committed in advance to the defence of the mechanistic philosophy often express serious doubts as to whether the gap can be bridged within the framework of present-day physical principles. Thus Professor von Bertalanffy of the State University of New York has heavily criticised the notion that, given a long enough time, almost anything can happen:

> Stanley Miller *et al* experimentally simulated the conditions which presumably prevailed in the early history of the earth and showed that amino-acids and other organic compounds may be formed. But this is something different from the assertion that, given only sufficient time, any chemical configuration which is possible, may naturally have been formed by random events. A pair of nylon stockings is, in its chemical structure, much simpler than a structure of nucleic acid chains, but we do not expect to find any nylons formed by 'spontaneous generation' and 'reaction at random' (82, p. 79).

It may also be pointed out that the synthesis of amino-acids and other compounds by Miller and his successors did *not* occur 'at random': it was the result of a set of physical and chemical conditions carefully arranged by conscious, intelligent beings, namely the experimenters themselves. Oddly enough, this point is often overlooked when Miller-type experiments are cited as evidence for the spontaneous origin of life. Miller's work was based on certain assumptions relating to conditions on the earth about three thousand million years ago; but were these assumptions valid? In their book *Origin and Development of Living Systems*, Brooks and Shaw outline the 'primitive soup' theory of abiogenesis, and point out that, whatever detailed mechanism one assumes for the self-assembly of life, it must have taken millions of years, during which time the primitive soup contained large concentrations of highly

nitrogenous matter (amino-acids, purines, pyrimidines etc).
Now such compounds are readily absorbed on a variety of rock
and clay particles, so we would expect to find evidence of their
existence in the form of massive deposits of 'nitrogenous cokes',
that is, materials produced by the action of heat and pressure
upon rocks containing absorbed nitrogen compounds.

If there ever was a primitive soup, then we would expect
to find at least somewhere on this planet either massive
sediments containing enormous amounts of the various nitrogenous organic compounds ... or alternatively in much
metamorphosed sediments we should find vast amounts of
nitrogenous cokes. In fact no such materials have been found
anywhere on earth. Indeed to the contrary, the very oldest
of sediments ... contain organic matter very much of the
sporopollenin type and degradation products of such materials, especially a variety of alkanes and fatty acids and
derivatives. Sediments of this type are extremely short of
nitrogen (19, p. 359).

Later on the same writers point out that another requirement
of the spontaneous formation theory is the existence of a
reducing atmosphere (that is, one containing gases such as
methane rather than oxygen):

Again there is no evidence for such a reducing atmosphere,
although such evidence might be difficult to find since
reduced minerals, for example, might have been subsequently reoxidised. The sort of 'evidence' sometimes for-
warded, namely the reduced iron beds, is somewhat absurd
since the existence of living systems was well documented
before such beds were deposited and the beds themselves
are very likely reduced by living organisms (19, p. 360).

Such objections are formidable enough. Yet even if we
waive these difficulties and accept the existence of the reducing
atmosphere and the primitive soup, could life have arisen in
the manner suggested by the mechanists? Sir Frederick Gow-
land Hopkins, the discoverer of vitamins, once described the
origin of life as 'the most improbable and the most significant
event in the history of the universe', and there seems no reason
to disagree with him. In the Fremantle Lectures for 1963, the

Cambridge zoologist W. H. Thorpe discussed in some detail the question of the chance formation of living systems, and came to the conclusion that the formation of even the most elementary living organism in this way is wildly improbable:

> The event which produced living matter must have been highly improbable even under primordial conditions. Assuming that an aqueous solution of amino-acids had been formed, the next problem is how could these be built up into complex proteins or enzymes? Assuming that the concentration of each free amino-acid is kept at one M, the equilibrium concentration of a protein with 100 residues (MW about 12,000) is 10^{-99}M which represents 1 molecule in a volume 10^{50} times the volume of the earth. This appears to rule out the possibility of the formation of any protein by mass action, even in the presence of a catalyst.... Thus the formation of two or more molecules of any enzyme purely by chance is fantastically improbable (139, p. 37).

Some writers have looked at this problem from the standpoint of the Second Law of Thermodynamics (or the 'Law of Morpholysis' as Clark (26) has called it). This law states that all closed physical systems tend towards a state of maximum entropy, that is, a state of maximum *disorder*. The continuous rise in complexity and orderliness which we observe in the living world certainly *seems* to be in direct defiance of this law. Schroedinger (123) attempted to explain this by saying that organisms feed on 'negative entropy', that is, they extract order from their surroundings, but this would appear to be nothing more than an alternative description of the process rather than an explanation. Sir Julian Huxley, in his preface to Teilhard de Chardin's *Phenomenon of Man* (23), referred to evolution as an 'anti-entropic process', without apparently realising that such a description is equivalent to an admission that living things defy the laws of physics. Recently attempts have been made to answer the thermodynamic objections to the mechanistic theory by pointing out that classical thermodynamics was developed for *closed* physical systems, whereas what we really require is a thermodynamics for open systems—an 'irreversible thermodynamics'. It is argued that an open system may well have a state of decreasing entropy. The difficulty still remains, however, of explaining how such open systems came into existence in the first place:

> According to well-known experiments, the formation of amino acids and other organic compounds is well possible in an artificial 'primeval atmosphere', energy being provided by electric discharges. It may be that, given the necessary time, eventually macromolecules, including self-duplicating DNA molecules,have formed by chance in the organic 'soup' of the primeval ocean. What is at present quite inexplicable is why and how organic substances, nucleoproteins, or coacervates should have formed, against the second principle —systems not tending towards thermodynamic equilibrium but 'open systems' maintaining themselves at a distance from equilibrium in a most improbable state. *This would only be possible in the presence of 'organising forces'* leading to the formation of such systems (Bertalanffy, 82, p. 73. Italics added).

A similar point has been made by H. H. Pattee, a Stanford University physicist, who writes:

> In the language of physics, matter is 'organised' only by the 'energy of interaction' or equivalently by the 'forces' which act upon it. For example, the structure or organisation of the solar system is largely the result of gravitational interaction or forces, the structure of molecules is partly the result of electric forces, and the structure of nuclei depends on nuclear forces. A few other types of forces are known, and all types may be combined in a great variety of ways, but as yet there is no clearly recognised special force or special combination of interactions or forces which can be uniquely associated with living organisations (148, p. 271).

An alternative way of viewing the problem is provided by Information Theory. In order to construct any patterned system, whether it is a house, the picture on a television set or a virus particle, it is not sufficient merely to have the necessary raw materials. A certain quantity of *information* is required so that the materials may be assembled in the correct order. Engineers express the quantity of information in terms of binary units, or 'bits'. Thorpe (139), following Linschitz and Morowitz, estimates the information content of a bacterial cell to be of the order of 10^{12} bits, and points out that even the information content of an amoeba must be 'several orders that of the information store of the most advanced computer' (p. 38). If the solar system developed by condensation from a 'primordial nebula', whence came the tremendous amount of information which we find in living creatures? A gas is the most *random* system known to science: the amount of information contained in the chaotic movements of gas molecules is negligible; yet according to the mechanistic theory we are to suppose that the living world with all its complexities (and this includes man with his cities, his transport and communications systems, and his space rockets!) has arisen from purely chance events occurring in a slowly cooling gaseous system. The mechanist is forced to assume that, somehow, the information was all there to start with:

> Ordered matter has thus evolved through a hierarchy of stages of self-assembly. Due to repeated reproductive cycling and infrequent but multitudinous mutations, *information available at the outset* has expanded to permit a vast array of diverse types of informational macromolecules and derived systems. These systems collectively represent what we recognise as life (Fox, 49, p. 12. Italics added).

This is in fact the modern version of the old preformationist myth: all the properties of living matter were already present, presumably in some sort of coded form, in the very atoms from which the solar system was formed. This will seem hardly conceivable to anyone except a determined mechanist. It is certainly not conceivable to Thorpe.

> If we consider the process of cosmic evolution from a primordial nebula through the solar system allowing, in its turn, organic evolution to take place ... we can say that the result has been, in the universe as we know it, a stupendous increase of order—that is to say, a stupendous increase of information (139, p. 38).

The information contained in a living organism is, of course, transmitted to its offspring by means of the genetic code; that is, it is encoded in the sequences of purine and pyrimidine bases which form part of the structure of the DNA molecules. As these molecules have the ability of self-replication, the coded information can be copied many times and passed on to succeeding generations during reproduction. One of the most remarkable discoveries of modern times concerns the *universality* of this code; it has been found that the same base sequences determine the same amino-acids in all organisms, ranging from the microscopic colon bacillus at one extreme to man at the other. Any fully satisfactory theory of the origin of life must also account for the origin of the code. Jacques Monod admits that it is 'exceedingly difficult' to imagine how the code could have originated, but suggests two possibilities:

a. Chemical—or, to be more exact, stereochemical—reasons account for the structure of the code; if a certain codon was 'chosen' to represent a certain amino acid it is because there existed a certain stereochemical affinity between them; or else

b. The code's structure is chemically arbitrary: the code as we know it today is the result of a series of random choices which gradually enriched it (92, p. 135).

Even so, Monod, with his unrivalled knowledge of the intricacies of cellular chemistry, does not seem to be too happy about the classical theory of the origin of life:

It might be thought that the discovery of the universal mechanisms basic to the essential properties of living beings would have helped solve the problems of life's origins. As it turns out, these discoveries, by almost entirely transforming the question ... have shown it to be even more difficult than it formerly appeared (92, p. 132).

We have now taken a critical look at the mechanistic theory of the origin of life (sometimes termed the 'Haldane-Oparin' theory), and we may summarise the results as follows:

(a) There is no real evidence that the necessary initial conditions, namely the presence of a reducing atmosphere and a primitive 'soup', ever existed on this planet. On the contrary, there is some evidence that they did not.

(b) Many physicists and mathematicians have come to the

conclusion that the random formation of even the simplest self-replicating unit is wildly improbable. Their arguments suggest that we must look for some outside influence, some 'organising force' or factor, not at present recognised by orthodox science.

(c) Investigations based on the principles of thermodynamics and information theory give no support to the mechanist theory, but on the contrary, make it appear even less plausible.

(d) Recent advances in molecular biology have shown that the cellular mechanisms are far more intricate than was thought to be the case even a few years ago; and consequently, the possibility that they could have arisen by chance in the absence of any kind of organising factor, seems exceedingly remote.

These conclusions may come as a surprise to those who have been brought up to believe that the 'primitive soup' theory is virtually an established fact. For years now the theory has been cited over and over again in biological text-books, including those intended for quite young schoolchildren, as though it were on the same footing as, say, the atomic theory in chemistry. Actually, as we have seen, there is no *factual* support for it whatever : it is a purely speculative theory made to seem plausible by the avoidance of detailed analysis and repeated confident assertion. 'The acceptance of this theory and its promulgation by many workers who have certainly not always considered all the facts in great detail has in our opinion reached proportions which could be regarded as danger-ous,' write Brooks and Shaw (p. 355). Dangerous indeed: for the constant authoritative assertions of the mechanists have the effect of stifling thought and suppressing criticism. They prevent men from searching in other possible directions for an answer to the problem of the origin of life.

If the current mechanistic theory fails to account satisfac-torily for the origin of life, how does it fare when confronted with the problem of life's subsequent development? The orthodox view is that all the forms of living organisms have arisen as the result of natural selection acting upon random mutations, but there is an increasing number of biologists who feel that this cannot be the whole story. Sir Alister Hardy (60) describes a number of phenomena which are difficult to account for in orthodox terms. It is obviously not possible to discuss all of these here, but we will consider some of the more important ones.

The first of these is the problem of homologous organs, which, says Hardy, is 'absolutely fundamental to what we are talking about when we speak of evolution,' yet which now appears to be inexplicable in terms of modern biological theory. The older text-books on evolution make much of the idea of homology, pointing out the obvious resemblances between the skeletons of the limbs of different animals. Thus the 'pentadactyl' limb pattern is found in the arm of a man, the wing of a bird, and the flipper of a whale, and this is held to indicate their common origin. Now if these various structures were transmitted by the same gene-complex, varied from time to time by mutations and acted upon by environmental selection, the theory would make good sense. Unfortunately this is not the case. Homologous organs are now known to be produced by totally different gene complexes in the different species. *The concept of homology in terms of similar genes handed on from a common ancestor has broken down*, says Hardy. The most striking evidence on this point comes from Morgan's experiments with *Drosophila*; when a pure line of flies bearing the 'eyeless' form of the gene is inbred, within a short time perfectly formed eyes appear, produced apparently by a kind of co-operative effort on the part of the other genes. Koestler has a pointed comment to make on this phenomenon :

> The traditional explanation of this remarkable phenomenon is that the other members of the gene-complex have been 'reshuffled and re-combined in such a way that they deputise for the missing normal eye-forming gene'. Now re-shuffling, as every poker player knows, is a randomising process. No biologist would be so perverse as to suggest that the new insect-eye evolved by pure chance, thus repeating within a few generations an evolutionary process which took hundreds of millions of years. Nor does the concept of natural selection provide the slightest help in this case. The recombination of genes to deputise for the missing gene must have been co-ordinated according to some overall plan.... (79, pp. 133-4).

Something similar to this is also suggested by D'Arcy Thompson's work on the shapes of animals, quoted by Hardy. Thompson found that the shapes of animals belonging to the same zoological group are often related to one another in a simple mathematical way: the shape of one species can be obtained from the shape of another by a simple distortion of the spacial coordinates. This again suggests some overall 'plan' rather than the result of random mutations selected by a changing environment.

Other writers besides Hardy have drawn attention to the difficulty of explaining the existence of homologous organs in terms of the modern theory of heredity. Thus, the distinguished embryologist Sir Gavin de Beer writes:

> It is now clear that the pride with which it was assumed that the inheritance of homologous structures from a common ancestor explained homology was misplaced; for such inheritance cannot be ascribed to identity of genes....
> But if it is true that through the genetic code, genes code for enzymes that synthesise proteins which are responsible (in a manner still unknown in embryology) for the differentiation of the various parts in their normal manner, what mechanism can it be that results in the production of homologous organs, the same 'patterns', in spite of their *not* being controlled by the same genes? I asked this question in 1938, and it has not been answered (10, p. 16).

Or again, from Dr Thorpe:

> It seems, however, that recent developments in genetical theory can no longer envisage the fairly static gene-pool or 'gene-cluster' which is maintained intact over long periods of evolutionary time and is responsible for the slowly changing development of organs .... of which we have fossil and recent evidence. Now it is suggested that these constant systems may exist only in our imagination and that the genetic control of the development of such homologous organs may shift relatively rapidly while the organ remains the same! This seems to me to raise a quite fantastic difficulty.... (82, p. 432).

The study of embryology only serves to accentuate the difficulty presented by genetics: not only are homologous organs not controlled by the same or similar genes, but they may also arise from *totally different parts of the developing embryo*:

> Structures as obviously homologous as the alimentary canal in all vertebrates can be formed from the roof of the embryonic gut cavity (sharks), floor (lampreys, newts), roof and floor (frogs), or from the lower layer of the embryonic disc, the blastoderm, that floats on the top of heavily yoked eggs (reptiles, birds). It does not seem to matter where in the egg or the embryo the living substance out of which homologous organs are formed comes from. Therefore, *correspondence between homologous structures cannot be pressed back to similarity of position of the cells of the embryo or the parts of the egg out of which these structures are ultimately differentiated* (de Beer, 10, p. 13. His italics).

It must be emphasised that in drawing attention to the difficulties inherent in the concept of homology we are not merely sniping away at some minor feature of the orthodox theory of evolution. The notion of homologous organs is so fundamental that any doubt cast upon it must inevitably tend to undermine the whole structure of neo-Darwinian theory. But what of the experimental evidence for natural selection? Experiments with bacterial cultures have shown quite clearly that Darwin's principle of 'survival of the fittest' certainly does operate within such cultures, leading, for example, to penicillin-resistant strains of staphylococci. Furthermore, the well-known work of Dr Kettlewell with the peppered moth, and many of the examples of animal camouflage described by Hardy, provide clear evidence of the selective effect of the environment on at least some of the features of organisms. The trouble arises when we try to extend this principle to explain the *whole* of evolution, as Darwin did. We may accept the principle of natural selection, and yet still question whether it is sufficient to account for the emergence of entirely *new* structures with a higher order of complexity: in other words, we may question whether it can explain the *creativeness* we observe in the development of life.

Whereas it is clear that Darwinian selection will account for many of the differences between varieties of the same species ('micro-evolution'), can it also account for the emergence of entirely new species with a higher degree of organisation? Waddington wrote in 1958:

> .... a new gene mutation can cause an alteration only to a character which the organism had had in previous generations. It could not produce a lobster's claw on a cat; it could only alter the cat in some way, leaving it essentially a cat (7).

Dr R. E. D. Clark, in an earlier book, put the matter even more forcefully:

> .... it is easy to imagine that, occasionally, mutations might help individuals to adapt themselves to their surroundings, after which the mutants may replace their fellows as a result of natural selection. But to go further and to imagine that a series of changes, however long continued, would in the end create new and highly complex mechanisms, so making organisms more complex than they were before, would seem to be highly ridiculous (26, p. 132).

Nowadays the orthodox Darwinian would reply to this by pointing out that new species can arise through the physical separation of existing ones. Once a population is separated into two by some geographical barrier, random mutations and natural selection acting separately on each half will eventually cause the two to become so unlike that they can no longer interbreed, that is, they become two species instead of one (Hardy, 60, pp. 96-97). This argument is very persuasive as far as it goes. It explains how one species could become two, but it does *not* explain why either of the two should show any increase in complexity above that of the original. The problem here is not why species differ from one another, but why in the course of evolution they show a continuous increase in organisation. Why should a purely random process—mutation —combined with another presumably random process— environmental change—lead to a steadily increasing amount of order in the living world?

L. L. Whyte, in a book published in 1965 (165), challenged

the generally accepted view that mutations are entirely random with respect to the direction of evolution. He suggested that a process of *internal selection* operates on the mutated genes long before they have a chance to become permanently established in the species, so that deleterious genes are eliminated or forced to back-mutate, while advantageous ones are permitted to survive. Again, we seem to be back with the concept of an overall species plan to which new mutations must be made to conform, at least within certain limits.

G. A. Kerkut (77) lists seven basic assumptions made by evolutionists which are 'often not mentioned during discussions on Evolution'. They are as follows:

(1) the assumption that non-living things gave rise to living material, i.e. spontaneous generation occurred;

(2) the assumption that spontaneous generation occurred only once;

(3) the assumption that viruses, bacteria, plants and animals are all interrelated;

(4) the assumption that the Protozoa (one-celled organisms) gave rise to the Metazoa (multi-celled organisms);

(5) the assumption that the various invertebrate groups are interrelated;

(6) the assumption that the invertebrates gave rise to the vertebrates;

(7) the assumption that within the vertebrates the fish gave rise to the amphibia, the amphibia to the reptiles, and the reptiles to the birds and mammals.

Kerkut points out that many evolutionists confine themselves entirely to the seventh of these assumptions; in fact, most of the evidence for the evolutionary theory is only evidence for assumption (7), not for the remaining six. He also points out that the seven assumptions are, by their very nature, *incapable of experimental verification* : they are assumptions about events which we presume must have happened at some time in the distant past.

It should be clear by now that what is loosely called the 'theory of evolution' is more in the nature of a particular *attitude* to biology rather than a scientific theory in the strict sense. The neo-Darwinians make quite a number of separate assumptions. Some of these are certainly true, others are doubtful, and some are clearly false. There is certainly no good reason to accept the dogmatic assertions of the mechanistic biologists that they have solved the mystery of the origin and development of life, even in broad outline. In fact, there are clear signs that some important factor has been overlooked; and it may well turn out (as so often before in the history of science) that the missing factor is the one which will completely transform the whole of our outlook.

15. Mechanism in the Melting Pot

At this point we can imagine the mechanistic biologist replying somewhat as follows:

> I agree with you that some molecular biologists and evolutionists have been over-confident in their assertions that the fundamental problems of life have been solved. I am fully aware that there are serious, perhaps fatal, difficulties surrounding the Haldane-Oparin theory of the origin of life, and that the neo-Darwinian theory of evolution may need modification. I am even prepared to concede the reality of some of the puzzling phenomena of parapsychology. However, none of these things gives me any cause to doubt the essential validity of the mechanistic approach. Around the frontiers of advancing science there are always areas where our understanding is incomplete, and there are always some people who will seize upon these areas as a justification for introducing some kind of metaphysical entity—a god of the gaps. Experience shows however that as our understanding of nature increases, so the gaps are filled, one after another, and the anti-mechanist must remove his god to still more remote regions. The successful explanations have always turned out to be mechanistic, and I have every confidence, therefore, that one day a completely mechanistic description of the origin, evolution and functioning of living matter will be achieved. Even psi-phenomena will be incorporated into an enlarged system of physical theory, and the 'ghost in the machine' will have been exorcised for ever.

This is a persuasive argument, and we have already seen how many people who would otherwise have insisted on the presence of some kind of spiritual reality permeating the living world have been driven to accept it. However, if we examine it more carefully we see that it is not quite as reasonable as it appears. It seems to be based on one or other of two implicit assumptions:

(a) that we have *a priori* knowledge that the real world is, by its very nature, mechanistic;

(b) that the nature of scientific enquiry is such that it must inevitably pursue only mechanistic explanations, any other kind being 'unscientific'.

Let us consider the first of these points. If we assume that we know in advance that we live in a mechanistic universe, then of course it is reasonable to seek for purely mechanistic explanations of all the phenomena within it. But do we, in fact, possess such *a priori* knowledge of the nature of things, or is this merely an *assumption* which the mechanists have skilfully conditioned us all into accepting without conscious reflection? No doubt our mechanist friend would agree that he is here making an unprovable assumption, but he would insist that it is an assumption which has been amply justified in practice. For if nature is *not* mechanistic, how can we explain the brilliant successes of geneticists, molecular biologists and others who, boldly disdaining any kind of vitalism, set about their work on the assumption that they are dealing with purely physical systems operating according to the known laws of chemistry?

Before we answer this point, let us consider the following passage from Sir Arthur Eddington's book *The Nature of the Physical World*:

If we search the examination papers in physics and natural philosophy for the more intelligible questions we may come across one beginning something like this: 'an elephant slides down a grassy hill-side....' The experienced candidate knows that he need not pay much attention to this; it is only put in to give an impression of realism. He reads on: 'The mass of the elephant is two tons'. Now we are getting down to business; the elephant fades out of the problem and a mass of two tons takes its place. What exactly is this two tons, the real subject-matter of the problem?.... Two tons *is* the reading of the pointer when the elephant was placed on a weighing-machine. Let us pass on. 'The slope of the hill is 60°.' Now the hill-side fades out of the problem and an angle of 60° takes its place. What is 60°? There is no need to struggle with mystical conceptions of direction; 60° *is* the reading of a plumbline against the divisions of a protractor. . . . And so we see that the poetry fades out of the problem, and by the time the serious application of exact science begins we are left with only pointer readings (40, p. 245).

Thus Eddington suggests that physics operates by *abstracting* from the real world only those aspects of it which can be expressed as pointer-readings : of the reality behind the pointer-readings science knows nothing. Calculations with pointer-readings inevitably lead us to more pointer-readings. In the example given above, we eventually calculate the time of descent of the elephant, which is a pointer-reading on the dial of our watch.

Could it be, then, that mechanistic science has been so successful merely because *it has abstracted from the real world only those aspects of reality which are susceptible to mechanistic analysis*, and ignored all the others? We are all familiar with the political enthusiast who reads only those newspapers which happen to support his point of view! If we take a human being, ignore all those aspects of him which cannot be expressed in the language of physics and chemistry (his consciousness, purpose, will etc.), and pursue our investigations as though he were a physico-chemical machine, then we shall find only evidence which supports the machine-theory of man. Like the reader of the political newspaper, we find only a reflection of our own preconceived opinions. There is good reason for supposing that western science has done something very similar to this: the strenuous attempts still being made to resist the evidence of parapsychology (even to allegations of widespread fraud) are surely indications of the determination of some scientists to prevent anything non-physical from penetrating the defences they have erected around their chosen fields. It is hardly to be wondered at, therefore, that these same scientists assure us that all the phenomena of life can be explained in purely physical terms. David Bohm has put the matter succinctly :

.... it is as important to ask the right kind of question as it is to find the answers to the question by observation and experiment. Thinking within a fixed circle of ideas tends to restrict the questions to a limited field. And, if one's questions stay in a limited field, so also do the answers. Thus, nature itself is apparently confirming our assumption that the general framework of current ideas is in principle complete and exhaustive, requiring only detailed development before leading to a full understanding of everything in the universe (148, p. 39).

It is instructive to compare this sobering comment, by a modern physicist, with the previously-quoted statement of Jacques Monod in which he asserts that the 'central concept' of modern biology is the sole conceivable hypothesis, never to be overthrown! (cf. p. 191)

So effective has been the conditioning of modern man against belief in anything non-physical that many modern thinkers find it literally impossible to conceive of anything not made of matter. Thus the geneticist Dobzhansky, criticising Driesch's notion of an *entelechy* in living things, writes:

> An immaterial or, indeed, supernatural telos must eventually somehow stoop down to the material and natural levels if it is to produce effects observable on these levels. Will the entelechy turn out to be some very powerful enzyme or a novel form of radiation? Enzymes and radiations are, however, substances or energies (34, p. 26).

The answer to this is that the entelechy need not turn out to be anything *material* at all: it could be an entity in its own right, with properties quite different from those of matter as we know it. Of course, it must *interact* with matter, if it is to produce observable effects of the physical level. Dobzhansky is correct to that extent. But this is not the same thing as saying that *entelechy* itself must be material. Dobzhansky's feeling that somehow all real entities *must* be susceptible to physical description is nothing more than a reflection of the *Zeitgeist*, and illustrates the domination exerted by the mechanistic philosophy upon modern thought. In the same book, Dobzhansky considers what would happen if parapsychologists produced 'incontrovertible proofs' of the existence of psi phenomena, and suggests, rather like Coulson, that we should then have to look for some new physical force or form of energy.

'The immaterial must sooner or later be brought down to the physiological and hence the material level,' he asserts, and refers to this bringing-down process as an 'ineluctable necessity'. While we may readily agree that psi will eventually manifest its presence by producing some change in the physical world (the fall of a die in a PK experiment, for example), this does not necessarily imply that the entity producing the effect must be explicable in physical terms. There is no logical reason why we should not believe in a dualistic world if such a belief appears to fit the facts. A dualistic view would acknowledge the existence of both mind and matter as irreducible components of reality, and seek to explore the ways in which these two fundamental entities interact with each other.

The second implication inherent in mechanistic thinking is that, whether or not there exists any kind of spiritual (i.e. non-physical) reality, science as such can have nothing to do with it. In an earlier chapter we saw how Watson tried to purge psychology of all metaphysical concepts such as purpose, thought and consciousness, so that it could become truly 'scientific'. Monod takes a similar view:

> The cornerstone of the scientific method is the postulate that nature is objective. In other words, the *systematic* denial that 'true' knowledge can be reached by interpreting phenomena in terms of final causes—that is to say, of 'purpose' ... the postulate of objectivity is consubstantial with science, and has guided the whole of its prodigious development for three centuries. It is impossible to escape it, even provisionally or in a limited area, without departing from the domain of science itself (92, p. 31).

It may seem strange that a geneticist should be insisting so strongly on the 'objectivity' of science in a century when physicists have become acutely aware of the impossibility of separating the observer from his observations. However, the belief that science *must* proceed according to mechanistic assumptions is very widespread. As we pointed out in a previous chapter, those who support a religious interpretation of reality are often content to allow the scientist to pursue his materialistic path provided that, in return, he refrains from making assertions about spiritual matters:

Men of science are quite right to try to reduce nature to laws which *appear* mechanical; the more they try, the more they discover, on strictly scientific lines, that the search ends in agnosticism—that a stage is reached when the notion of an automatic machine gets them no further; that scientific research does not 'explain' life and can produce no evidence to contradict the Christian doctrine of the immortal soul (Williams, 163).

The whole procedure in science is a mechanistic one and as far as the purely scientific aspect is concerned, this is perfectly legitimate.... It is when the biochemist, having reached some definite conclusion, maintains that he has thereby solved the mystery of life and unlocked the last door that, we retort, he is still far from any ultimate explanation (Greenwood, 56).

But is it true that the mechanistic approach is the only one that is 'perfectly legitimate' in science? The habit of partitioning reality into a spiritual region which is the province of religion and a material region which is the sole concern of science, may be nothing more than a hangover from the Victorian conflicts between science and religion. Parapsychology, of course, cuts right across any such partitioning, which perhaps partly explains why its findings have been treated with such disdain by scientists and theologians alike. Parapsychologists do *not* subscribe to the belief that science can offer no evidence on such matters as the existence and immortality of the soul; on the contrary, they assert that such topics can, and must, be investigated by all the techniques that science can muster. They insist that scientific method provides a means of investigating the non-material just as much as the material, although they acknowledge that such investigation is bound to be difficult. Because of their unique approach, parapsychologists have been accused on the one hand of trying to import superstitious notions into science, and on the other of blasphemously dabbling in things which should be left to revealed religion. Thus, Dean Inge condemned psychical researchers for 'trying to prove that eternal values are temporal facts, which they can never be,' while Archbishop Temple wrote:

... I cannot ask that so-called Psychical Research should cease. But I confess I hope that such research will continue to issue in such dubious results as are all that I am able to trace to it. (*Nature, Man and God*, 1951.)

The present writer believes that there is nothing whatever about the scientific method that restricts it to any particular set of assumptions or to any particular kind of phenomenon. Scientific procedures can be applied to the investigation of an apparition no less than to the study of a spiral nebula or a bacillus. Nor need science be committed in advance, as Monod would have it, to the exclusion of concepts such as mind and purpose. Scientists proceed by making careful observations and setting up and testing hypotheses. It is this empirical-inductive approach which characterises a particular piece of work as 'scientific', not the subject-matter with which it deals. In the course of their work, scientists must feel free to formulate any hypotheses which are capable of being tested by observation and experiment: if such hypotheses involve concepts such as 'mind', 'soul' or 'consciousness', there is no reason to regard them with any more contempt than we usually accord to the physicists' concepts of space-time curvatures, energy fields and matter waves. The chief requirements for a scientific theory are that it should be logically consistent, and it should be in accordance with observed facts. It should also be *predictive*, that is, capable of suggesting new facts which can then be experimentally verified. Provided that these requirements are met, there is nothing to prevent the scientist from postulating the existence of immaterial entities or principles. Science must not allow herself to be confined within the barriers erected by materialistic philosophers.

So far, then, we have criticised the mechanist theory of life on the following grounds:

(1) that, despite strong claims to the contrary, it fails to provide a satisfactory explanation of the origin and evolution of living systems: its apparent success in this area arises partly from the ignoring of important facts which run contrary to the theory;

(2) that it completely ignores the existence of such aspects

of reality as consciousness, free-will and purpose, of which we have direct introspective awareness. It attempts to dismiss such phenomena as illusory, and to stigmatise their study as 'unscientific';

(3) that it ignores, or attempts to dismiss as fraudulent, all the findings of parapsychology.

Although mechanistic thinking still predominates among biologists, there is evidence that an increasing number of them are becoming dissatisfied with the orthodox text-book theories. On April 25th and 26th 1966 the Wistar Institute of Anatomy and Biology, Philadelphia, held a symposium whose proceedings were published the following year under the title *Mathematical Challenges to the Neo-Darwinian Interpretation of Evolution*. The symposium was chaired by Sir Peter Medawar, who said in his introductory remarks:

> ... the immediate cause of this conference is a pretty widespread sense of dissatisfaction about what has come to be thought of as the accepted evolutionary theory in the English-speaking world, the so-called neo-Darwinian Theory (93).

In the autumn of 1968 Arthur Koestler organised, in the Austrian village of Alpbach, another symposium of scientists who were 'critical of the totalitarian claims of the neo-Darwinian orthodoxy'. This meeting seems to have been sparked off by a remark of Dr Thorpe to the effect that there is 'an undercurrent of thought in the minds of perhaps hundreds of biologists' who find it difficult to accept the current reductionist theories of life and mind (82). One of the participants in Koestler's symposium was Professor C. H. Waddington of Edinburgh University, who had himself been responsible for organising a series of symposia from 1966 onwards at the Villa Serbelloni, Lake Como, under the auspices of the International Union of Biological Sciences. The outcome of these meetings was the publication of three volumes of papers entitled *Towards a Theoretical Biology*, and a number of the papers in these volumes are highly critical of the prevailing reductionist-mechanist approach. Some of them have been quoted elsewhere in this book. It seems, therefore, that a sizeable minority of scientists are already dissatisfied with the picture presented in most of the official text-books.

If we reject mechanism, what can we put in its place? It seems that there are only two alternatives: either we must revert to some form of vitalism, or we must adopt an *organismic* approach of the kind suggested by von Bertalanffy (17). Those who support the organismic viewpoint see it as a kind of 'third way' distinct from, and superseding, both mechanism and vitalism. According to Bertalanffy, both mechanists and vitalists made the mistake of approaching the living organism as if it were a 'sum of parts and machine-like structures' (17, p. 19). Thus they failed to take into account those very features which are characteristic of living, as distinct from non-living, systems: order, organisation and self-regulation. Aware of the limitations of the machine-theory, the vitalists sought to save it by introducing demon-like entities to operate the machine, or to repair it when damaged. However, by taking such a step the vitalists had, in effect, abandoned scientific explanation altogether. To search for a 'ghost in the machine' is, in Bertalanffy's view, to separate oneself from the strict canons of scientific enquiry. If we had not made the initial mistake of thinking of organisms as machines, the ghost would not have been necessary!

To replace mechanism and vitalism, Bertalanffy envisages a general systems theory which will determine the laws governing the living system *as a whole*, rather than concentrating upon its components. In contrast to the behaviourists who see the organism as an essentially passive automaton, responding mechanically to outside stimuli, Bertalanffy sees it as a continually *active* system. An important characteristic of such living systems is that they are *hierarchically* ordered: the organism is composed of organs, which are composed of tissues, which are composed of cells, which are composed of organelles, which are composed of macromolecules, and so on. The needs of the system as a whole exert a controlling influence over the lower members of the hierarchy; when they fail to do so we have disease, as in the unchecked growth of cancer cells. By developing a general theory of hierarchical systems, Bertalanffy and his followers hope to account for those characteristics of living matter which are inadequately expressed by the analytical, reductionist approach.

As one might expect, Jacques Monod rejects Bertalanffy's theory rather scornfully. 'How far would a Martian engineer get if, trying to understand an earthly computer, he refused, on principle, to dissect the machine's basic electric components which execute the operations of propositional algebra?', he asks (92, p. 80). The answer is, surely, that he could get a very long way. It is perfectly possible to understand the basic laws which govern the functioning of a computer without having the faintest idea of how, electronically, the individual components function. A competent amateur, equipped with a circuit diagram and a soldering iron, could without difficulty construct an efficient computer, even though he might have no idea how a gate or a flip-flop works. No adherent of the organismic theory would deny that a knowledge of the individual components is both useful and necessary to a full understanding of the living organism. Nevertheless, he would insist that the way in which the parts interlock, the *circuit diagram*, is the crucial factor:

> ... if you ask what is the 'secret' of a computing machine, no physicist would consider it any answer to tell you what everyone already knows—that the computer obeys all the laws of mechanics and electricity. If there is any secret, it is in the *unlikely constraints* which harness these laws to perform highly specific and reliable functions. Similarly, if you ask what is the secret of life, you will not impress most physicists by telling them what they already believe—that all the molecules in a cell obey all the laws of physics and chemistry. The real mystery, as in any machine, is in the origin of the highly unlikely and somewhat arbitrary constraints which harness these laws to perform specific and reliable functions (Pattee, 149, p. 117).

Undoubtedly the systems-theory approach is a very useful one which is already bearing fruit in many fields of biology, psychology and medicine. Cybernetics, one of its earliest manifestations, made its entry into biology some years ago, bringing with it the useful concepts of feed-back and homeostasis. Today we may accept without quibble Bertalanffy's general point that it is the way in which the parts of an organism work together, rather than their fine structure, which reveals the essential distinction between living and non-living things. A deeper understanding of the laws governing such systems of organised complexity would be of inestimable value to all the life sciences. Nevertheless, we may reserve the right to question whether even the organismic approach is capable of fully accounting for the phenomenon of life. It seems unlikely that a 'general theory of systems' could explain, for example, how such a highly improbable structure as a living cell came into existence in the first place; and it seems even more unlikely that it could explain the phenomena of consciousness and self-awareness.

Let us return to Monod's imaginary Martian, struggling to comprehend the workings of an earthly computer. By adopting a mechanistic, analytical approach he will begin to understand the structure and functioning of the electronic components as isolated units. If he then proceeds to investigate how these components are linked into a coherent system, he will gain an even deeper insight into the working of the device. However, no amount of detailed study of the fine structure or functioning of the system will tell him *how the machine came into existence in the first place*. He will realise, from the sheer complexity of the thing, that it could not have arisen by chance. Since he is an intelligent being, he will inevitably draw the conclusion that this machine was constructed for a specific purpose by some other beings possessing the property of intelligence like himself. However, an examination of the computer alone will tell him very little about its creators, or the purpose for which it was created. He will realise that it is capable of performing complicated mathematical calculations; but whether it was intended to compute the path of a guided missile or to analyse a country's income-tax returns will remain obscure. In short, some of the most important questions about the machine cannot be answered by an examination of the mechanism alone.

No matter how much the mechanists may try to dodge the issue by appealing to the twin goddesses of Chance and Natural Selection, there remains, both in the individual living organism and throughout the biosphere, a fantastic degree of creative organisation. It would seem to be incredibly naïve to suppose that all this somehow 'just happened'. In a previous chapter we quoted Bertalanffy and Pattee as stating that the formation of such systems would be possible *only in the presence of organising forces* (p. 143). Thorpe, reflecting on the development of the biosphere, wrote of the 'stupendous increase of information' involved. Despite more than a hundred years of Darwinism, it seems that the most important characteristic of life—its amazing *creativeness*—remains totally unexplained. Twentieth-century science, still paying its ritual homage to the shades of Darwin and Mendel, cannot bring itself to admit that Paley was right after all. Unable to accept, for dogmatic reasons, that the existence of design implies the activity of an intelligent designer, the modern theoretician finds himself at a total loss to understand how anything as complicated as a living organism could have come into existence.

We have yet to consider the most despised of all the approaches to biological theory : that of vitalism. Today, even the mention of the word brings a faintly contemptuous smile to the lips of most biologists; yet many of the great biologists of previous centuries were vitalists, and vitalism continued into our own century through the writings of Driesch. Most modern biologists object to it on the grounds that it really explains nothing. Thus, Dobzhansky refers to it as a 'sham solution of biological riddles' (34, p. 25) and G. R. Taylor as a 'pseudo-explanation' :

> Chief of the pseudo-explanations which have bedevilled biology has been *vitalism*—the attempt to explain the mysterious by postulating some ill-defined force capable, by definition, of doing whatever was seen to be done. The healing of wounds was thus attributed to a *vis medicatrix naturae* or healing force of nature. Today we know it to be based on lymphocytes, antibodies and other explicable mechanisms. The history of biology is the story of the gradual abandonment of such question-begging explanations (137, p. 347).

It is difficult not to feel a considerable degree of sympathy with this view. Certainly in the past all sorts of vaguely-defined entities have been invented by those with a mystical turn of mind and few, if any, of these imaginative creations have survived the forward march of science. Nevertheless, we must point out that the fact that an entity cannot be precisely defined and explored by the techniques of present-day science is no proof that it does not exist. As we have seen, there is a widespread feeling among physicists and theoretical biologists that somehow or other, the 'vital principle' needed to explain the phenomenon of life has escaped their net. For more than a hundred years scientists have been busily exorcising the ghost in the machine; yet as soon as their backs are turned, he re-appears in some new guise to haunt the margins of their text-books!

In the closing chapter of their book, Brooks and Shaw point out that there is a big difference between regarding the living system as a machine *with qualifications*, and regarding it as a machine without any qualifications. 'If we could look at a motor car factory in which all the people were invisible we should see what we might think was a living system creating and recreating itself over and over again, then suddenly (new model) mutating to a form which perhaps was more powerful or safer or possessing other useful features which might apparently seem to arise by some process of natural selecti n' (19, p. 368). The analogy is a striking one; and the authors suggest it may be much closer to reality than we are inclined to think:

> The cell, in spite of its intricacies, is very much a collection of both physical and chemical nuts and bolts. Whether it was or is produced and subsequently perpetually driven by some little known celestial force either for pleasure or some other unknown purpose may not readily be open to objective study, but nevertheless it is a possibility that cannot be ignored.

How seriously we should take such an idea is a matter of opinion; but we must certainly consider it very strange that such a notion can even be hinted at in a serious text-book written by well-qualified scientists in the 1970s. Many scientific rationalists believe that Darwin disposed once and for all of the old idea of a purposeful, creative power behind the living world. How odd, therefore, that this idea should still linger in the minds of highly educated scientists more than a century later.

16. Order from Chaos: the Reality of Mind

John Smith is living on his own, as his family have gone to stay with relatives for a few days. Before leaving for the office on Monday morning, he glances into the children's nursery and notices a number of lettered blocks strewn all over the floor. Muttering complaints about the untidy habits of his offspring, he locks up the house and sets off for work. When he returns home in the evening, he happens to glance into the nursery again. To his astonishment the blocks are no longer strewn randomly around the room, but are now arranged in a neat line, so that the letters on their faces spell out the word PARAPSYCHOLOGY.

What will John Smith do? One thing is absolutely certain : he will *not* attribute the arrangement of the blocks to chance, or to some blind physical force. He knows that no amount of shaking and shuffling by earth tremors or other environmental agents would produce such a highly ordered arrangement. Most probably he will suspect that his wife, or one of the children, has returned unexpectedly and is playing a trick on him. Let us suppose that careful investigation proves this to be false; what other hypotheses will he consider? He may think that perhaps a mischievous neighbour entered the house and arranged the blocks, and he will begin to look for signs of illegal entry. The important point is this : whatever alternative hypotheses John Smith may consider, they will all involve the existence of a being or beings with *conscious intelligence*. It is just conceivable that a talented engineer might have built a machine capable of entering the house and arranging the blocks : indeed robots with very similar abilities have been constructed in several laboratories. However, the machine could only have come into existence if a human being, *conscious* of what he was doing and possessed of a definite *purpose*, had built and programmed it to carry out its specific task. The purposiveness of the machine is a secondary purposiveness, derived from the existence of a conscious purpose in its creator.

As a last resort, our perplexed citizen might have to fall back on a paranormal explanation. Yet even if he concludes that the children's blocks were arranged by some kind of poltergeist, he will still be obliged to attribute to the mysterious entity some kind of purposeful intelligence; for only an intelligent *mind* can produce order out of chaos. Dr R. E. D. Clark has pointed out that the whole of scientific progress has been built upon the belief that orderliness does *not* arise spontaneously. When a scientist comes upon an example of order in nature, he immediately seeks for an explanation:

> Only when it was realised that natural forces could not make order spontaneously was it possible for science to begin. Science was impossible so long as each interesting new example of order—a beautifully shaped crystal, cloud formation, striations on rocks or the form of waves on water— could be ascribed to self-ordering principles in nature (26, p. 151).

Of course there are a number of instances in the inorganic world where order *seems* to emerge spontaneously out of chaos: crystallisation is an example of this. However, close examination shows that what is actually occurring in all these cases is really a separating out of a particular kind of orderliness which was already present in the system. In fact, the overall degree of orderliness always *decreases*, in accordance with the Second Law of Thermodynamics. In the living world, the development of a chicken from an egg might seem to be an example of a highly ordered system emerging from a less ordered one; however, modern genetics has shown that this too is merely an example of a pre-existing order becoming visible. If the molecular biologists are correct, all the information needed to produce the chicken was already present in the highly ordered DNA molecules of the chromosomes*.

---

* Some physicists, e.g. Elsasser, have questioned whether such an enormous quantity of information can all be stored in structures as small as the DNA molecules without serious loss due to thermal noise. See the discussion in Thorpe, 139, p. 39.

As Clark forcefully points out, nothing of a factual nature that we know about matter, life or evolution would lead us to suppose that evolution could ever, in the strict sense, be constructive or creative. According to physics, matter ought *not* to organise itself into increasingly complex structures; yet in the course of the evolution of life upon this planet it has quite definitely done so. Like John Smith, we are confronted with the unexpected appearance of order out of chaos: only here it has occurred to a far more staggering degree. We too are forced to conclude that we are here witnessing the activity of *mind*; for in the whole universe the only entity of which we have any direct knowledge which is capable of producing order of this kind (albeit on a smaller scale) is a conscious human mind. Whether or not the physical universe as a whole reveals the activity of a 'cosmic mind', we can hardly avoid postulating some such entity to explain the existence of the biosphere.

For many years now, scientists and philosophers have been reluctant to accept the existence of mind as a distinct entity, chiefly because this implies a dualistic model of the world. One of the most powerful psychological drives in man is the urge towards the unification of experience, and this has provided an important incentive for scientific exploration. Thus, chemists were delighted when it became possible to explain the properties of the hundred or so chemical elements in terms of the behaviour of a much smaller number of fundamental particles inside the atom. Physicists were equally pleased when Einstein was able to prove that matter and energy were merely different forms of the same thing. Ideally, we would like to be able to reduce all the varied phenomena of the universe, living and non-living, to a single cosmic principle or law from which everything else could be derived by straightforward logical deduction. Unfortunately, there is no reason to suppose that nature will always conform to our wishes, and we *may* find that we are living in a world composed of a number of independent, irreducible entities.

Let us, then, assume a dualistic model of reality, and see whether it can be made to fit the facts. We may tentatively suggest the following postulates:

(1) the universe contains two distinct entities, matter and mind;

(2) we have direct awareness of mind through introspection, and we thereby discover certain properties of it, such as consciousness, purpose and free-will;

(3) we have no direct awareness of matter. We deduce its existence from the evidence brought to us through the sense-organs. By comparing the evidence from different senses, and by the use of sense-extending instruments such as the microscope and the telescope, we are able to construct theories about the physical world. These theories suggest that the 'real' world outside our bodies may be very different from the naïve picture presented by our unaided sense-organs;

(4) matter and mind are capable of interacting with one another;

(5) when matter is not interacting with mind, it shows a tendency towards increasing disorder;

(6) we infer that mind has interacted with matter whenever the information content of a physical system shows an increase which cannot be attributed to chance, or to the transfer of information from another physical system.

These postulates might provide us with a sort of rough framework on which to develop a more precise theory. At this stage there are inevitably a lot of questions remaining unanswered : for example, what are the conditions which must be fulfilled before mind can interact with matter? Obviously matter does not always respond to the purposes of mind, otherwise paranormal healings and psychokinetic effects would be everyday occurrences. Presumably there are certain definite conditions which must be satisfied before these phenomena can occur, and these conditions should be discoverable by research. Since orthodox science has largely turned its back on the problem of mind, the task of elucidating the properties of mind-matter interactions falls to the parapsychologist. Indeed, we might redefine parapsychology as the science of mind-matter interactions.

How can a dualistic theory help towards an understanding of the evolution of life? At this point it seems to be necessary to recognise that, just as we can speak of matter in a general sense (meaning the whole material universe), and also refer to a particular *piece* of matter (such as a stone), so we may also use the word 'mind' in a general or restricted sense. We can thus distinguish between mind-at-large, which we will write with a capital *M*, and the individual minds of human beings. We may then suppose that, in the beginning of life upon earth, Mind interacted with certain molecules present on the cooling planet, bringing into existence highly improbable configurations of matter. In effect, the creation of life involved the transfer of information from Mind to matter, just as the mischievous intruder in our parable story transferred information (i.e. knowledge of the sequence of letters in the word PARA-PSYCHOLOGY) to the lettered blocks. Once a self-replicating organism had been created, it would not be necessary for Mind to intervene to maintain it in existence. The various homeostatic devices built into the living system would ensure its survival.

From time to time, accidental variations would occur in the hereditary material of the primitive organism. If such variations led to a decrease in efficiency, they would be eliminated by natural selection. However, such a process could not create entirely new structures with a greatly increased degree of orderliness, so we must suppose that Mind intervened on a number of occasions throughout the course of evolution, thereby bringing into existence increasingly complex organisms. It seems that the general tendency has been to produce organisms which are self-regulating to a very high degree, so that the necessity for Mind-intervention is reduced to a minimum. When an organism has been injured or afflicted with disease, a number of highly intricate automatic repair systems come into action, so that in most cases Mind does not need to intervene to produce healing. However, the repair mechanisms do not always succeed in restoring the organism to health, and on these occasions Mind may interact directly (i.e. psychokinetically) with the material systems of the body, thereby initiating a so-called 'paranormal' healing. It may be important to note that, on this theory, there could be two different kinds of paranormal healings : those produced by the individual mind of the patient, and those produced by that greater Mind whose activity is responsible for the whole progress of life upon this planet. Some forms of faith healing seem to be of the first kind, whereas some of the Lourdes miracles may fall into the latter category.

Since *purpose* is a characteristic of Mind, we are entitled to ask what is the purpose behind the creation and development of the biosphere. Since we are assuming that the individual human mind shows similar characteristics (although on a smaller scale) to the great Mind, we may seek for an analogy in the human artist's urge to create new forms. Imagine a pianist who has been stranded in the jungle. As the weeks go by he learns the techniques of mere survival: how to make clothes and a shelter for himself, and how to obtain food. All the time he longs to have a musical instrument with which to express his creative needs. Gradually, by trial and error, he manages to construct some primitive tools: with these, he begins to build himself a piano. His first attempts are all crude failures. He has many difficulties to overcome, such as finding the right kinds of wood, obtaining suitable material for the strings, etc. However, he keeps on trying, every now and again inventing some new technique which brings him gradually nearer to his goal. Eventually, after years of effort, he succeeds in producing a playable instrument. Now he can forget the technical details and concentrate upon the creative task of producing fine music. It is important to note that the machinery of the instrument must be sufficiently perfect to respond easily to his touch: if he is to compose and perform great works of art, he must be able to forget the mechanical aspects of the generation of sound, and concentrate entirely on the actual sound *patterns* he wishes to produce.

This rather trivial analogy may help us to understand the purpose behind the creation of life. We may imagine that Mind has been striving, over vast periods of time, to produce a living organism capable of expressing its own creative desires. In Man, something very close to this has at last been achieved. The human brain is a computer of sufficiently advanced design to operate the day-to-day running of the body without requiring much attention from the mind. The cerebellum is equipped with programmable circuits which enable it to compute the exact sequences of muscle contractions necessary to carry out complicated actions such as walking, swimming, type-writing and ballet-dancing. The mind is thus freed to concentrate on making the important decisions, such as *which* actions are appropriate in particular circumstances. It is also free to deal with categories of decision which lie right outside the scope of any computer, such as decisions about right and wrong (ethics), good and bad (art), holy and profane (religion).

At first sight it may appear that what is being proposed here is more in the nature of a system of theology than a scientific theory. Is not our concept of Mind merely another name for God? Even if that were true, the author would be quite unrepentant. The deep division between science and theology which began over a hundred years ago has not been particularly helpful to either of these two disciplines: on the contrary, it seems to have left them both with a heap of unsolved and unsolvable problems. However, we must reflect carefully before we equate the concept of Mind with the theologian's notion of God, for there are important differences between the two. The theologian attributes certain *infinite* properties to his God; he is described as omnipotent, omniscient, and of infinite goodness. Now the Mind which reveals itself in the development of life on this planet is clearly not omnipotent, otherwise it would have assembled perfectly designed organisms directly from the dust of the earth without having to go through the long process of trial and error which we call evolution. If the biosphere reveals the activity of a god, he is clearly not the Almighty God of the Christian scriptures. Rather, he seems to be an Experimenter-God, constantly trying out new kinds of living structures, and sometimes making serious mistakes. In its creativeness and in its vast superiority to any individual human mind, the Mind behind evolution obviously resembles the God of the Judaeo-Christian tradition; yet unless we can account for the presence of error and disease in the living world by some additional postulate (such as the existence of a Devil) the two concepts cannot be equated. For the present, it would seem to be best to retain the concept of a creative Mind behind evolution, without attributing to it such absolute qualities as would convert it into a God.

The dualist theory provides a reasonably comprehensive explanation of most of the phenomena of parapsychology. Like all interactions, the interaction of mind with matter might be expected to induce changes in both. In the case of mind, this reveals itself in an awareness of some aspect of the material system acted upon: in other words *clairvoyance*.

In the case of matter, a change in the patterning of the material system is observed, and we say that *psychokinesis* has occurred. Clairvoyance and PK are therefore aspects of the same event : a mind-matter interaction. Precognition is a much more difficult phenomenon to explain : we can only assume that mind operates, at least in part, outside the space-time continuum of the physical world. Of course, this is not really an *explanation* of precognition—to achieve that we need to construct a completely new theory of the nature of time. Perhaps the most hopeful approach would be the construction of a two-dimensional theory of time, similar to that proposed by the philosopher C. D. Broad.

Telepathy provides us with a rather interesting problem; for if the dualist theory is correct, the telepathic transmission of a piece of information from person A to person B might be due to any one of three different mechanisms :

(1) A's mind acting psychokinetically upon the neurones in B's brain;

(2) B's mind drawing the information clairvoyantly from A's brain;

(3) the information passing directly from A's mind to B's mind.

There is no doubt that Myers, who invented the term 'telepathy', originally intended it to describe processes of type (3), although later he realised the possibility of a type (1) mechanism. In view of the considerable body of evidence for the existence of clairvoyance and PK which has accumulated since the time of Myers, it may now seem that (1) and (2) are more likely mechanisms than (3). At any rate, in the present state of our knowledge (or ignorance) there is no conceivable experiment which can be designed to discriminate between the three possibilities, and J. B. Rhine has suggested, therefore, that the telepathy problem should be shelved for the time being. It is of course possible that there is more than one kind of telepathy, and there is some evidence from spontaneous cases which supports this view. On the other hand, when we understand more about the mind-matter relationship the distinctions between the three types may be seen to be meaningless.

The problem of the relationship between mind and brain is one which has baffled philosophers and scientists for centuries.

According to the dualist-interactionist theory advocated here, it is merely a special case of the general problem of mind-matter interactions. In a book published in 1952, the distinguished Australian neurophysiologist J. C. Eccles suggested that the brain acts as a highly sensitive detector of very weak psycho-kinetic influences. Each nerve cell (neurone) is linked to the next via the minute structures known as *synaptic knobs*: a nerve impulse reaching one of these knobs causes the release of a chemical substance known as a *transmitter*, which crosses the minute gap between the synaptic knob and the next cell. A small PK influence exerted at the synaptic knobs could be amplified through the nerve-cell network which forms the cerebral cortex: 'There is thus in the active cortex a mechanism that could effectively amplify by thousands of times minute effects exerted on the individual synaptic knobs, provided of course ... these influences have some "meaningful" pattern and are not random' (39, p. 278).

If Eccles is correct, the brain functions rather like a radio receiver, tuned to the rather weak transmissions of a particular mind entity. We have already suggested, in fact, that the whole purpose of evolution was to create just such a receiver: only when Mind had succeeded in producing a sufficiently sensitive receiving instrument could it fully express its creativity in the world of matter. We must remember, however, that the interaction is a two-way one. If it is true that the individual human mind expresses its will by acting psychokinetically upon the neurones of the physical brain, the converse state-ment—that any change in the brain neurones will bring about a change in the state of mind—must also be true. The dualist should not be dismayed by the evidence which shows that mental states are profoundly affected by drugs, electric shocks and brain damage: that is exactly what one would expect if the interaction theory is true. On the other hand, the dualist theory suggests other possibilities which are not envisaged in the simple mechanist theory. For example, it might be possible to weaken the hold of an individual mind on the corresponding brain, allowing other minds (incarnate or discarnate) to take possession of it. Such a weakening might occur in certain trance states, or through ingesting certain drugs. The phenomena of spiritualism point strongly to such a possibility, although it cannot be said to have been scientifically established. Yet another possibility, which is engaging the attention of an increasing number of people in the western world, is expressed in the ancient oriental belief in reincarnation : on a dualist theory it is clearly possible that a discarnate mind might enter into a relationship with a newly created brain.

If any theory is to be acceptable, it must provide a satisfactory explanation of all the facts accounted for by previous theories, it must explain some phenomena which are *not* explicable by those theories; and it must not conflict with any other known facts. Judged by these criteria, the dualist-interactionist theory stands up rather well. It does not conflict with any of the facts discovered through the mechanist approach to life, and it predicts the occurrence of some new facts which are incompatible with mechanism. Most important of all (since it provides a crucial test of the theory) the dualist theory predicts the occurrence of psi phenomena. Since the individual human mind can interact with the atoms of the corresponding brain, there is no reason why it should not interact with other physical systems also. PK and clairvoyance are thus merely external manifestations of the same mind-matter interaction that is happening all the time in the living brain. The only problem which the theory fails to solve is why a particular human mind remains so firmly attached to a particular brain—in other words, why paranormal phenomena are comparatively rare. Perhaps the physical organism is still not sufficiently developed for the mind to be able to leave it unattended for long periods without incurring a risk of damage. It is possible that the growing research into 'out-of-the-body' experiences may throw some light on this question.

Of course there are many who will automatically reject any form of interactionism, merely because it resembles beliefs which have been held by adherents of most of the world's religions for several thousand years. Such people have an image of a 'pure' science, standing proudly aloof from anything which smacks of religion, superstition, witchcraft or occultism. To suggest that there might be even the smallest grain of truth in any one of these things puts them immediately on the defensive : they rush to man the barricades, fearing a return to all the horrors of the Dark Ages. But science, if it is to be the impartial pursuit of truth rather than the propagation of a system of dogma, must be prepared to investigate phenomena which lie outside the framework of existing theories. Truth is often to be found in the most unsavoury places, and we shall not make much progress if we are afraid of dirtying our laboratory overalls. A purely dogmatic science, confined within the mental limitations of the mechanistic philosophy, can be no more acceptable to the twentieth century mind than a purely dogmatic religion. Modern man has at last begun to realise that infallibility, from whatever source, is a myth; for all our knowledge is imperfect and provisional. That, as Bronowski says, is the human condition; and it is within that condition that all our philosophy, science, and religion must operate.

Epilogue: Parapsychology and the Future

One hundred and sixteen years ago Charles Darwin initiated a Great Schism between science and religion. Until that time, scientists had felt no inhibitions about referring to the Creator in their scientific writings, nor had theologians hesitated to utilise the latest scientific discoveries in their discussions of the nature of God and man. Today no scientific paper would be accepted for publication in any of the 'establishment' journals if it contained any mention of God, immortality, or the human soul; for it has become almost universally accepted that science must confine itself to strictly materialistic hypotheses. This restriction is supposed to be an indication of the 'objectivity' of science, although why it should be regarded as objective to refuse to think about certain aspects of reality is not at all clear. True, it may be *difficult* to obtain direct evidence for the reality of entities such as the soul; but no more so than it is to demonstrate the existence of positrons, muons, and neutrinos. In fact, the Great Schism seems to have had an unhealthy effect upon both religion and science: it has driven theology away from all contact with the natural world, and confined scientific thinking within the straitjacket of materialism.

Today, there are signs that many of the old inhibitions are disappearing. A new generation, looking with troubled eyes at the hydrogen bombs, the guided missiles, and the cylinders of nerve gases, has begun to wonder whether we can any longer afford the luxury of a purely 'objective' science. There has been a marked shift of interest away from the physical sciences towards those sciences whose aim is the study and betterment of mankind: medicine, economics, psychology, sociology. At the same time there has arisen a new willingness to look afresh at the beliefs and practices of the ancient religions. On every bookstall can be found an amazing variety of paperback texts on religious and quasi-religious topics, from modern Christian writers such as C. S. Lewis and J. B. Phillips to ancient oriental classics such as the *Bhagavad gita* and the *Tibetan Book of the Dead*. In the United States, psychologists have at last begun to break free from the dead hand of behaviourism, and all the techniques of modern science are being brought to bear upon phenomena which would once have been contemptuously dismissed as illusory, or at any rate regarded as lying outside the province of science. Thus mysticism, out-of-the-body experiences, psychedelic visions, prophetic dreams, Yoga and Zen meditation, and of course, ESP and PK, are all being examined in a new and refreshing spirit of open-mindedness. Here in Britain, the same spirit of impartial enquiry is demonstrated by Sir Alister Hardy's Religious Experience Research Unit, which was established at Oxford University a few years ago, and which has already begun to produce some interesting and potentially important results. In short, what seems to be happening is the gradual emergence of a new science or group of sciences concerned with the *spiritual* components of man's being: that is, with those non-material factors which have been tragically ignored by the older sciences. If this is so, then we may look forward to the day when the spiritual sciences will take their proper places alongside the physical, the biological and the psychological. Each has something important to tell us about the nature of reality; but none is complete in itself. If we are to obtain a satisfactory synthesis, to discover (in Tyrrell's words) the conclusion to which the *whole* body of knowledge points, we need to explore the spiritual world as thoroughly and impartially as we have already explored the physical world. Parapsychology, once the despised outcast of a materialistically-orientated orthodoxy, may now claim pride of place among the spiritual sciences; for it was parapsychology which pioneered the exploration of the world beyond the senses.

What benefits may we expect to accrue to mankind as the spiritual sciences develop? Perhaps an analogy may not be out of place here. Until quite recently, very little factual knowledge was available concerning the nature and development of the sex instinct in man. During Victorian and Edwardian times an incredible amount of human misery was generated by sexual ignorance, prejudice and dogma, and as a result many thousands of human lives were spoilt by unnecessary burdens of fear, guilt and neurosis. One has only to think of the cruel mechanical contraptions which were fastened to the bodies of some children to prevent masturbation, of the equally cruel threats of disease and hell-fire used for the same purpose, or of the savage punishments meted out to homosexuals and other deviants, to realise the extent of this suffering. Today we live in a kinder society, thanks to a small group of pioneers who had the courage to break through the old taboos, and subject the forbidden topics to impartial scientific investigation. Largely due to the work of such determined explorers as Alfred Kinsey, we now know a great deal more about human sexuality, and with increased knowledge has come a greater degree of sympathy and tolerance. Kinsey and his fellow researchers *dared to extend the use of scientific method into areas from which it had been previously excluded*; and the result was a great enhancement of the quality of human life.

In our modern society it is the *religious* instinct, rather than the sexual, which has been powerfully repressed. Twentieth-century man has been made to feel almost ashamed of his religious impulses. For over a hundred years, all the massive prestige of 'science' has been used to persuade him that religion is nothing more than an outdated superstition, that life is the accidental result of certain chemical reactions, and that he is merely an intellectually overgrown ape. Through all the media of communication, over and over again, the message has been propagated: that life is meaningless, that death is the end of all things, and that the only sensible course of action is the pursuit of pleasure for its own sake. Yet in spite of this continuous torrent of materialist propaganda, the religious instinct remains. Just as sexual behaviour persisted in spite of Victorian attempts at suppression, so the religious impulses of modern man continue to express themselves, sometimes in bizarre and unhealthy forms. Despite the contempt with which religion is regarded in some intellectual circles, the vast majority of mankind still seeks relief from the misery of the existential vacuum through ritual, sacrament and prayer. Now at last we are witnessing the extension of scientific procedures into these spiritual areas of human experience: is it too much to hope that the result will be a deepening of understanding which will lead to yet another advance in the liberation of the human spirit? Already progress has been made. Although parapsychology has not found any evidence to support the specific propositions of any one religion, it has at least destroyed the basis of the old dogmatic materialism. In Rhine's words, it has shown that the universe does not conform to the prevailing materialistic concept; it is a universe in which it is *possible* to be religious. To those who are seeking for a glimpse of the promised land, this may seem a small achievement; but we must not be impatient. For thousand of years mankind has been trying to answer the really important questions about life by appealing to 'infallible' authorities of one sort or another. Religion, politics and science share at least one characteristic in common: as time goes by their discoveries tend to become hardened into dogmas which are then perpetuated by their followers, often with extraordinary intellectual arrogance, and sometimes cruelty. Gradually we are beginning to realise that the appeal to authority and dogma gets us nowhere in the long run. The only way to a proper understanding lies through the slow, patient unravelling of factual data. This is the method of science, and it is astonishing that we have for so long refrained from using it to attack the most important questions about human life. Now that parapsychology has broken through the barriers erected by both dogmatic religion and mechanistic science, we may be on the verge of a new revolution in human thought, comparable to those brought about by Copernicus, Newton, Darwin and Einstein. We can only wait and see.

References

(1) ANDERSON, M. L.: A precognition experiment comparing time intervals of a few days and one year. *J. Parapsychol.* 1959, *23*, pp. 81-9.

(2) ANDRÉ, E.: Confirmation of PK action on electronic equipment. *J. Parapsychol.* 1972, *36*, pp. 283-93

(3) ARTLEY, B.: Confirmation of the small-rodent precognition work. *J. Parapsychol.* 1974, *38*, pp. 238-9 (abstract).

(4) BACKSTER, C.: Evidence of a primary perception in plant life. *Int. J. Parapsychol.* 1968, *10*, pp. 329-48.

(5) BARKER, J. C.: Premonitions of the Aberfan disaster. *J. Soc. Psych. Res.* 1967, *44*, pp. 169-81.

(6) BARKER, J. C.: *Scared to Death*. Frederick Muller, London, 1968.

(7) BARNETT, S. A. (Ed.): *A Century of Darwin*. Heinemann, London, 1958.

(8) BARRINGTON, M. R.: A free response sheep/goat experiment using an irrelevant task. *J. Soc. Psych. Res.* 1973, *47*, pp. 222-45.

(9) BECHTEREV, W.: 'Direct influence' of a person upon the behaviour of animals. *J. Parapsychol.* 1949, *13*, pp. 166-76.

(10) DE BEER, G.: *Homology, An Unsolved Problem*. Oxford Biology Readers, 1971.

(11) BELOFF, J.: *The Existence of Mind*. Citadel Press, New York, 1962.

(12) BELOFF, J.: *Psychological Sciences*. Crosby Lockwood Staples, London.

(13) BELOFF, J. (Ed.): *New Directions in Parapsychology*. Elek Science, London, 1974.

(14) BELOFF, J. & BATE, D.: Research report for the year 1968-9. *J. Soc. Psych. Res.* 1970, *45*, pp. 297-301.

(15) BELOFF, J. & BATE, D.: An attempt to replicate the Schmidt findings. *J. Soc. Psych. Res.* 1971, *46*, pp. 21-31.

(16) BELOFF, J. & EVANS, L.: A radioactivity test of psychokinesis. *J. Soc. Psych. Res.* 1961, *41*, pp. 41-6.

(17) BERTALANFFY, L. VON: *Problems of Life*. Harper & Brothers, New York, 1960.

REFERENCES 245

(18) BLACK, S.: Mind and Body. William Kimber, London, 1969.
(19) BROOKS, J. & SHAW, G.: Origin and Development of Living Systems. Academic Press, London & New York, 1973.
(20) BROUGHTON, R. & MILLAR, B.: An attempted confirmation of the rodent ESP findings with positive reinforcement. Unpublished manuscript.
(21) CARREL, ALEXIS: Man, the Unknown. Penguin Books, 1948.
(22) CATTELL, R. B.: Psychology and the Religious Quest. London, 1938.
(23) DE CHARDIN, T.: The Phenomenon of Man. Collins, London, 1959.
(24) CHAUVIN, R. & GENTHON, J.-P.: Eine Untersuchung über die Moglichkeit Psychokinetscher Experiemente mit Uranium und Geigerzähler. Zeitschr. f. Parapsych. 1965, 8, pp. 140-7.
(25) CHURCH INFORMATION BOARD: Report of the Archbishops' Commission on the Church's Ministry of Healing. 1958.
(26) CLARK, R. E. D.: Darwin: Before and After. Paternoster Press, London, 1950.
(27) COLEMAN, W.: Biology in the Nineteenth Century. Wiley & Sons, New York & London, 1971.
(28) COULSON, C. A.: Science and Christian Belief. London, 1954.
(29) CRANSTON, R.: The Mystery of Lourdes. Evans, London, 1956.
(30) DALTON, G. F.: Comments on W. G. Roll's paper on precognition. J. Soc. Psych. Res. 1961, 41, p. 183.
(31) DALTON, G. F.: Letter in J. Soc. Psych. Res. 1971, 46, pp. 148-9.
(32) DARLINGTON, C. D.: Genetics and Man. Allen & Unwin, London, 1964.
(33) DINGWALL, E. J., GOLDNEY, K. M. & HALL, T. H.: The Haunting of Borley Rectory. Duckworth & Co., 1956.
(34) DOBZHANSKY, T.: The Biology of Ultimate Concern. Fontana, 1971.
(35) DRIESCH, H.: The History and Theory of Vitalism. Macmillan, London, 1914.
(36) DRIESCH, H.: The Science and Philosophy of the

Organism. Black, London, 1929.

(37) DUNNE, J. W.: *An Experiment with Time*. Black, London, 1927.

(38) DUVAL, P. & MONTREDON, E.: ESP experiments with mice. *J. Parapsychol*. 1968, 32, pp. 153-66.

(39) ECCLES, J. C.: *The Neurophysiological Basis of Mind*. Oxford, 1952.

(40) EDDINGTON, A. S.: *The Nature of the Physical World*. Everyman Edition, 1935.

(41) ELGUIN, G. H. & BÄCHLER, O.: Psychokinese und experimentelle tumorentwicklung. *Zeitschr. f. Parapsych*. 1967, 10, pp. 48-61.

(42) EVANS, C.: Long Dream Ending. *New Scientist*, 20th March 1969, pp. 638-40.

(43) EVANS, C.: Parapsychology – what the questionnaire revealed. *New Scientist*, 25th January 1973, p. 209.

(44) EXTRA, J. F. M.: GESP in the rat. *J. Parapsychol*. 1972, 36, pp. 294-302.

(45) EYSENCK, H. J.: *Sense and Nonsense in Psychology*. Penguin Books, 1957.

(46) EYSENCK, H. J.: Personality and extra-sensory perception. *J. Soc. Psych. Res*. 1967, 44, pp. 55-71.

(47) FISK, G. W. & WEST, D. J.: ESP tests with erotic symbols. *J. Soc. Psych. Res*. 1955, 38, pp. 1-7.

(48) FISK, G. W. & WEST, D. J.: Dice-casting experiments with a single subject. *J. Soc. Psych. Res*. 1958, 39, pp. 277-87.

(49) FOX, S.: In the beginning ... life assembled itself. *New Scientist*. February 27th 1969, pp. 450-2.

(50) FRANKL, V. E.: *Psychotherapy and Existentialism*. Souvenir Press, 1970.

(51) FREUD, S.: *Beyond the Pleasure Principle*. A. & C. Boni, New York, 1922.

(52) FREUD, S.: *The Future of an Illusion*. Hogarth, London, 1928.

(53) GRAD, B., CADORET, R. J. & PAUL, G. I.: An unorthodox method of treatment in wound healing in mice. *Int. J. Parapsychol*. 1961, 3, pp. 5-24.

(54) GRAD, B.: A telekinetic effect on plant growth I. *Int. J. Parapsychol*. 1963, 5, pp. 117-33.

(55) GRAD, B.: A telekinetic effect on plant growth II. *Int.*

J. Parapsychol. 1964, 6, pp. 473-98.

(56) GREENWOOD, W. O.: The teaching of biology in religion. *Religion in Education*, 1938, 5, No. 4.

(57) HALL, T. H.: *The Spiritualists.* Duckworth, London, 1962.

(58) HANSEL, C. E. M.: *ESP: A Scientific Evaluation.* C. Scribner's Sons, New York, 1966.

(59) HARALDSSON, E.: Subject selection in a machine precognition test. *J. Parapsychol.* 1970, 34, pp. 182-91.

(60) HARDY, A. C.: *The Living Stream.* Collins, London, 1965.

(61) HARDY, A. C., HARVIE, R. & KOESTLER, A.: *The Challenge of Chance.* Hutchinson, London, 1973.

(62) HARRIS, S. & TERRY, J.: Precognition in a water-deprived Wistar rat. *J. Parapsychol.* 1974, 38, p. 239 (Abstract).

(63) HASTINGS, R. J.: An examination of the Borley report. *Proc. Soc. Psych. Res.* 1969, 55, pp. 66-175.

(64) HEYWOOD, R.: G. W. Fisk and ESP. *J. Soc. Psych. Res.* 1973, 47, pp. 24-30.

(65) HUMPHREY, B. M.: *Discrimination between high- and low-scoring subjects in ESP tests on the basis of the form quality of their response drawings.* Ph.D. dissertation, Duke University, 1946.

(66) HUTCHINSON, L.: Variations of time intervals in pre-shuffle card-calling tests. *J. Parapsychol.* 1940, 4, pp. 249-70.

(67) HUXLEY, J.: *Religion without Revelation.* London, 1927.

(68) JAMES, W.: *Psychology, briefer course.* Holt & Co., New York, 1892.

(69) JANIK, J. & KLOCEK, R.: A biochemical approach to ESP. *J. Parapsychol.* 1970, 34, pp. 276-7 (Abstract).

(70) JEVONS, F. R.: *The Biochemical Approach to Life.* Allen & Unwin, London, 1964.

(71) JOHNSON, R. V.: Letter in *J. Parapsychol.* 1972, 36, pp. 71-2.

(72) JUNG, C. G.: *Modern Man in Search of a Soul.* London, 1933.

(73) JUNG, G. C.: *Memories, Dreams, Reflections.* Fontana, London, 1967.

(74) KAHN, S. D.: Studies in extrasensory perception. *Proc. Amer. Soc. Psych. Res.* 1952, 25, pp. 1-48.

(75) KANTHAMANI, B. K. & RAO, K. R.: Personality character-istics of ESP subjects. II. The combined personality measure and ESP. *J. Parapsychol.* 1972, *36*, pp. 56-70.

(76) KANTHAMANI, B. K. & RAO, K. R.: Personality character-istics of ESP subjects. III. Extraversion and ESP. *J. Parapsychol.* 1972, *36*, pp. 198-212.

(77) KERKUT, G. A.: *Implications of Evolution*. Pergamon, Oxford, 1960.

(78) KNIGHT, M.: Theoretical implications of telepathy. *Penguin Science News.* 1950, *18*, pp. 9-20.

(79) KOESTLER, A.: *The Ghost in the Machine*. Hutchinson, London, 1967.

(80) KOESTLER, A.: *The Case of the Midwife Toad*. Hutchinson, London, 1971.

(81) KOESTLER, A.: *The Roots of Coincidence*. Hutchinson, London, 1972.

(82) KOESTLER, A. & SMYTHIES, J. R. (Eds): *Beyond Reduc-tionism*. Hutchinson, London, 1969.

(83) KUHLMAN, K.: *I Believe in Miracles*. Lakeland, London, 1968.

(84) LACK, D.: *Evolutionary Theory and Christian Belief*. Methuen, London, 1957.

(85) LESHAN, L.: *The Medium, the Mystic, and the Physicist*. Turnstone, London, 1974.

(86) LYTTELTON, E.: *Some Cases of Prediction*. Bell & Sons, London, 1937.

(87) MCDOUGALL, W.: *Body and Mind: a History and Defence of Animism*. Methuen, London, 1911.

(88) MACKAY, D. M. (Ed.): *Christianity in a Mechanistic Universe*. Inter-Varsity Fellowship, London, 1965.

(89) MEDHURST, R. G. & SCOTT, C.: A re-examination of C. E. M. Hansel's criticism of the Pratt-Woodruff experiment. *J. Parapsychol.* 1974, *38*, pp. 163-84.

(90) MITCHELL, A. M. J.: Home-testing ESP experiments. *J. Soc. Psych. Res.* 1953, *37*, pp. 155-64.

(91) MITCHELL, A. M. J. & FISK, G. W.: The application of differential scoring methods to PK tests. *J. Soc. Psych. Res.* 1953, *37*, pp. 45-61.

(92) MONOD, J.: *Chance and Necessity*. Fontana Books, 1974.

(93) MOORHEAD, P. S. & KAPLAN, M. M. (Eds): *Mathematical*

Challenges to the Neo-Darwinian Interpretation of Evolution. Wistar Institute Press, Philadelphia, U.S.A. 1967.

(94) MORRIS, R. L.: Psi and animal behaviour: a survey. *J. Amer. Soc. Psych. Res.* 1970, *64*, pp. 242-60.

(95) MYERS, F. W. H.: *Human Personality and its Survival of Bodily Death.* Longmans, London, 1902.

(96) OSIS, K.: Precognition over time intervals of one to thirty-three days. *J. Parapsychol.* 1955, *12*, pp. 82-91.

(97) OSIS, K.: A test of the occurrence of a psi effect between man and the cat. *J. Parapsychol.* 1952, *16*, pp. 233-56.

(98) OSIS, K. & FOSTER, E.: A test of ESP in cats. *J. Parapsychol.* 1953, *17*, pp. 168-86.

(99) OSIS, K. & TURNER, M. E.: Distance and ESP: a transcontinental experiment. *Proc. Amer. Soc. Psych. Res.* 1968, 27, pp. 1-48.

(100) OSIS, K., TURNER, M. E. & CARLSON, M. L.: ESP over distance: research on the ESP channel. *J. Amer. Soc. Psych. Res.* 1971, *65*, pp. 245-88.

(101) PARKER, A.: ESP in gerbils using positive reinforcement. *J. Parapsychol.* 1974, *38*, pp. 301-11.

(102) PRICE, G. R.: Summary of article 'Science and the Supernatural'. *J. Soc. Psych. Res.* 1955, *38*, pp. 176-9.

(103) RANDALL, J. L.: Experiments to detect a psi effect with small animals. *J. Soc. Psych. Res.* 1971, *46*, pp. 31-9.

(104) RANDALL, J. L.: Card-guessing experiments with schoolboys. *J. Soc. Psych. Res.* 1974, *47*, pp. 421-32.

(105) RANDALL, J. L.: An extended series of ESP and PK tests with three English schoolboys. *J. Soc. Psych. Res.* 1974, *47*, pp. 485-94.

(106) RAO, K. R.: *Experimental Parapsychology.* C. Thomas, Springfield, Illinois. 1966.

(107) RHINE, J. B.: *Extra-Sensory Perception.* Faber, London, 1935.

(108) RHINE, J. B.: *The Reach of the Mind.* Faber, London, 1948.

(109) RHINE, J. B.: Location of hidden objects by a man-dog team. *J. Parapsychol.* 1971, *35*, pp. 18-33.

(110) RHINE, J. B. & FEATHER, S. R.: The study of cases of 'psi-trailing' in animals. *J. Parapsychol.* 1962, *26*, pp. 1-22.

(111) RHINE, J. B. & RHINE, L. E.: *An investigation of a*

'mind-reading' horse. *J. Ab. & Soc. Psychol.* 1929, 23, pp. 449-466.

(112) RHINE, J. B. & RHINE, L. E.: Second report on 'Lady', the 'mind-reading' horse. *J. Ab. & Soc. Psychol.* 1929, 24, pp. 287-92.

(113) ROLL, W. G.: The problem of precognition. *J. Soc. Psych. Res.* 1961, 41, pp. 115-28.

(114) ROSE, L.: *Faith Healing.* Penguin Books, 1971.

(115) RYLE, G.: *The Concept of Mind.* Hutchinson, London, 1949.

(116) SCHMIDT, H.: Precognition of a quantum process. *J. Parapsychol.* 1969, 33, pp. 99-108.

(117) SCHMIDT, H.: Clairvoyance tests with a machine. *J. Parapsychol.* 1969, 33, pp. 300-6.

(118) SCHMIDT, H.: A PK test with electronic equipment. *J. Parapsychol.* 1970, 34, pp. 175-81.

(119) SCHMIDT, H.: PK experiments with animals as subjects. *J. Parapsychol.* 1970, 34, pp. 255-61.

(120) SCHMIDT, H.: Comparison of PK action on two different random number generators. *J. Parapsychol.* 1974, 38, pp. 47-55.

(121) SCHMIDT, H. & PANTAS, L.: Psi tests with internally different machines. *J. Parapsychol.* 1972, 36, pp. 222-32.

(122) SCHOUTEN, S. A.: Psi in mice: positive reinforcement. *J. Parapsychol.* 1972, 36, pp. 261-82.

(123) SCHROEDINGER, E.: *What is Life?* Cambridge University Press, 1944.

(124) SCHULTZ, D. P.: *A History of Modern Psychology.* Academic Press, London, 1960.

(125) SCHWEITZER, A.: *My Life and Thought,* London, 1933.

(126) SCOTT, C. & HASKELL, P.: 'Normal' explanation of the Soal-Goldney experiments in extrasensory perception. *Nature.* 1973, 245, pp. 52-4.

(127) SIDGWICK, A. S. & SIDGWICK, E. M.: *Henry Sidgwick—a Memoir.* London, 1906.

(128) SMITH, J.: Paranormal effects on enzyme activity. *J. Parapsychol.* 1968, 32, p. 281 (Abstract).

(129) SMITH, N.: Replication studies: a neglected aspect of psychological research. *American Psychologist,* 1970, 25, pp. 970-5.

(130) SMITH, B. M. & HUMPHREY, B. M.: Some personality characteristics related to ESP performance. *J. Parapsychol.* 1946, *10*, pp. 169-89.

(131) SOAL, S. G.: Reply to article by G. R. Price. *J. Soc. Psych. Res.* 1955, *38*, pp. 179-84.

(132) SOAL, S. G. & BATEMAN, F.: *Modern Experiments in Telepathy.* Faber, London, 1954.

(133) SPENCER BROWN, G.: *Probability and Scientific Inference.* Longmans, London, 1957.

(134) SPINKS, G. S.: *Religion in Britain since 1900.* London, 1952.

(135) TARG, R. & PUTHOFF, H.: Information transmission under conditions of sensory shielding. *Nature.* 1974, *251*, pp. 602-7.

(136) TAYLOR, G. R.: *The Biological Time-Bomb.* Panther Books, London, 1969.

(137) TAYLOR, G. R.: *The Science of Life.* Thames & Hudson, London, 1963.

(138) TAYLOR, J.: *The Shape of Minds to Come.* Michael Joseph, London, 1971.

(139) THORPE, W. H.: *Science, Man and Morals.* Methuen, London, 1965.

(140) THOULESS, R. H.: Thought transference and related phenomena. Discourse to the Royal Institution, December 1st 1950.

(141) THOULESS, R. H.: Letter in *J. Soc. Psych. Res.* 1969, *45*, pp. 91-2.

(142) THOULESS, R. H.: Experiments on psi self-training with Dr Schmidt's precognitive apparatus. *J. Soc. Psych. Res.* 1971, *46*, pp. 15-21.

(143) TYRRELL, G. N. M.: *The Personality of Man.* Penguin Books, 1946.

(144) ULLMAN, M., KRIPPNER, S. & VAUGHAN, A.: *Dream Telepathy.* Turnstone, London, 1973.

(145) VAN OVER, R. (Ed.): *Psychology and Extrasensory Perception.* Mentor Books, 1972.

(146) VASILIEV, L. L.: *Experiments in Mental Suggestion.* Institute for the Study of Mental Images, Church Crookham, Hants. 1963.

(147) WADDINGTON, C. H. (Ed.): *Towards a Theoretical*

Biology, Vol. 1. Edinburgh University Press, 1968.

(148) WADDINGTON, C. H. (Ed.): *Towards a Theoretical Biology, Vol. 2.* Edinburgh University Press, 1969.

(149) WADDINGTON, C. H. (Ed.): *Towards a Theoretical Biology, Vol. 3.* Edinburgh University Press, 1970.

(150) WADDINGTON, C. H.: *The Nature of Life.* The Scientific Book Club, London, 1961.

(151) WADHAMS, P. & FARRELLY, B. A.: The investigation of psychokinesis using beta particles. *J. Soc. Psych. Res.* 1968, *44*, pp. 281-8.

(152) WARNER, L. & CLARK, C. C.: A survey of psychological opinion on ESP. *J. Parapsychol.* 1938, 2, pp. 296-301.

(153) WARNER, L.: A second survey of psychological opinion on ESP. *J. Parapsychol.* 1952, *16*, pp. 284-95.

(154) WATKINS, G. & WATKINS, A. M.: Possible PK influence on the resuscitation of anaesthetised mice. *J. Parapsychol.* 1971, *35*, pp. 257-72.

(155) WATSON, J. B.: *Behaviourism.* University of Chicago Press. Revised Ed., 1930.

(156) WEATHERFIELD, L. D.: *Psychology, Religion and Healing.* Hodder, London, 1951.

(157) WELLS, R. & KLEIN, J.: A replication of a 'psychic healing' paradigm. *J. Parapsychol.* 1972, *36*, pp. 144-9.

(158) WEST, D. J.: Home-testing ESP experiments. *J. Soc. Psych. Res.* 1953, *37*, pp. 14-25.

(159) WEST, D. J.: *Eleven Lourdes Miracles.* Duckworth, London, 1957.

(160) WEST, D. J. & FISK, G. W.: A dual ESP experiment with clock cards. *J. Soc. Psych. Res.* 1953, *37*, pp. 185-97.

(161) WICKES, I. G.: Book review. *J. Soc. Psych. Res.* 1956, *38*, pp. 375-6.

(162) WILLIAMS, M. & WILLIAMS, M.: Report to the Southern California Society for Psychical Research, June 5th 1970.

(163) WILLIAMS, R. E.: Biology and Christian Belief. *Religion in Education,* 1939, 6, No. 2.

(164) WOOD, G. H. & CADORET, R. J.: Tests of clairvoyance in a man-dog relationship. *J. Parapsychol.* 1958, 22, pp. 29-39.

(165) WHYTE, L. L.: *Internal Factors in Evolution.* Tavistock Publications, London, 1965.

Index